*Will the Corporation Survive?*

# Will the Corporation Survive?

John L. Paluszek

Foreword by Elliot L. Richardson

Reston Publishing Company, Inc.
A *Prentice-Hall Company*
Reston, Virginia

Library of Congress Cataloging in Publication Data
Paluszek, John L
  Will the corporation survive?
  Includes bibliographical references.
  1. Industry—Social aspects—United States.
2. Corporations—United States.   3. Industry and state
—United States.   I. Title.
HD60.5.U5P35           658.4'08           77-5730
ISBN 0-87909-894-5
ISBN 0-87909-893-7 pbk.

*To my wife, Jean*

© 1977 by Reston Publishing Company, Inc.
*A Prentice-Hall Company*
Reston, Virginia 22090

*All rights reserved. No part of this book may be reproduced in any way, or by any means, without permission in writing from the publisher.*

10  9  8  7  6  5  4  3  2  1

Printed in the United States of America

# Contents

FOREWORD ix
ACKNOWLEDGMENTS xiii

## THE SETTING

1 A HISTORIC CONFLUENCE 3

2 CORPORATE MANAGERS PROPHESY 7
Large Companies See Evolution, 8
Another View: More Government Control, 11
"Small" Companies: New Moves to Satisfy Public Demands, 14

## THE ATTACK

3 THE "PAYMENTS" STAIN 21
The Revelations, 21
Early Results, Proposed Remedies, 24
   General Policies, 29
The Long-Term Effect, 30
The Practical and the Philosophical, 33

## 4 THE NEW VALUES POOL — 35

## 5 THE CHANGING WORLD AROUND BUSINESS — 53
The Velocity of Change (If You Don't Like the News, Come Back Tomorrow), 54
Big Government Growing Bigger, 55
The New American Political Leadership, 57
The Inflation-Cum-Unemployment Fallout, 60
The New Challenge of Organized Labor, 64
Decay at the Center, 68
The Courts' New Reach Into Your Pocketbook, 71
Income Redistribution in America, 73
The Evolution of a Global Economic Order, 77

## 6 ATTACKS ON THE SYSTEM — 83
Recent Activist Organizational Developments, 86
Recent Activist Accomplishments, 89
The Remaining Demands, 93

## 7 ONE-ON-ONE: THE ISSUE ATTACKS — 103
Equal Employment Opportunity, 103
Other Employee-Related Problems, 108
The Environment, 111
A Safer Place to Work, 120
Safer Products More Honestly Sold, 122
Attack on the Multinationals, 125
Accountability/Disclosure, 129

# THE RESPONSE

## 8 THE EMERGING CORPORATE MODEL — 135
State of the Art, 138
Effect of Economic Downturn, 139
Sources of Help, 140
A Road Map for Future Corporate Social Responsiveness, 141
A Comparison of American, British, and European Economic Community (EEC) Companies, 143

## 9 THE CORPORATE FUTURISTS — 149
Identifying Major Impact Points, 160
Challenges to Business Values, 163

| | | |
|---|---|---|
| 10 | **TOWARD A NEW WORKPLACE** | 171 |

Restructuring Work Time, 173
   The Shorter Work Week, 174
   Flexitime, 175
   The Changing Worklife, 176
Reorganizing Work, 176
   Job Enrichment, 177

| | | |
|---|---|---|
| 11 | **THE ENVIRONMENTAL BRIDGE** | 181 |
| 12 | **MORE SIGNS OF CORPORATE STIRRING** | 191 |

The Board Goes Social, 191
Courage to Ask—and Tell—"How Are We Doing?" 195
   Measurement, 195
   Disclosure, 197
More Hope for the Employee, 198
   The Corporate Ombudsman, 198
   Affirmative, Affirmative, 199
   Security and Privacy, 199
   Helping with Employees' Problems, 200
Struts for the Environmental Bridge, 202
   Taking the Initiative, 203
   The Sweet Confluence, 204
Care for the Consumer, 204
And a Bit of Miscellany, 205
   Lending a Hand, 205

## WILL THE CORPORATION SURVIVE?

| | | |
|---|---|---|
| 13 | **RELATING WITH THE PUBLIC** | 213 |

Understanding Media, 224
   Media Reflect Not Life But a Slice of Life, 225
   Media Magnification Makes a Subject Bigger Than Life, 226
   The Winds of Change are Beginning to Cool Media, Too, 230
   The Great Majority of Journalists are Honest, Objective, Hard-Working Professionals, 231
"What Should We Do—Just Sit There and Take It?" 232
   Taking the Initiative, 233
   Attacked? Reply! 233
   Asked for an Interview? Cooperate, 234
   Practical Advice on Strategy From a "Radical," 235

This Is the Age of Communications Feedback, 235
What About All Those Economic Education Campaigns? 236
Finally, Stop Crying Wolf, Wolf! 237
Science in the Public Interest, 238
   A Scientific "Supreme Court"? 240
   And Other Courts, 242
The New Corporate Manager, 243
Issue Management—A Case History, 245
   Rationale, 245
   The Management Technique, 245
   Issue Roster, 246

## 14  THE CORPORATION IN A SELF-CORRECTING SOCIETY   251

The Self-Correcting Society, 253
A Personal Postscript, 254

# *Foreword*

During most of 1976, it was my good fortune to serve as Secretary of Commerce, a department whose activities are so diverse as to suggest a governmental conglomerate. Yet there were threads of cohesion running through the departmental fabric, including the broad question of the corporation's role in contemporary American society.

Whether in the context of corporate social responsibility generally, or in numerous more specific issues—the need to eliminate so-called questionable corporate payments abroad, the response of United States business to the Arab boycott of Israel, the cost-benefit analysis of government regulation, and so on—the pattern was clear enough: much more is expected of business today than to develop, produce, and market its products. Business, and I refer chiefly to big business, today is expected to look well beyond its traditional functions and to take into account the impact its activities will have on the environment, the consumer, the health and safety of its employees, and a series of ethical questions which cut across cultural lines.

As Secretary of the department viewed by business as its representatives within the federal government, I frequently met with and appeared before members of this departmental constituency to discuss this trend. I heard their pleas again and again: something has to be done to get government, as well as activist groups of various kinds (the media, the academic community, and labor) off their backs.

Executives of major enterprises expressed a willingness—sometimes even a desire—to "do what is right." "But," they added, "somebody is going to have to tell us what that is." This frustration stemmed from the increasing and often competing demands which government and society today make upon them—demands that they at one and the same time produce the safest possible product, with zero damage to the environment, and that they employ the maximum number of people and sell their product at the lowest possible price.

Business is capable of achieving such goals individually, and perhaps several of them at once. But seldom is it possible to satisfy *all* of these claims at once. Briefly put, business is being whipsawed between competing claims.

How much is it worth to us to eliminate that final five percent of pollutants from an almost-completely-clean river? Should it be done irrespective of the cost, irrespective of the other uses—job creation, improved product quality, a safer working environment—for which the same capital might be applied? These questions need to be answered by society generally, not by business.

A Commerce Department study found that environmental regulations now in effect will increase the aggregate energy consumption of the steel industry by ten percent above what would be required to achieve eighty-five percent of the environmental protection contemplated by the regulations. This increased energy consumption has implications in terms of dependence on foreign oil, and is a contributor itself to increased pollution. Job losses and higher consumer prices are other potential negative results.

Cleaning up the environment is a national goal. So is conserving energy. This is an instance in which the two goals clash, with business caught in the middle.

To what extent should U.S. companies be bound by U.S. customers in their dealings abroad? At what point do regulations become unreasonable, adding more to society's cost than to its benefit? What kinds of products should we allow American business to export to Communist countries?

A corporation has a responsibility to its shareholders, to its bondholders, to its employees, to its customers, and to its community. These responsibilities differ and at times conflict. Where do the priorities lie?

Business leaders seek clear answers to such questions, and often fail to get them because such answers are difficult to give. The vehicle through which these questions must be resolved is our democratic process, which exists to establish guidelines for the trade-offs that most certainly are required. But unfortunately in the debate thus far, there has been a surplus of emotion and a shortage of reason. Self-righteous, simplistic, and ideological harangue has too often been substituted for balanced consideration.

The result has been an increasing polarization, pitting those identified as supporters of the "public interest"—protectors of the environment, consumer, and so on—against backers of "private interests," as if the two were so neatly and simply opposed. In reality, of course, the public interest is of broad dimension, encompassing not only environmental protection but also job creation, not only assuring worker health and safety but also providing goods and services at a reasonable cost.

We are working with limited resources always, cannot do everything at once, and must necessarily balance one set of costs and benefits against another. In short, we must make difficult choices.

Part of the answer is more effective education of the public on the nature of these choices so the people can participate more meaningfully in the democratic process. I sought to make one small contribution to this process while at the Commerce Department by establishing a Secretary's Advisory Council consisting of several dozen leaders of business, labor, education, and consumer groups. The Council met quarterly to debate in open session such topics as corporate social responsibility, regulatory reasonableness, and capital formation.

I was pleasantly surprised at the extent of common ground that existed within such a broadly based group. There was the statement, for example, by Rodney C. Gott, Chairman of the Board of AMF, Inc., summing up much of the discussion on corporate responsibility:

> If you want to be academic, it seems to me that we passed through at least two periods of capitalism. I guess you would call the first "Entrepreneurial Capitalism," in which men were giants, and the second "Managerial Capitalism," in which corporations became giants. We are at the end of that right now and are entering a new phase of capitalism. You can give it all the names you want, but some people call it "Humanistic Capitalism," "Environmental Capitalism," or "Social Capitalism," and I am all for it.

This change is precisely what John Paluszek is writing about in *Will the Corporation Survive?* It is a book which pulls together most of the significant thinking on the subject and presents it in a coherent and balanced fashion. One is struck in reading it by the myriad pressures exerted upon business today which did not exist even a decade or two ago. The fact that there is enough material to fill a lengthy section on contemporary attacks on business is itself significant.

The corporation today is challenged to live by international codes of conduct, to rebuild our decaying cities, to fight unemployment, to clean up the environment, to support the arts, to hold down prices, to provide equal opportunity for employees without discriminating in reverse and without fueling inflation, to disclose information once considered privileged, to defend itself against a multitude of critics, and not incidentally to provide goods and services that are the marvel of the world.

Will the corporation survive? Those who hope so can take some solace in the author's amendment of the original title, which was to be *Can the Corporation Survive?*

The key question, of course, is not simply whether the corporation will survive at all. I assume that it will. The question is in what form it will survive, a question which should be of interest to all Americans, not only those in the business world. For there is a political as well as an economic and sociological aspect to this issue. Yes, business must change to meet changing conditions. Yes, outside pressures on business are here to stay and will likely increase. No, government is not likely to be out of our lives, or those of our businesses, soon.

But as we go about the task of assuring a responsive corporate structure, we must remember that political freedom and economic freedom are intertwined. Only if the corporation survives as an economically free vehicle of capitalism will we be able to maintain our individual liberties.

The corporation, like other structures within our society, is responsive to public opinion. It is becoming more responsive all the time. Perhaps the major contribution of this book is to document that fact.

*Elliot L. Richardson*

# *Acknowledgments*

The author wishes to express his indebtedness to the AMACOM division of American Management Associations for its support in the preparation of the national survey of corporate executives that forms the core of this book, as well as for the permission to use the survey's conclusions in this volume. Dale Tarnowieski was particularly helpful in the execution of the survey and the analysis of its results. David McDermott, then editor-in-chief, was kind enough to secure permission for reuse here.

Equally important, there is no way that a book of this kind can be researched and written by someone maintaining a regular employment schedule without great depths of understanding from those who are closest to him. To my family and to my associates in business, I say thank you for such understanding.

Next, a special note of thanks to James E. Post, Assistant Professor of Management Policy at Boston University, whose numerous suggestions improved the text appreciably.

Finally, I extend my gratitude to the talented workers who transformed a virtually unreadable set of manuscript notes into the handsome volume you now hold: to researcher-typists Patricia Paluszek, Linda Greenberg, and Kathy Pohl; to my editors at Reston/Prentice-Hall; and to the many other good people involved in the design, production, and marketing of this maiden effort.

J.P.

# *The Setting*

# 1

# A Historic Confluence

"We have reason to ask whether the corporation as we know it . . . will survive into the next century." The scene, Detroit, late November 1974. The American economy was under assault by the twin jackhammers of high inflation and high unemployment. It wasn't Ralph Nader speaking. Nor was it any of several dozen radical economists who might well have felt emboldened to announce the collapse of capitalism. It was Reginald H. Jones, chairman and chief executive officer of the General Electric Company. His audience: members of the elite Detroit Economic Club and their guests.

Jones is by no means alone in his concerns about the future of the corporation. In recent years a fast growing list of powerful minds and influential names—among them Robert Heilbroner and Daniel Bell, Barry Commoner and Michael Harrington—have discussed at length what they feel are fatal flaws in the corporate system.

Clearly, the corporation, which touches us all, is under attack as never before.

A historic confluence now threatens the corporation's very existence. Simultaneously, it is under attack because of changing social values, rapidly growing government regulation, environmental degradation and resource depletion, embarrassing revelations of how business has sometimes been conducted both here and abroad, high inflation with high unemployment, public interest groups with new vigor and influence, and powerful consumer media unsympathetic to business.

Some business leaders say, "What else is new? The corporation has been under attack for 100 years. It has experienced dismemberment in the trustbusting era, straight-jacket regulation under the New Deal and constant attack since then. The tinkering never stops."

Undeniably true. But what is being proposed here in the mid-1970s is no mere tinkering with what has been called "the greatest engine of human progress ever developed." The issue now is whether the engine requires an overhaul, or indeed, whether it's time for this society to develop an entirely *new* engine.

This book is written primarily for an "extrabusiness" audience, that is, for students who are still pursuing formal education as well as for those beyond that point in life who simply take knowledge or opinion where they find it. In short, it may well be of interest in academic institutions, but I hope that consumers, environmentalists, and journalists as well as scientists, government regulators, and social critics will all find it worth their time.

The "business" audience? Yes, there may well be some interest there, too, but certainly of a very different kind. Few experienced and well-read business leaders will find this report on how business is reacting to new social pressures "news." There have been hundreds of books and articles on this and related subjects in recent years. But because this book is a *distillation* of much of this information it may also be useful in corporate circles. The business leader may well want to see how his or her firm stacks up against some of the norms I suggest. Too, the catalogue of current social pressures on business that we will present may well contain a few pressures that the business leader has overlooked.

For both types of reader, the message of this book is this: Look carefully at the business community. Something is stirring in the corporation—in the way it relates to people, be they employees, shareholders, customers, or neighbors in the community or in society generally. In many corporations there is under consideration—and, in some, under development—a new ethic, a new way to do business. It now appears that the corporations that survive into the 1980s will not only embrace that ethic but effectively communicate the fact of that embrace.

I confess that I approach the task of writing this book with a bias.

I am a professional communicator. As a former magazine editor, I have worked in the public relations field for 17 years. I believe very strongly in the power of communications. I believe in *planned* communications programs that are carefully reasoned and implemented, and I believe in two-way communication where feedback becomes an element in policy formation. I am not naive enough to believe that all the highly complex problems of this advanced society can be easily solved if people will simply talk to one another. But I do believe that business leaders and critics of business have not been talking nearly frequently enough nor well enough.

I present this caveat because from time to time in this book I will suggest approaches to the corporation's current problems that only a professional communicator *would* suggest. In fact, the central proposition of this book is that the corporation's current plight is largely the result of its inability to relate to its public. The communications problem is not peripheral; it is central. Educators, engineers, lawyers, accountants, scientists, and others may well disagree with my emphasis. So be it.

It seems appropriate at the outset to tour with the reader the borders of this book. The title of this book could easily generate a library of information. So I have carefully circumscribed the area I will cover in this manageable volume.

First, by "corporation" I mean the American corporation based in this country (although it may well have foreign subsidiaries), owned largely by American shareholders, with the bulk of its manufacturing and marketing operations here, and, most important, responsible to the American public and American government agencies. I will from time to time refer to European and other corporate models but only for the sake of comparison.

Two other limitations: I will survey some of the macro-issues of this decade as they have an impact on the corporation, but only in general terms. A few macro-issues not covered—such as competition from planned economies and state enterprises backed by national treasuries—are indeed threats to the survival of the American corporation, but consideration of these would take us well beyond the natural scope of this discussion. I will also present a selection of recent corporate initiatives to illustrate that something indeed is stirring in the corporate evolutionary process; however, I will not bury you with a list of the myriad "social responsibility" programs, large and small, that various corporations have announced in recent years.

You may be interested to know that the original title of this book was *Can* the Corporation Survive? However, after research and reflection, I have concluded that if it moves quickly enough in the right direction, the corporation can indeed survive and even prosper. But *Will* the Corporation Survive? is another question entirely. To try to answer that question, I have attempted to probe the minds of business leaders across the country. How serious, *in their eyes,* is the current assault on the corporation? Can this institution adapt sufficiently and in time? What changes are already underway? What social pressures do they see on the horizon?

The answers have provided a nucleus for this book. For in the final analysis, the answer to the question *Will the Corporation Survive?* rests with business leaders themselves. If these leaders are able to foresee and respond to the demands of a changing society, the corporation will not only survive, it *will* prosper. However, it is surely not enough to ask business leaders what *they* think about the corporation's future in society. So I will report on a wide variety of opinions and events that will ultimately bear on the issue of corporate survival.

I will tell you now that based on all these data, I have concluded that the widely heralded death of the corporation, like the "God is dead" talk of a few years ago, is premature. If the corporation does indeed pass, it will be because American business leaders have underestimated the current threat.

Meeting that threat is a tall order, but it is doable, when we consider how the corporation has already evolved over the decades.

In the theme words of an old "holocaust" novel, "There is still time, brother [sister]." But not much time.

# 2

# Corporate Managers Prophesy

In recent years, just about every kind of social critic—academician, student, journalist, politician, leaders of public interest organizations, and the average citizen—has been heard from on the subject of how corporations should better serve society.

In mid-1975, under the auspices of the American Management Associations, I asked American business leaders across the country what *they* thought about the subject. In the largest known national survey of American business executives on the future of business in our society, we asked corporate presidents to share their opinions with us. The survey generated 644 usable replies (about 13 percent of the questionnaire recipients) from presidents of companies large and small, in manufacturing and in services, in every section of the country.*

One of the most significant findings was how concerned these executives are about the future of the corporation. We asked for their reaction to Reginald Jones's statement, "We have reason to ask whether the corporation as we know it will survive into the next century. . . . The corporation itself must change, consciously evolving into an institution adapted to the new environment."

A little over 68 percent of the respondents agreed with the statement. And as an indication that we had indeed hit a raw nerve, almost

---

* AMA Survey Report, "Business and Society 1976–2000," John Paluszek, New York, N.Y.: American Management Associations, 1976.

all the 439 executives who agreed with the statement added strong words in support of it. Their thoughts provide a cornucopia of business leaders' visions of business in our society in the foreseeable future.

Taken as a whole, the executives who responded to the AMA survey agreed with Jones's analysis of the threats to the private enterprise system, but they were less optimistic about things turning out the way they would prefer. The traditional executive discomfort with the unknown was not far beneath the surface of their replies. Even when they acknowledged the need for corporate reform, they felt uncomfortable with the likelihood of that reform being *imposed* upon them.

Here are selected, typical responses grouped in three categories generally representing large, medium, and small companies.

### LARGE COMPANIES SEE EVOLUTION

Respondents from large companies (5,000 or more employees) appeared confident that the current system can adapt to new and emerging social pressures. Among the dominant thoughts expressed by these respondents:

- The corporation has gone through several basic stages of evolution—the era of trustbusting and the New Deal regulatory period among them—and has adapted successfully as soon as the new ground rules became clear in each case.

- There is a need for legitimization of the "corporate social responsibility" function within American companies in order to anticipate and deal with the diverse social demands on the corporation expected in the years ahead.

- The successful business of the future will be more responsive to the interests of the individual—employee, customer, or neighbor. This emerging corporate philosophy will have significant and widespread implications for management structure, corporate ownership, and board participation.

- Corporations must effectively communicate to the public the burden of rapidly increasing governmental regulation—a burden that is in most cases passed on to the consumer in the form of increased prices.

## What Presidents of Large Companies See as the Future of Business in American Society

(Selected Comments from Respondents in Companies with 5,000 or More Employees)

"I believe that there must be a change in the measurement of performance of a corporation to reflect social responsibility. If this does not occur, the conflicting demands placed on the corporation cannot be balanced by management in an understandable way. If this change in measurement occurs, then corporations will restructure themselves to meet the demands."

President, age 30–39
25,000 + employees
transportation communications company

"I feel that we may move toward broader ownership of the corporation. Also, I am more certain we will see more 'participative management' or more involvement of employees in the decision-making processes of the corporation."

President, age 40–49
25,000 + employees
merchandising: wholesale/retail company

"I tend to agree with Mr. Jones as the phenomenon of change is constant. The corporation of 1975 is not the same as we knew it in 1950 or as we perceive it to be in 2000. Media mobility, affluence . . . a realization that there is a limit on resources . . . the freedom and equity movements of minority groups will continue to influence corporate activity. The corporation of the year 2000 will be more closely monitored by public and private sources. Corporate plans must consider the possibility of slower growth rates. Possibly the most significant 'change' will be the expression of corporate concern for the individual."

President, age 40–49
25,000 + employees
manufacturer of industrial goods

"We expect that the major change in the structure and operation of the corporation will be the formal legitimization of corporate responsibility as a function of the corporate organization. More and more, managers will be picked and evaluated on bases beyond operational competence; they will be expected to exhibit sensitivity to, and problem-solving ability in, public problems."

President, age 60 or over<br>
25,000 + employees<br>
merchandising: wholesale/retail company

"Corporation management must become less arbitrary in the use of its power and more responsive to the concerns of its many publics, including employees and communities in which it functions."

President, age 40–49<br>
10,000–24,999 employees<br>
manufacturer of industrial goods

"My projection: (1) Public interest will play a larger role both in policy-making and operations. (2) The 'social audit,' however defined ultimately, will be a reality. (3) Products will have to demonstrate their social value, as well as their social costs."

President, age 50–59<br>
10,000–24,999 employees<br>
manufacturer of consumer goods

"Coming: Greater public ownership; more group decision-making; more 'freeform,' less hierarchy; more authority based on competence, less authority based on position; greater diffusion of responsibility; more involvement; increased operating interface between corporations and governments (including supranational governments such as EEC, UN)."

President, age 60 or over<br>
10,000–24,999 employees<br>
manufacturer of industrial goods

"While profit maximization must continue for survival, a more social orientation must evolve to help end the social inequities in our communities and to recognize the need to enhance the working environment of our employees to give them a greater feeling of contribution and self-worth."

President, age 50–59<br>
10,000–24,999 employees<br>
finance/real estate insurance company

> "We are drifting into socialistic modes and will have much nationally controlled (by government) industries."
>
> President, age 30–39
> 5,000–9,999 employees
> merchandising: wholesale/retail company
>
> "What's ahead? Professional directors—more ownership by employees—wider decision making in management—more flexibility in jobs and responsibilities—increased visibility of women and minorities in middle and upper management."
>
> President, age 40–49
> 5,000–9,999 employees
> manufacturer of consumer goods

**Figure 2-1**

## ANOTHER VIEW: MORE GOVERNMENT CONTROL

Survey respondents from medium-sized companies (500 to 4,999 employees) also had some distinctive points of view on the emerging business/society interface. Even more than their large-company counterparts, these executives fear the likelihood of creeping—or, worse, galloping—socialism. Many deplore the threat of increasing government regulation and feel that the private enterprise system may disappear in the decades immediately ahead. Some, however, are quite ready to turn this threat into opportunity. There is a readiness among the executives of some medium-sized companies to take the initiative on social pressures to preclude the need for additional government action. Such management, it is thought, will lead the way in broadening employee involvement in decision making and ownership.

However, these respondents also perceive a price to be paid for such a business transformation. This price may well be profits. More than a few respondents in this category refer to "sacrificing some responsiveness to stockholders," the likelihood of more "cooperatives and nonprofit corporations," and depressed standards of return on investment—developments that in themselves could bring on a whole new cycle of attacks on the private enterprise system.

## How Presidents of Medium-Sized Companies Expect the Business/Society Interface to Change

### (Selected Comments from Respondents in Companies with 500 to 4,999 Employees)

"I'm not optimistic about the future of business enterprises. I believe that there will be an increasing trend toward socialization in our country that will eventually turn the business sector into an extension of government."

> President, age 30–39
> 2,500–4,999 employees
> merchandising: wholesale/retail company

"I foresee increasing concern for public policy balancing the interests of shareholders with the broader interests of the society within which we operate."

> President, age 30–39
> 2,500–4,999 employees
> finance/real estate/insurance company

"I would expect the public corporation to turn more and more into a public body [that is] less and less responsible to its stockholders."

> President, age 50–59
> 2,500–4,999 employees
> manufacturer of industrial goods

"The 1976–2000 time period relates to the need for our society and the Western world to learn to live with changing obligations in which performance will be emphasized rather than growth. . . . Perhaps new measures of corporate performance would be appropriate—the question is how does that make stockholders happy?"

> President, age 50–59
> 2,500–4,999 employees
> finance/real estate/insurance company

"The corporation must change the manner in which it is perceived even if this means changing its structure."

> President, age 40–49
> 500–2,499 employees
> manufacturer of industrial goods

"Corporations must resist actions and legislation that increase government controls on them. Frankly, I don't see this happening and really believe that our country will become a socialized welfare state by 2000."

President, age 40–49
500–2,499 employees
business services/consulting firm

"It is my opinion that we will become more and more under government control, and the corporation must, therefore, have a better voice in government to make the controls and guidelines workable instead of having them imposed by some bureaucrat."

President, age 60 or over
500–2,499 employees
finance/real estate/insurance company

"Social responsibility programs can no longer be peripheral. They must be an integrated part of any company objectives if the company is to continue to exist."

President, age under 30
500–2,499 employees
restaurant company

"I forecast policies to (1) bring labor into the management of corporations and (2) place the interest of employees before the interest of owners in major decisions."

President, age 50–59
500–2,499 employees
manufacturer of industrial goods

"Hopefully, we will see more enlightened self-interest on the part of our corporations—leading to recognition of the goals of corporate social responsibility, with actions such as increased employee involvement, including stock offerings, real (not superficial) participative management, and flexibility of the work situation."

President, age 40–49
500–2,499 employees
manufacturer of industrial goods

**Figure 2-2**

## "SMALL" COMPANIES: NEW MOVES TO SATISFY PUBLIC DEMANDS

The survey also produced a large number of comments on the future of the corporation from the presidents of firms with one to 499 employees. As might be expected, opinions vary more in this group than in the first two groups. Although agreeing that socialism, "federalism," and nationalization are to be avoided at all costs, most of the executives of small businesses who responded to the survey nevertheless feel that business must make significant new moves toward satisfying emerging public demands—"as long as the tail doesn't wag the dog," as one of them put it. In addition, they hold these opinions:

- There is a real need for the development of new instruments to better understand public expectations. Until such instruments are developed, business executives may have to rely on government agencies and Congress to convey the *vox populi*.

- Smaller companies, with their flexibility, may be the hope of American business in the future as it tries to adapt to new public demands.

- Greater corporate accountability to the public is virtually assured.

- Consumer groups will continue to grow in influence, and a new government social audit arm—the Internal Social Responsibility Service?—is a distinct possibility.

- More staff people—and therefore higher overhead costs—will be needed to handle the increasing demands of the federal government.

- The corporation will continue its evolutionary course, but perhaps more as a mutant than as a straight-line descendant of its ancestors.

## What Presidents of Small Companies Foresee for the Relationship Between American Business and Society

(Selected Comments from Respondents in Companies with One to 499 Employees)

"At present, the world turmoil, economic and political, including severe dislocations of markets and political institutions, will lead to greater control over corporate activity to force conformance with public goals and national requirements."

> President, age 50–59
> 100–499 employees
> finance/real estate/insurance company

"With present attitudes in many government areas I seriously question whether free enterprise as we have known it can change swiftly enough to survive to 2000."

> President, age 50–59
> 100–499 employees
> merchandising: wholesale/retail company

"We must learn to accept criticism—learn to understand public expectations and satisfy them."

> President, age 50–59
> 100–499 employees
> business services/consulting firm

"Large corporations that exercise control over key resources will move toward being nationalized. Companies that operate in the area of energy, communications, military contracts, foreign trade, etc., will have to serve the public interest more and shareholders less. This will result in small businesses being the only 'free enterprise' left."

> President, age 30–39
> 100–499 employees
> manufacturer of industrial goods

"Consumers will play a major role in the activities of all corporations, primarily through increased social leverage. There will be increased employee involvement in corporate affairs and increased corporate involvement and investment in social activities."

President, age 40–49<br>
100–499 employees<br>
finance/real estate/insurance company

"The corporation must take a leadership position so that it does not seem to be reacting to government or special interest group pressures. The public must be educated to understand the cost of these programs."

President, age 50–59<br>
100–499 employees<br>
merchandising: wholesale/retail company

"The corporation must resist surrendering to all social and regulatory changes brought to bear upon it by well-meaning, but uninformed, zealots. Social responsibility can be integrated into the existing structure, but if the 'tail wags the dog' it is unlikely that most businesses can survive."

President, age 40–49<br>
25–99 employees<br>
educational/nonprofit company

"There will be more government control to the extent that one can even visualize board members being government-appointed—social responsibility representatives and an IRS-type reporting and audit arm of the government solely involved with social responsibility. Maybe with the same initials transposed—Internal Social Responsibility Service."

President, age 40–49<br>
25–99 employees<br>
business services/consulting firm

"Business will become a public sector entirely controlled and supervised by agencies of government, which in turn will be believed to represent the people."

President, age 30–39<br>
25–99 employees<br>
merchandising: wholesale/retail company

"I foresee that (1) larger corporations will have international instead of national allegiances; (2) those that don't will be under increasing pressures to be directed by the state; (3) the influence of employees in the decision-making process will be greater; and (4) there will be greater difficulty in securing capital for new ventures."

> President, age 50–59
> 25–99 employees
> finance/real estate/insurance company

"Just as the lack of foresight by business forced the formation of labor unions at the end of the nineteenth century, lack of foresight will force the formation of strong consumer groups in the next 25 years. These groups will cause corporations to weigh the effects of their products and services on society, as well as the financial effect. Material shortages will force a more reasonable approach to ecology."

> President, age 30–39
> 25–99 employees
> business services/consulting firm

"Corporations are entities created by the state; they may be taken away by the state. Therefore corporations must evolve along the general lines wished by, perhaps, the U.S. House of Representatives, assuming that the American public, though more or less imprecisely, elects people to that body who reflect their current wishes."

> President, age 40–49
> less than 25 employees
> agricultural company

"Nothing short of a complete reversal of most corporate actions will allow the corporation to survive. Corporations will become smaller and weaker or will cease to exist."

> President, age 30–39
> less than 25 employees
> finance/real estate/insurance company

"There must be a general dedication by business, completely within the framework of our capitalistic democracy (including the profit motive) to the total attainment of social justice. Only then can the corporation survive."

> President, age 50–59
> less than 25 employees
> business services/consulting firm

> "I doubt if the superlarge multiindustry corporations (including multinationals) will be permitted by society in the future. Concentrations of power not accountable to the general electorate will be less and less acceptable."
>
> President, age 40–49<br>less than 25 employees<br>business services/consulting firm

**Figure 2-3**

If, as in the old adage, critics of the corporation have been "trying to get the mule's attention by hitting him over the head with a club," they have certainly succeeded in recent years. There is little doubt that corporate executives are now aware of the threat to the corporate system. The survey responses document that awareness, but the responses also hint at a far more significant recent development. Corporate management has begun to stir. New structures, new programs, new commitments are in development or already in place.

Will this be enough to forestall radical surgery?

To begin to answer that question, we must first consider what kind of scapel—some would say dagger—is now pointed at the corporate body.

# The Attack

# 3

# The "Payments" Stain

> "The widespread utilization of illegal payments could represent the most serious challenge ever to confront our competitive free enterprise system."
>
> —John R. Evans
> Commissioner, Security and
> Exchange Commission,
> October, 1976 (1)

Of all the current threats to corporate survival, none is as sensational, serious, and far-reaching as the revelations of "illegalimproperquestionable" political and commercial payments by corporations in this country and abroad. Illegalimproperquestionable is a symbol of the blur that characterizes the entire discussion.

It will be some time before the fallout of these payments can be properly assessed. Nevertheless, it is already possible to see in broad outline just how significant the payments issue has become. To do so, it is necessary to examine a number of ingredients in this complex witches' brew.

Let's look at these fundamental aspects of the payments issue: the nature of the revelations; early results and proposed remedies; and, most significant of all, the likely long-term effect of the payments revelations.

### THE REVELATIONS

We must be precise about several different kinds of corporate payments which, in too many reports, have been lumped together without adequate distinction.

- One type of payment revealed is the *illegal* campaign contribution made in the United States to political candidates.

- Another, very different, type of corporate payment is the *legal* political contribution, usually a *campaign contribution*, made in various countries around the world. These payments—let's call them "general" campaign contributions—are unrelated to specific services.

- Still another kind of payment, also occurring abroad, is that made to a political figure in connection with a *specific service* rendered to the corporation.

- Finally, there are the corporate payments to foreign "agents," well-connected private individuals able to deliver services or contracts deemed valuable to the corporation.

These are by no means insignificant distinctions. For one thing, they present a cardinal point of the discussion: Some corporate payments under attack were *legal*, others were not. Few if any business apologists are defending the *illegal* payments.

Now we move into more murky waters. Critics of the corporate payments contend that many of the payments that were technically legal were improper or questionable. Some even brand such payments immoral.

"This whole destructive episode," writes *Fortune* editor Walter Guzzardi, Jr., "has come about because of a kind of dislocation between our laws and the temper of our times. We are going through a moral seizure, in which any reluctance to disclose everything to an investigative body is immediately equated with a base desire to cover up. An emerging American ethic is judging business to be deficient because it does not adhere to new and sweeping principles of conduct. Those ill-defined principles somehow go beyond the law, and seek to blend in morality and international standards of behavior as well." (2)

Furthermore, Guzzardi might have added, those "new and sweeping principles of conduct" are being applied well after the fact.

Guzzardi's article illustrates just how murky the legal-but-questionable payments matter can get:

> Grohman [Robert Grohman, president of Levi Strauss International] supplies an interesting perspective as he explains some of the general difficulties that his industry confronts abroad. "The general problem in the apparel industry is related to the movement of goods across frontiers," he says. "Fashion clothing may lose its value if it is late. Delays can cost you 80 percent. In the Far East, trucks may not run right. Goods just don't seem to make it onto ships. Shipments fall off cranes. Enforcement around the docks is nonspecific. Maybe you estab-

lished abroad with the help of a local law firm. Then the firm sets up as your representative. You tell them what you are shipping and they represent you to see that things run smoothly. You are properly billed for services rendered. Are you paying a sophisticated bribe instead of a crude one? That is a very hard question to answer."

Others defending such legal payments abroad have raised the questions of whether many such payments represent extortion rather than bribery and the pervasiveness of such practices by foreign corporations. Business critics say these are irrelevancies. "If it's 'wrong,' you just don't do it."

Perhaps it *is* that simple. But the executive on the daily firing line of international trade who must make the subjective judgment of wrongness at least deserves understanding rather than outright condemnation.

It is useful in this regard to distinguish between business ethics in *this* country and the questionable dealings that take place in international trade. In many of the lands where Americans now do business, a free market economy has never existed. "Agents' fees" that *are* bribes are strongly related to the traditions of many of these countries. If business executives are in error in paying such fees, it is not an error that corrupts innocence. If there is guilt in such action, there is enough to be shared—not only with those accepting such payments but quite often with officials of our own government's international trade agencies who know full well about such traditions.

Incidentally, in a recent survey of religious leaders, a major newspaper concluded that business executives seeking guidance on this subject are "unlikely to receive many clear signals from the nation's moral shepherds."

The extortion angle received increasing attention as revelations of the payments wore on. After many months of condemning corporate executives involved in illegalimproperquestionable payments, the *Washington Star* editorialized that the relationship of the Netherlands' Prince Bernard with Lockheed in a payments scandal "illustrates the two sided nature of the shame that must attach to the Lockheed abuses. . . . There are at least two sides to every story of international business corruption." (3)

At about the same time, a *New York Times* "Op-Ed" article by Leonard Silk of the *Times*' editorial board opined that "government officials and legislators who solicit improper corporate payments are at least as culpable as the businessmen who make them. Many businessmen feel that they are more the victims of political shakedowns— and some 150 [later the number of corporations disclosing *questionable* payments grew substantially] corporations have now admitted making illegal political contributions—than voluntary bribers." (4)

This kind of journalistic reexamination of illegalimproperquestionable payments, useful as it is, came too late to forestall a wave of public indignation that has generated both immediate and long-term effects on the American corporation.

### EARLY RESULTS, PROPOSED REMEDIES

Perhaps the most immediate, direct, and dramatic effect of the payments scandal was the wrecked careers of the business executives caught up in this unfortunate series of events. Bob R. Dorsey, ousted chairman of Gulf Oil, reportedly forfeited bonuses and stock options valued at $1.35 million. (5) A number of such executives have admitted that in hindsight the payments were serious mistakes.

With respect to his company's foreign political payments, a leading oil executive has stated publicly: "I don't know of any matter in my 30-odd years with the company that has caused this company more concern and more grief and more sorrow." A top executive of another company that admitted illegal domestic political contributions told shareholders at an annual meeting: "We have paid dearly for this mistake."

A few top executives involved in the payments controversy seem to have weathered it in fine style. For example, Thomas V. Jones, chairman of the Northrop Corporation, who pleaded guilty to charges of having made $150,000 in unlawful contributions to Richard Nixon's 1972 campaign, is as powerful and successful as ever. Company directors who chastised Jones and briefly removed his title say that he has ended whatever bribery existed at Northrop. Others say that his performance outweighed his wrongdoing.

However, according to the *New York Times*, for many executives the price of such involvement was not only fines and the loss of stature or position within their companies, but also being relegated to the status of pariahs within the business community: "Businessmen who have lost high-level jobs at major corporations in the aftermath of bribery and payoff scandals are also being dropped from the boards of directors of other companies. For such executives, the loss of outside directorships—which reinforce their bank accounts and their egos—has been one of the fringe disasters of being caught in the recent spate of payoff scandals." (6)

Of course, these American businessmen were not the only ones to suffer serious personal and career setbacks in the aftermath of the payments scandals. When all is said and done, castles may crumble not only in The Netherlands and Japan but in countries such as Venezuela and Iran, each of which has undertaken investigations of high-ranking officials who have dealt with multinational firms.

The payments revelations have had broader early results as well. For one thing, they have brought to top management's direct attention practices that in some corporations "just growed up" over decades. The furor that has resulted has removed any doubt about the public's view of the propriety of such actions. As a result, a number of major corporations have issued clear-cut policy statements or disseminated to employees newly articulated codes of ethics that in many cases deal not only with the payments question but also with a variety of other business ethics issues. In these companies—including the Bendix Corporation, Celanese Corporation, E.I. duPont de Nemours & Co., and Firstmark Corporation to name a few—management expectations are now on record. At the same time the employee has protection from harassment by superiors if his or her ethical decision works against the company's commercial interest.

Some major companies such as IBM and Texaco, Inc. have had such written guidelines for some time. The Norton Company, which has had such a code since 1963, nevertheless issued an updating memo in light of recent developments.

The Norton memo, signed by Chief Executive Officer Robert Cushman, included these points:

1. In matters relating to company business, employees should place the interests of the company ahead of his or her own personal interests. They should place the interests of society ahead of those of the company.
2. The use of corporate or subsidiary funds or assets for any unlawful or unethical purpose is strictly prohibited. When in doubt, talk to your immediate superior.
3. Although the practice may be lawful in some nations, no funds or assets are to be used for political contributions.
4. No undisclosed or unrecorded fund or asset of the corporation or any subsidiary shall be established for any purpose.
5. No false or artificial entries shall be made in the books or records of the corporation or its subsidiaries for any reason, and no employee shall engage in any arrangement that results in such a prohibited act.
6. No payment on behalf of the corporation or any of its subsidiaries shall be approved or made with the intention or

understanding that any part of such payment is to be used for a purpose other than that described by the documents supporting the payment.

7. Any employee having information or knowledge of any unrecorded fund or asset or any prohibited act shall promptly report such a matter to the chief auditor of the corporation.

8. Employees are prohibited from bribing or causing others to bribe public officials to advance, promote, or expedite company interests. We define a bribe as anything such as money, property, or a favor offered or given to someone to induce that person to act dishonestly or where the size or amount could be considered unusual in relation to the value received.

9. We want our product quality, value, and service to be the means to acquire business. We will not "buy business" by offering users or potential users of our products incentives which might be considered as putting them under obligation or where entertainment or a gift is an amount in excess of levels deductible in determining U.S. income taxes. We are not trying to eliminate the use of tips and gratuities, the practice of which differs from one country to another, but the burden of properly identifying them rests with the donor. (7)

Carl Gerstacker, then chairman of Dow Chemical Company, put much of this in a nutshell when he told an interviewer, "I think honesty is not only good morals and ethics, but it's more profitable. If you pay bribes, the money comes from somewhere." (8)

Another early result of the payments revelations was increased scrutiny of business ethics at many of the nation's graduate and undergraduate business schools where many of the business leaders of the 1980s and 1990s are now being trained. There was no unanimity on the matter. A study of business students at the time of peak interest in the payments issue concluded that there were significant differences in the way such payments were perceived by these students. According to the study, women undergraduates were more concerned with the morality of the payments and more vocal in condemning them. Experienced executives enrolled in advanced management programs were most sympathetic. Night school graduate students and male undergraduates fell somewhere in between.

At about the height of the payments scandal, Donald C. Carroll, dean of the Wharton School at the University of Pennsylvania, told a group of financial writers and editors: "We've heard a great deal during the past year on illegal campaign contributions, inside trading, embezzlement, bribes, kickbacks, cheating on expense accounts and the like. . . . Our feeling is that such misbehavior as we have seen is frequently based on failure of the misbehaver to understand the consequences— the long-run consequences— . . . on society. If we can get across to our students how their organizations interact with this rather complex structure of politics and society, then indeed they will exercise their own values wisely."

Similarly, some business leaders felt it appropriate to comment on payments and ethics in academic settings. In delivering the 1976 "Annual Business Leadership Lecture" at the University of Michigan's Graduate School of Business Administration, Thomas A. Murphy, Chairman of General Motors, offered this analysis:

> You students have a right to demand an explanation, as do thousands upon thousands of business people and business organizations in our country whose reputations have been tarnished unjustly by the actions of a guilty minority. To the extent that violations of law were involved, there can be no excuse—explanations or rationales, perhaps—but no excuse. If the laws are onerous, we should seek their sensible modification or elimination, but we must not violate them—not ever, under no circumstance. If competition includes a contest in illegality, then we must refuse to compete—and I am positive I speak for the great majority of the American business community when I say that.
> 
> . . . But . . . we must recognize that other actions, such as political contributions which are illegal for a corporation in this country, may in another country not only be legal but indeed a respected custom. We must not be so provincial—or so arrogant—as to imagine that our laws in the United States must be binding upon the business community in another country—any more than their laws, if different from ours, should be binding here.
> 
> Obviously, this question of ethics is a many-faceted one. But as a guide, what we as businessmen, and what you as future business people, must understand—if you do not already—is that the good of our company, our stockholders, and our employees is not the supreme good. *As great as our responsibilities as a steward may be, our responsibilities as a moral person are greater.*

Nevertheless, proposals for new regulation of American companies' activity abroad came thick and fast. Fundamentally, they are of two types—increased disclosure of payments and making certain foreign payments illegal under American law.

Increased disclosure of questionable payments is certainly coming. The Securities and Exchange Commission is championing new disclosure procedures as the deterrent to such payments in the future. As to exactly what should be disclosed, there are many suggested approaches. However, it is likely that the traditional disclosure standards of corporate financial statements—*materiality*—can also serve effectively in the matter of payments.

William R. Mette, Jr. and Charles A. Werner, partners in the accounting firm of Alexander Grant & Company, have presented *Business Week* readers with a useful summary of the key aspects of materiality, especially as they might apply to the payments question:

> The basic question for a company to ask is: What is the significance of this payment? Or more simply: Does it matter? Specifically, these are some of the factors that determine materiality in financial statements:
>
> - The direct monetary effect of the act. The American Institute of Certified Public Accountants has suggested that there is a presumption that 5% or more of some appropriate denominator (for instance net earnings) should be treated as material.
> - The contingent monetary effects that might be involved—fines and other damages.
> - Contingent losses. If the acts might lead to expropriation of assets, loss of contracts, or strictures on operations, this would be material.
> - The effect on operations. Are significant amounts of revenues or earnings involved? And does the payment increase or reduce the risks?
> - The extent to which top management is involved. An otherwise trivial act could be material if top management can be blamed for it. (9)

The debate over what corporations should disclose will most likely go on for some time. Unworkable suggestions (such as the proposal for disclosure of all corporate payments over $1,000 that appeared in one Senate bill) as well as unenforceable proposals will undoubtedly crop up whenever the political pot boils.

The pot was boiling, of course, during the 1976 presidential election campaign. Many Democrats argued for direct criminal sanctions while the Republican administration, led by Elliot L. Richardson, chairman of the specially formed Task Force on Questionable Corporate Payments Abroad, supported stricter disclosure and an international agreement. The debate did not end with the presidential campaign.

However, one important new procedure business leaders *will* have to live with is the prohibition of falsification of corporate accounts. It is, after all, one thing to have taken an action that is deemed by some to be unethical but that is not illegal; it is another if the action *is illegal* either in a host country or in the United States. And it is another dimension entirely when, having taken the action, the company conceals it from regulatory agencies.

Other federal agencies have entered the picture. The Internal Revenue Service asks: If corporate bribes at home and abroad were hidden from the SEC, were they also disguised on corporate tax returns as ordinary and necessary business expenses? The Federal Trade Commission staff asks an equally obvious question: Are companies that pay political and commercial bribes to gain competitive advantage engaging in unfair competition that violates antitrust laws?

Potentially the most significant *early* result of the payments scandal is the code of conduct for multinational companies agreed to by the 24 member countries of the Organization for Economic Cooperation and Development. Although the code covers much more than corporate payments, it is widely acknowledged to have come into being as a direct result of the corporate payments controversy. The historic agreement, actually a series of voluntary guidelines subscribed to by the governments of the OECD member nations, nevertheless represents the corporate responsibilities these governments expect their corporations to accept. In return, the governments have agreed to a framework of responsibilities for fair treatment of the multinational companies, granting that as far as possible multinationals will be treated on the same basis as local companies. The code has been praised by such American trade groups as the United States Council of the International Chamber of Commerce and the Emergency Committee for American Trade. If it works, it will be the best thing to come out of the payments scandal.

Here are the parts of the code bearing on the payments question:

## General Policies

Enterprises should . . .

7. Not render—and they should not be solicited or expected to render—any bribe or other improper benefit, direct or indirect, to any public servant or holder of public office;

8. Unless legally permissible, not make contributions to candidates for public office or to political parties or other political organizations;

9. Abstain from any improper involvement in local political activities. (10)

The OECD code applies, of course, only to the 24 Western governments who are members of the organization. Whether it contains the basis for worldwide ethical business standards remains to be seen. The United Nations, through its Centre on Transnational Corporations, is attempting to develop a global code of conduct. In a report to the U.N. Secretariat, the Centre indicated that a draft of such a code may be in hand by the spring of 1978. (11)

## THE LONG-TERM EFFECT

In terms of corporate vulnerability, the payments scandal could not have come at a worse time. As one influential daily, Long Island's *Newsday*, editorialized in mid-1975:

> Right now, opinion polls indicate an erosion of public confidence in business's ability to function as the mainspring of the American economic system. . . . Condoning widespread scandals at a time of 9.2 percent unemployment is like throwing gasoline on an already burning barn: It could consume the free enterprise system. In a democracy like ours, after all, public opinion is always the master in the long run. (12)

The seemingly unending parade of payments accusations and admissions had, after all, reached public attention in the wake of disclosure of entanglement of a number of corporations with surreptitious operations of the Central Intelligence Agency, questionable corporate tax evasion and money-laundering activities through Swiss banks, increasing unease over the domestic and international munitions industry, and corporate involvement in the overthrow of the Chilean government. Former U.S. Ambassador to Chile, Edward Korry, has charged that high U.S. officials urged such corporate involvement in the 1960s.

In addition, in the same period the American public had been exposed to charges of grain shipment frauds, charges of laxity by a leading accounting firm in audits conducted for a half-dozen major corporations, and charges that a leading automobile manufacturer ordered wholesale firings in one of its regional sales organizations as a result of "years of improper relationships with auto component suppliers."

And as these headlines began to fade just a bit, still another kind of payments scandal was beginning to make news—interindustry kickbacks. The SEC began an investigation of several industries including the nation's breweries and construction companies allegedly involved in rakeoffs, rebates, and other forms of commercial bribery. (In 1974, the

U.S. Chamber of Commerce had estimated that such illegal payments probably totaled some $3 billion annually.)

What would the American people make of all this? How long would it be before the stain would fade? To what advantage would corporate critics put all these revelations?

It didn't take long to find out.

An unprecedented wave of stockholder suits against companies involved in illegal, questionable, or improper payments were filed in short order. By early 1976 the Gulf Oil Company had been sued by nine shareholders, Exxon Corporation by three (Exxon, incidentally, has announced that it will no longer make political contributions even where legal), and a number of other companies by one or two. Nor was money the only thing sought by the plaintiffs. Far more important, many of the suits were filed to effect significant structural changes in the corporations under fire.

John R. Phillips of the Center for Law in the Public Interest, which was instrumental in getting the Northrop Corporation and the Phillips Petroleum Company to agree to such structural changes, was quoted by the *New York Times* to this effect:

> The traditional legal remedy for corporate misbehavior is to sue for money damages. We're doing something far more drastic. We're asking for structural reforms. We're getting a lot of requests from lawyers all over the country asking for the settlement documents in the Northrop and Phillips cases. That's why we filed the cases. We wanted to create a model. (13)

The legal grounds for the suits included alleged false and misleading proxy materials "which omitted to state material facts," the maintenance of phony and off-the-books accounts, breach of fiduciary duty, and waste of corporate assets.

Predictably, Ralph Nader was in the fray early and often. With his colleague Mark Green, he wrote a *Wall Street Journal* "think piece" that used the payments scandal as a launching pad for a particularly vituperative attack on American business: "Not perhaps since the robber baron era, and certainly not since the 1930s . . . has America witnessed such an epidemic of corporate corruption." (14)

Nader then proceeded to lay out a course of proposed action to "help ensure that the potential costs of corporate crime outweigh its perceived benefits." The proposals included a Justice Department Division on Corporate Crime; five-year disqualification of officers, directors or partners convicted of willful corporate-related violations; a full-time board of "outside" directors (persons with no connections with the companies); removal of company indemnification of executives pleading *nolo contendere* in criminal suits or found liable in civil lawsuits; and regularly issued federal compliance reports listing, among other things, company violations and the corrective action required and taken. In October 1976 the Justice Department in cooperation with the Securities and Exchange Commission formed a special task force to press criminal charges in corporate bribery cases.

The *Wall Street Journal*, for its part, drew the attention of its readers to the Nader-Green piece by editorializing that "We are happy to have Mr. Nader and his colleague Mark Green discuss the problem of corporate ethics in our columns today." (15) It added, "We would like to add one count they have somehow overlooked. Bribery is an assault on the price mechanism that produces an uneconomic allocation of resources."

Finally, in terms of assessing the long-term impact of the corporate nightmare the payments scandals represent, one need only consider the corporate structural reforms put in place since the scandal erupted. Although we will look at such reforms in greater depth in a later chapter, the following observations belong here.

A few years ago, when Arthur Goldberg was a director of Trans-World Airlines, he insisted that the only way he, as a nonmanagement director, could assess whether the company was meeting its social obligations as well as its financial obligations was to have a staff to study and report on all corporate affairs bearing on the question. His advocacy of this interpretation of the outside director was so strong—and so completely unacceptable to the TWA board—that he resigned.

For several years, the concept of the outside director went virtually nowhere. However, in the wake of the payments scandal, one company, Phillips Petroleum, now has a board with a majority of outside directors. And more outside directors and strengthened audit committees appear to be in the wings in many major corporations.

Item—John J. McCloy, writing "On Corporate Payoffs" in a recent issue of the *Harvard Business Review*:

> Many companies are strengthening the staffs of the internal audit function not only in numbers but also in professional expertise. In one company, for example, where disclosure of illegal business activities during the past two years embarrassed the CEO and the board, the head of internal audit was made a corporate vice president who is to report to the chairman of the board. His staff of accountants was augmented with lawyers and former FBI agents. The job function of internal audit was enlarged to include the detection of fraud and other illegal activities. (16)

Item—The New York Stock Exchange, in the late summer of 1976, circulated a proposal to its members that would require all listed companies to establish audit committees dominated by outside directors to check the corporate books to prevent, among other things, repetition of illegal, questionable, or improper payments. An exchange researcher indicated at the time of the proposal that a sampling of the 1,500 firms listed on the exchange indicated that 966 already fulfilled the requirement of the proposal.

## THE PRACTICAL AND THE PHILOSOPHICAL

What then is the net-net after this sorry experience for the American business community? Perhaps it can be stated on two levels—the practical and the philosophical.

On the practical level, like it or not, American business leaders are now operating in a new environment. New values have coalesced and are being applied to those leaders' decisions and actions. They must consider a standard for determining the "right" thing to do in many ethically fuzzy areas. Perhaps the most workable standard in this age of disclosure—voluntary and involuntary—is, "Would you do it if you knew it would be on page one of tomorrow morning's newspaper?" Increasingly, the chances are that it just might be there the next day.

But critics of business must also be practical. They must comprehend that a management with the best intentions has control over headquarters staff, domestic operations, and wholly-owned subsidiaries. It has less control over joint ventures, distributors, dealers, licensees, and agents.

On the philosophical level, we present this offering to the business community from a recent *New York Times* editorial:

> Business needs to help create a social climate in which it can perform effectively with the trust and understanding of the community—not one in which it is able to have its way on every specific issue in which it has a direct interest. Obviously, business's perspective and goals will not always coincide with those of other groups and business has every right to present its own views clearly and forcefully; but business can win public trust only if it recognizes that other social interests are as legitimate and proper as its own and if it takes account of the broader public interest in reaching its own decisions. (17)

Finally, commentary from one of America's most respected industrialists, J. Irwin Miller, chairman of Cummins Engine Company:

> A complex, interacting, interdependent world such as ours is today cannot function without a considerable amount of restraint on the part of each member of each group. When individual businesses will not restrain themselves voluntarily in the public

interest, restraints will inevitably be imposed upon all business by law. . . .

Our performance will have to be beyond reproach even to be perceived as being merely acceptable. (18)

## REFERENCES

1. *New York Times*, October 6, 1976.
2. Guzzardi, Walter Jr. "An Unscandalized View of Those 'Bribes' Abroad," *Fortune*, July 1976, pp. 118–182.
3. *Washington Star*, September 1, 1976.
4. *New York Times*, August 31, 1976.
5. *New York Times*, September 30, 1976.
6. *New York Times*, May 6, 1976.
7. Cushman, Robert. "The Norton Company Faces the Payoffs Problem," *Harvard Business Review*, September–October, 1976, p. 7.
8. "Why Dow is Rated One of the World's Best-Managed Corporations," *The Environment Monthly*, May, 1976, p. 12.
9. Mette, William R. Jr., and Werner, Charles A. "Stopping Illegal Corporate Payments," *Business Week*, July 26, 1976, p. 19.
10. "Excerpts from OECD Text on Conduct Code," *New York Times*, May 27, 1976.
11. "Transnational Corporations: Issues Involved in the Formulation of a Code of Conduct," New York, N.Y.: Centre on Transnational Corporations, United Nations, p. 4.
12. *Newsday*, October 3, 1975.
13. "Stockholders Versus Payoffs," *New York Times*, March 14, 1976.
14. "What to Do About Corporate Corruption," *Wall Street Journal*, March 12, 1976.
15. "Mr. Nader and Mr. Insull," *Wall Street Journal*, March 12, 1976.
16. McCloy, John J. "On Corporate Payoffs," *Harvard Business Review*, July–August, 1976, pp. 14–160.
17. "The New Integrity," *New York Times*, April 26, 1976.
18. "The Greer/Kandel Report," *Newsday*, February 6, 1977.

# 4

# The New Values Pool

> "The deepest challenge comes from a basic shift in the values and beliefs that undergird our society. . . . Increasingly, Americans distrust the market system and demand that government step in to assure them of economic benefits."
>
> —Reginald Jones,
> Chairman of the Board and
> Chief Executive Officer,
> General Electric Company (1)

American values are changing—rapidly.

Within that simple statement resides the core of the threat—and, yes, the opportunity—now facing the American corporation.

In our survey of American businessmen, one of the more revealing things they told us is that they cannot seem to be sure who really speaks for Americans today. Is it elected officials only? Is it the media? Do the public interest groups really have a significant constituency and a mandate to represent that constituency? In short, what does the American public want of business?

In fact, the AMA survey concluded that the issue of "What is expected of us?" is the greatest problem American business leaders face in meeting their social responsibilities. And it is not simply a matter of determining what mainstream values are today. What will be the predominant values of five, ten, and twenty-five years from now?

There are, of course, many people ready to offer opinions on where American values are heading. It will be helpful to discuss *sociopolitical* values first and then *personal* values.

One point of view on the change in sociopolitical values has come from the distinguished journalist J. F. ter Horst:

> There is a radicalism abroad in America these days that is reminiscent of the spirit of revolution that gave birth to the Declara-

tion of Independence. . . . It is not a call to arms, but it is definitely a call for change in society and government. Everywhere we look, our venerated institutions are under attack for lack of performance or for poor performance—our family structure, the churches, our schools, the corporate and financial structure, the government at every level. And these attacks are not coming from the usual quarters, the political extremists on the left or right, but more significantly from the long-suffering, basically unpolitical middle group in America. When radicalism is defined as advocating a break with established ways and traditions, then there are more radicals among us today than at any time since the nation's birth. What we are experiencing is a national frustration with our past efforts to achieve America's exalted purpose—life, liberty and the pursuit of happiness. . . . The goal is nothing less than to recapture the country from big government, big business, and Big Brother. . . . There is a certain naïveté about such radicalism. It may be no more practical than the radicalism of the "new right," but that's what the Tories also said about the band of radicals who signed the Declaration of Independence and whom we now call Founding Fathers. (2)

Some will say that ter Horst's observations on the spread of the radical ethic in America are a few years late. After all, the campuses are relatively calm as most students contend for places in the system and not for choice spots on the barricades from which to attack it. A 1975–76 study of college students' attitudes sponsored by the Carnegie Council on Policy Studies in Higher Education concluded that, compared with results of a similar study in 1969, students had become much more moderate on academic policy, race relations, and the use of violence to achieve political goals. The civil and human rights organizations seem somehow less visible than they were just a few years ago. Environmentalist and consumerist public interest groups have largely moved out of the street and into the courtroom (and, many say, with much more effect).

There is, of course, a long if uneven radical tradition in the United States. In spurts and pauses, we have produced the original Revolutionists themselves followed by the abolitionists, the organizers of American labor, the suffragettes, and the war protesters of the sixties—each group radical in its time but representing values now widely accepted as mainstream.

A parenthetical word about the American Revolutionists: There is a point of view, most recently expressed editorially by *Fortune* magazine, that the "radicalism" of the Founding Fathers is commonly overstated or misunderstood:

> When the Declaration as a whole is viewed in context, in the light of what led up to it, the impression of radicalism fades away. . . .
> For them, the object of their revolution . . . was to change the government, not to transform society. . . . As historian Edmund Morgan observes, the American Revolution began "as a dispute over the security of property." That was the gut issue in the prolonged and intricate quarrel concerning the British government's efforts to tax the colonists.
> . . . In our time, we are accustomed to specious playing-off of "human rights" versus "property rights." The distinction would have made no sense at all to Americans two hundred years ago. To them, property rights were human rights—fundamental human rights. (3)

Whether or not the Founding Fathers should be thought of as radicals, there seems to be reason to believe that there is a gradual increase in interest in and commitment to radical political philosophy among Americans. Radicals themselves say this is so. According to some of its leaders, the radicalism of the 1960s is simply in hibernation. Rennie Davis has stated, "This generation [of radicals] is completely hidden, like a Trojan Horse, in this country. We are now in every aspect of every institution. . . . It wouldn't take much to pull it all together." Kirkpatrick Sale estimates that there are now 2 to 3 million Americans who call themselves radical for life. Other radical leaders such as Tom Hayden feel that "the radicalism of the sixties is the common sense of the seventies." (Hayden, aided by his wife Jane Fonda, ran a vigorous but unsuccessful campaign for the Democratic nomination for the U.S. Senate in 1976; it is hard to imagine the Tom Hayden of the 1960s participating in the system as a candidate for electoral office seeking, as he did, the nomination of one of the two major parties and receiving considerable support within it. David Harris, another famous "radical" of the 1960s, received the Democratic nomination for Congress in California but was defeated in his attempt to unseat Congressman McCloskey.)

Some may think of the current process in terms of Hegelian thesis-antithesis producing a new synthesis, in this case, a more leftward synthesis. If we are witnessing so fundamental a process, Louis Banks may have presented us with a revealing snapshot of this historic flow. Banks, who is Thomas Henry Carroll Ford Foundation Visiting Professor in the Graduate School of Business Administration at Harvard University, recently wrote in du Pont's *Context* magazine:

> I have asked three succeeding groups of second-year Harvard Business school students—many of them mortgaged to the

hilt to be corporate leaders themselves—to relate this role [of powerful executive in a highly profitable multinational company] to their expectations. The one consistent theme of response is that they put higher premium on their individual values than on "making it" in corporation terms that conflict with those values.

. . . A theme from one . . . [who is] conservative in general outlook: "I feel that a company must be positioned within two dynamic continuums: social demands and company operating demands, and there must be a continual re-evaluation of the fit. When the fit has become static and non-responsive, my association with the company will become a personal embarrassment, and my performance and loyalty will also start to shake." (4)

Even more illuminating is a report from the legal profession that young lawyers are looking askance at the corporation. An article in a recent issue of *Juris Doctor—The Magazine for the New Lawyers* reported on a survey of its readers. (5) Of 1,250 respondents, "46 percent think corporation profits are too high . . . and half . . . think that many of the largest companies ought to be broken up for the good of the nation."

One of the interesting manifestations of the changing sociopolitical values is the growth of what might be called "alternative media," especially print media. Many publications generated by the social strife of the 1960s have not only survived that era but prospered. Dozens of "alternative" periodicals—the number depends on your standard for *mainstream* media—are published in this country, mainly in weekly newspaper format.

*Rolling Stone*, largely a product of the Vietnam era, might perhaps be considered a granddaddy of many such publications. Today, with its millions of readers, great financial success, and less controversial content, it may be considered more mainstream than alternative. In its wake have come new publications such as the national magazine *New Times*, founded in 1973 and reporting a circulation of over 300,000. A few interesting statistics on *New Times*: Readers' median age is 29. Some 86 percent of the subscribers have been to college. And corporate America is beating a path to the *New Times* advertising pages; in 1976 the magazine had the second best ad page percentage increase in magazine publishing (*New Times* was also the downfall of Earl Butz). In this era of fractionation of print media, with audiences being more precisely identified, the interests and values of a more leftward-leaning generation are being served by a sizable editorial capability—which, not incidentally, is being run for the most part *for profit*. Perhaps the ultimate in this field was reached in late 1976 with the announcement that *You*, a new national monthly, would begin publication in early 1977.

*You*, according to its publisher, will be published for those many people in their twenties and thirties "who are tired of the Great American Dream and want to live life their own way."

Let's look at how such changing sociopolitical values can affect an industry. Perhaps the most dramatic example is the current debate over the American arms industry. (During the 1976 presidential campaign Senator Mondale suggested that this country, "once the arsenal of democracy," could simply become "the arsenal" unless we rethought our position on selling arms to the rest of the world.)

There is a lot at stake in this discussion. The United States is said to have sold almost $10 billion in arms in 1975, accounting for about 7 percent of our exports and generating some 350,000 jobs. The fortunes of some very large companies, such as McDonnell Douglas, Grumman, Lockheed, Northrop and their suppliers, are directly dependent on the arms trade.

The public debate in America on the morality of the arms trade is largely the result of the changing values we have been discussing. Some younger critics of the international arms trade, who also criticize American defense expenditures, were, after all, born after World War II and the Korean War. They, more than their elders, have read "revisionist" historians. For many, their only personal experience with an American military action was the nationally debilitating Vietnam conflict. Their attitudes, like all of ours, are largely conditioned by the point at which they entered the theater of life.

Young or old, the critics of the arms trade make some powerful arguments. A Senate Foreign Relations Committee recently warned that the nation's military sale program is "out of control." Others ask, in effect, whether we can be a champion of world peace and at the same time a leading supplier of weapons of war. And there is the threat of direct involvement in other nations' conflicts because many of the United States weapons sold abroad require American training and support staffs. The discussion is complex, involving as it does our balance of payments, foreign policy, and national security.

The point is that it is a discussion that would not have occurred as recently as 15 years ago. And it is a discussion based largely on emerging values that has tremendous potential impact on a significant segment of the American corporate world and all that it touches.

A personal example of changing values: fifty years ago, my father came to this country from Poland. Like most immigrants, he saw the United States as his best hope not only for a higher standard of living but also for a set of values and freedoms unavailable anywhere else in the world. He worked hard, moved upward into the American middle class, and was able to build an economic base from which his children might climb. In turn, with lucky breaks and some diligence, I have been able to rise a few steps higher on the American economic ladder. If my patriotism is not as idealistic as my father's, it is real nevertheless. I recognize both this country's achievements and its shortcomings.

I have a son who feels quite differently about the American society. A foreign policy that in any way seeks to influence the fortunes of another nation appalls him. The prospect of affluence holds little appeal for him. He sees racial injustice and says it should not be. He sees poverty and pollution and political and commercial corruption and says they should be eliminated. He is right. His social values are good. But he cannot possibly know how far we have come, just as I cannot fully appreciate the distance between Poland and the United States in the 1920s.

Perhaps most significant of all, the arms issue is an illustration of an increasingly held central value that *all* business leaders will have to deal with: Timothy Traverse-Healy, a British public relations counselor, recently suggested that we are seeing the application of the "Nuremberg Rule—the individual's ultimate responsibility for his own actions and indeed inactions" in a corporate situation.

George Cabot Lodge of the Harvard School of Business has written a seminal book on the subject of changing American values. In *The New American Ideology*, he argues that the traditional ideology of free enterprise is disintegrating and the transition to a new creed is putting great stress on American institutions. (6) The new ideology, Lodge suggests, will be based on these elements: "communitarianism" (succeeding individualism); subordination of property rights to rights of survival, health, and other basic needs; reduced competition in the interest of better service to the community; state planning of goals; and belief in the interdependence of all things.

Furthermore, Lodge and William F. Martin conducted a survey of readers of *Harvard Business Review* to determine whether those readers believed that emerging values of the kind described in *The New American Ideology* would dominate in 1985. The authors described the survey and results in the *Harvard Business Review* itself:

> The poll focused on two opposing ideologies: readers were asked to determine which one they (1) prefer, (2) find dominant in the United States today, (3) expect to dominate in 1985, and (4) believe would be more effective in solving future problems.
>
> The first ideology [Ideology I] enunciated by philosopher John Locke 300 years ago is the nucleus of the traditional "American way" extolling the values of individualism, private

property, free competition in an open marketplace and limited government. . . .

The second ideology [Ideology II] defines the individual as an inseparable part of a community in which his rights and duties are determined by the needs of the common good. Government plays an important role as the planner and implementer of community needs. (7)

The conclusions: not surprisingly, the *Harvard Business Review* readers strongly preferred the "traditional American way" ideology, found it dominant in the United States today, and believed it to be more effective in solving future problems.

However, almost three-quarters of the respondents—73 percent—anticipate that Ideology II will dominate in 1985. And in this connection, Cabot and Martin report that:

Many readers think that the transformation from Ideology I to II could lead to social disaster, with burdensome government interference causing the disintegration of business and loss of personal freedom. A minority accept the change with cautious optimism, acknowledging that many perplexing problems—including resource shortages, explosive population growth, and environmental degradation—can be resolved only within the framework of Ideology II.

In our potpourri of current value systems, let us now also include a point of view not often reported even in this era of ubiquitous media —the view of a self-styled "conservative black." Thomas Sowell is his name. A fellow at the Center for Advanced Study in the Behavioral Sciences, Stanford, California, Sowell recently offered these opinions on the current American scene:

Once it is realized that "liberal" and "conservative" are simply arbitrary designations for opposing political teams . . . we can turn to the substance of the issues between them. . . . A so-called "conservative" is nothing more than a dissenter from the prevailing liberal orthodoxy. A "radical" would simply be someone who carries the liberal orthodoxy to further extremes. . . .

Why would a black man dissent from the prevailing liberal orthodoxy, and especially on such radical issues as busing, "affirmative action" and the like? The question itself shows how pervasively the mass media have stereotyped and filtered the news. Most black people oppose busing. . . . The really crucial assumption behind involuntary busing is that some tangible benefit will result. . . . The hard evidence does not support any of these assumptions. . . . There is very little hard evidence that "affirmative action" has that net [beneficial] effect. . . .

> To be blunt, the poor are a gold mine. By the time they are studied, advised, experimented with, and administered, the poor have helped many a middle-class liberal to achieve affluence with government money. . . .
> How unusual is a so-called "black conservative"? Not very. . . . the great majority of blacks considered this country worth defending against foreign enemies and rejected violence as a means of achieving social change. A Gallup poll found that a substantial number of blacks regard the courts as too lenient on criminals. Still another survey found that more than three-quarters of the blacks describe themselves as "sick and tired" of hearing attacks on "traditional American values."
> So being a "black conservative" is not quite as distinctive as it might seem. (8)

What are the new *personal* values from which the sociopolitical Ideology II or its variants may spring?

An intriguing analysis of what may be the dominant personal value system before long has been offered by Tom Wolfe in "The ME Decade" in *New York* magazine. Wolfe uses religious terms, contending that we are now seeing "the upward roll (and not yet the crest) of the third great religious wave in American history." (9)

(For the curious, Wolfe's first wave was the great awakening of the 1740s led by New Light preachers such as Jonathan Edwards, and the second was the great awakening during the period between 1825 and 1850 characterized by "hoedown camp-meeting revivalism.")

Wolfe does not agree with the journalists who regard the new value systems as collectivist. Rather, he says, the current wave

> . . . begins with "Let's talk about Me." They begin with the most delicious look inward; with considerable narcissism, in short. . . . Whatever the Third Great Awakening amounts to, for better or for worse, will have to do with the unprecedented post-World War II American development: the luxury, enjoyed by so many millions of middling folk, of dwelling upon self. . . . the notion of "If I've only one life" challenges one of those assumptions of society that are so deep-rooted and ancient, they have no name—they are simply lived by. In this case: man's age-old belief in serial immortality.
> . . . Once the dreary little bastards started getting money in the 1940s, they did an astonishing thing—they took their money and ran. They did something only aristocrats (and intellectuals and artists) are supposed to do—they discovered and started doting on *Me!* They've created the greatest age of individualism in American history! All rules are broken! The prophets are out of business! Where the Third Great Awakening

will lead—who can presume to say? One only knows that great religious waves have a momentum all their own. Neither arguments nor policies nor acts of the legislature have been any match for them in the past. And this one has the mightiest, the holiest, rule of all, the beat that goes . . . Me . . . Me . . . Me. (9)

(While we're on the subject of self-gratification, note the appeal of *instant* gratification among Americans as demonstrated by the immediate and widespread popularity of those state lotteries introduced in recent years that offer "instant" identification of winners and losers.)

At first glance, Wolfe's heralding of the "greatest age of individualism" is in stark contrast to Lodge's prediction of a coming collectivism. What is more important, however, is that they have both identified a new supercommitment to improvement in the quality of life.

Let's use a familiar and, it is hoped, not obsolete social microcosm, the family unit, to illustrate. Generally, young adults in America are getting married later in life. If they have children at all, they are delaying the arrival of the first child and limiting the number of their children to two or three. The number of mothers who go out to work—to help support the family and/or for self-fulfillment—is increasing rapidly. In 1940 the United States had 3 million two-income families. In 1974 it had almost 19 million two-income families. All this is certainly connected with the desire for a better life and the increasing possibility of achieving it. If that family unit is itself moving toward such a standard, will it not demand that social obstacles—faulty products, befouled environment, injustices such as limited opportunity for women and minorities—be eliminated?

We may be seeing a new manifestation of a particularly American genius—the ability to combine idealism and materialism. What to call it? Idealistic Materialism? Materialistic Idealism?

Is the young American adult an unalloyed threat to business? Not at all.

I present to you Genevieve Atwood, 28, geologist for Ford, Bacon and Davis in Utah (as she is described in a recent *Scientific American* advertisement):

> Ms. Atwood, corporate geologist: "If the social benefit is there, we should exploit our resources. People think reclamation means simply making it all green again. But it's more subtle than that. If the hydrological conditions are stabilized, and the soil characteristics restored, the green will come and will stick. So why not mine it? It's a lot safer than underground mining."

Ms. Atwood, state legislator and women's rights advocate: "I decided to put my life to the 'fun test' and running for office came out on top. So I ran and won. I was surprised but not so surprised as my opponent. I don't mean to give the impression that politics is simply a lark. It may have started out that way but even the first campaign was straight 12-hour days. . . . one of my constituents said she opposed the ERA because the women who want it are trying to get away from children they can't stand. But then she made my day by saying to her daughter 'someday you could be a state representative, too.'" (10)

The corporate leaders who will survive and succeed in the next decade are already evaluating the entire American demographic mix of the 1980s. That mix is already apparent: More babies (with many more people entering the potential-parent stage, a new baby boom is likely even assuming zero population growth); fewer teenagers; fewer middle-aged citizens; and many more oldsters than today. What will be the value pool across this demographic spectrum? No one can say for sure, but one thing is certain—*"quality of life" in the here and now* will be a common denominator as never before.

There are those who are troubled by what they see as emerging values. William V. Shannon, the *New York Times* columnist, hardly a conservative, may have spoken for many such concerned observers when he recently wrote:

. . . Many conscientious parents are genuinely concerned whether [when sending their children to school] they may be delivering their children into enemy territory. Their concern is . . . the values and opinions, the tastes and expectations . . . quite different from those that loving parents try to inculcate. They comprise what may be called the "new sophistication."

These newer values arise from the adult society, are diffused through movies, records and magazines and enforced among older children and adolescents by peer group pressure. . . . The new sophistication involves introducing children at even younger ages to marijuana, hard drugs, alcohol and sexual experience. . . . The distinctive theme of this new sophistication is absence of restraint. (11)

There is more trouble in the emerging American paradise: we now have reason to believe that many Americans have "tuned out," "signed off," and dropped out of the American political system. As the 1976 presidential campaign began, a national poll by Peter D. Hart Research Associates made headlines by concluding that for the first time in American history, a majority of eligible voters—registered and unregistered—would not vote in that election. In November, a late rush of interest resulted in a turnout of about 54 percent of the eligible voters, above the level predicted by many experts, but the lowest percentage since 1948.

The nonvoting American public has traditionally been composed of the poorer, relatively unschooled citizen, but the Hart survey indicated that in 1976 the ranks of nonvoters was swelled by a significant number of middle-class voters who were purposely dropping out. The main reasons given: "candidates say one thing and do another"; "it doesn't make any difference who is elected because things never work right"; and "I just don't bother with politics."

Perhaps most significant of all, nonvoting inclinations are notably high among post-World War II voters who came of age in an era of protest and seem to feel that nonparticipation in politics is reasonable.

This political fatalism is dangerously similar to the attitude of citizens in the Russian collectivist society, as described by Hedrick Smith in *The Russians:*

> For the common man, politics and the power of the leaders are like the natural elements. No ordinary mortal—worker, peasant, intellectual, Party member—dreams of doing anything about them. They are simply a given fact, irresistible and immutable.

And, again:

> I remember listening to a Russian who . . . told me of his astonishment at the earnest idealism of American delegates [to an international congress]. "They take it so seriously," he said. "They really believe that they can do something about bringing peace and influencing political leaders. And we are so cynical—nothing will happen, nothing will change . . . what I mean is that they think they can actually affect politics. Are all Americans like that?" (12)

Apparently not.

Vietnam and Watergate still weigh heavily on the American psyche. Two sentences in C. D. B. Bryan's recent book, *Friendly Fire,* recounting the new attitude of an American family that lost a son in Vietnam are particularly relevant to the national mood:

> The Mullens' surviving son and daughters would never possess so naïve a confidence in this nation's purpose or its leaders. This, in a very real sense, is as great a tragedy as the loss of a son. (13).

But Bryan goes much further in assessing the damage of that tragic involvement:

> The intensity of their [the Mullens] indignation wasn't all that overwhelmed me. I was astonished, too, by the seemingly inexhaustible volume of sources that outrage fed upon. Local school board elections, telephone company stock manipulations, draft inequities, Nixon's Vietnamization policies, farm subsidy programs, the voting records of incumbent congressmen and senators, the machinations of the military-industrial complex, each seemed to contribute to some consummate proof of a conspiracy on the part of the United States government deliberately to deceive and defraud Mr. and Mrs. Oscar Eugene Mullen of La Porte City, Iowa. (13)

Intentionally or not, Bryan was writing about a sizable segment of the American public in the early 1970s.

And yet it may be that we are experiencing only a *temporary* national loss of self-confidence. The Bicentennial was an opportunity for national celebration, and it did have a cauterizing effect on many such wounds. But doubts linger.

The nonbusiness reader may be surprised to learn of the personal value osmosis taking place at the membrane between business and society. We will treat the coming metamorphosis of the *corporation* at some length in later chapters. Here, let's take a few quick glimpses of changing *individual* values and lifestyles in the corporation.

David Whitsett, a psychology teacher at the University of Northern Iowa, says that a new breed of employee, one that reflects a basic shift in our value system, has emerged in recent years. Whitsett, who presented his views at a 1976 Annual Personnel Conference of the American Management Association, says that the new breed of employee has an increased concern for the quality of day-to-day existence. "If employees continue to evolve in these directions and employers are unable to respond, the consequences are enormous. Our organizations will suffer further losses in productivity and the psychological consequences to the employees involved will have devastating impact." (14)

Not surprisingly, Whitsett says that these emerging value changes have been most evident among young employees. He concludes that the traditional value of judging things by results—a deeply entrenched American business value—is now in a state of flux. It is being replaced in part by a value associated with judging things, activities, and relationships by the amount of personal enrichment involved.

As a result of these value changes, it appears that workers—and indeed, managers—are becoming more loyal to their professions and less loyal to their employers. Arch Patton, chairman of a recent Presidential Commission on Executive, Legislative and Judicial Salaries and an experienced observer of executive style and substance, has written:

> One of the seldom-recognized by-products of the great industrial boom of the fifties and sixties was a devastating decline in the loyalty of an executive to his company. [Earlier] the "company interest" was accepted virtually without question. If a sales manager had to uproot his family . . . seven times in 10 years . . . the company need . . . far outweighed the effect of the moves on the executive's family. . . .
>
> [Now] many once-accepted "inconveniences" of corporate life are being reexamined as executives question company decisions in the light of their own interest. (15)

Patton sees an increasing likelihood of middle management unions formed by younger executives to protect against imposition of such inconveniences as well as for job security.

If that prospect would make some deceased captains of industry do a few pirouettes in their graves, consider how they might react to this recent development in the executive suite. According to *Business Week*, a variety of methods for coping with personal stress that a few years ago most business leaders would have labeled "for hippies only" are now increasingly popular at the office. "There is no doubt," *Business Week* reports, "that the new methods have been taking hold. Transcendental Meditation, or TM, was first brought to the United States 17 years ago by the Indian teacher Maharishi Mahesh Yogi. Only 200 Americans were trained before 1965. Today some 800,000 Americans have taken the official course in TM and as many as 30,000 people are signing up each month. Many are executives." (16)

Not far behind TM in executive favor, *Business Week* says, are yoga, encounter groups, transactional analysis, est (Erhard seminars training), biofeedback, and, yes, behavior modification.

If that's what is going on with establishment executives, what are the younger execs, the campus "enfant terribles" of the 1960s who nevertheless joined the corporate world, up to?

Again, *Business Week* may have the answer:

> What ever happened to the "radical college students" of the late 1960s? They turned out to be the best thing that has happened to U.S. business in a long, long time. . . . Yesterday's campus rebels, in fact, seem to have become today's business achievers. . . . The graduates value money for different purposes than their predecessors . . . but value it just as much . . . [and they] prefer to work for "socially responsible" companies but not to the point of leaving otherwise desirable jobs.

More typically, they channel their social impulses into after-hours projects. (17)

In recent years, I have come to know and respect a good number of young professionals in the public relations field. Many of these men and women, now in their mid-to-late twenties, were among the campus activists who gave business and the establishment in general a very hard time of it in the late 1960s and early 1970s.

I have often asked some of these young people how and why they left the barricades and joined the targets of their earlier attacks. One of the brightest of these, now a 27-year-old member of the public affairs staff of a national insurance trade association, recently told me this:

> First, you have to realize that in addition to our idealism, many of us were at a point in life where we had to be part of the action of the day. So we joined with some rather far-out people who seemed to have identified some major things that needed fixing in society.
>
> I started to move away from the group when I began to realize the complexity of the problems we were attacking. And I realized that the way-out leadership didn't have adequate answers, they just had oversimplified accusations. Call it a maturing process if you want to.

I was ready with the logical follow-up question: "And you realized that business was becoming more socially responsible, so you joined it?"

> No way. In my view today's "social responsibility" programs are band-aid projects. You don't see commitments to the really substantive matters like developing new methods of capital formation to spread the business base, do you? No, I joined the establishment because it can provide me with the resources to do some personally challenging work. And I'm rewarded rather nicely while doing something that really interests me.

Another less disillusioned young professional has a somewhat different point of view: "Corporations have all the resources. If you want to change society, get into the corporation and help decide how those resources are going to be used." The following points were made in a *Business Week* review of *What Really Happened to the Class of '65*, a book written by Michael Medved and David Wallechensky, 1965 graduates of Pacific Palisades High School:

> . . . many [1965 Palisades High graduates] still profess the same political and social ideology, if a bit diluted and more flexible, that gripped them in the 1960s. "Today, I've come to the point where I can have nice things and be comfortable without feeling like a traitor," says the lawyer. . . .

Clearly, it's still too early for a verdict on the class of '65. . . . Will these restless searchers now return to the fold, full of spirit and committed to achievement in the American way? It seems unlikely. Some, I think, will remain lost and even some of those in this book who claim to have found the right direction may be pausing only long enough to regain their energy and start their search again. (18)

The reviewer was Jeffrey Madrick, class of 1965 at Long Island's General Douglas MacArthur High School. His job when he wrote the review? He was the *Business Week* editor writing the "Inside Wall Street" column.

Interestingly, a number of well-known young activist leaders of the late 1960s and early 1970s have recently moved on to challenges growing out of their earlier activist organizations.

Elliot Weiss, executive director of the Investor Responsibility Research Center since its founding in 1972, left the organization in the fall of 1976 to write a book on the responsibilities of corporations to society.

Susan Gross, Weiss's sister, was communications director for the Project on Corporate Responsibility, which took over Campaign GM and directed other shareholder movements aimed at other companies. She moved on to handling public relations for the Council for Law in the Public Interest, which seeks financing for public-interest law firms. To Susan Gross, the shareholder movements were no longer as "dramatic" and consequently no longer as powerful. "But at least," she said, "they have become a regular part of the corporate agenda."

The executive director of the Project on Corporate Responsibility was Phillip Moore, who later practiced law in Washington and Maryland. He believes that, although the shareholder movement was valuable, legal action is a more practical course. Philip C. Sorensen, chairman of the project, is now teaching law at Ohio State University.

Theodore Jacobs, one of Ralph Nader's original "raiders" and the consumer advocate's major domo, became the staff counsel for the House subcommittee on Government Information and Individual Rights.

What kind of business management style will come out of all this? Richard Cornuelle thinks he may have the answer. In his book, *De-Managing America*, he offers the theory that our institutions—corporations among them—really run themselves. (19) They are guided by the ingenuity and initiative of the people who work in them, so these organizations would run more efficiently with less management and attain greater productivity by setting forth the results to be achieved and not the procedures to be followed.

Cornuelle says that such a final revolution is coming: "This 'revolution' is real, and it has enormous permanent power. . . . It aims not for the substitution of one authority for another, but for the final transformation of authority. It is moving on different fronts. Its weapons are self-discovery and self-expression."

Visionary? Perhaps. But 10 years ago, I would have bet a bundle against yoga in the executive suite.

## REFERENCES

1. Jones, Reginald H., Chairman and Chief Executive Officer, General Electric Company, in a speech delivered at Detroit Economic Club, Detroit, Michigan, November 25, 1974.

2. ter Horst, J. F., in his nationally-syndicated column, July 5, 1975.

3. "Misunderstanding the Spirit of '76," *Fortune*, July, 1976, p. 97.

4. Banks, Louis. "Business and the Rise of Individualism," *Context* magazine, published by E. I. du Pont de Nemours, No. 1, 1976, pp. 4, 5.

5. "Lawyers and the Corporation: A Creeping Cynicism," *Juris Doctor*, April, 1976, pp. 28–29.

6. Lodge, George Cabot. *The New American Ideology* (New York, N.Y.: Knopf, 1975).

7. "Our Society in 1985—Business May Not Like It," *Harvard Business Review*, November–December, 1975, pp. 143–150.

8. Sowell, Thomas. "A Black 'Conservative' Dissents," *New York Times Magazine*, August 8, 1976, pp. 14–46.

9. Wolfe, Tom. "The ME Decade," *New York* magazine, August 23, 1976, pp. 26–40.

10. Advertisement appearing in *New York* magazine, September 30, 1976, pp. 110, 111.

11. *New York Times*, September 8, 1976.

12. Smith, Hedrick. *The Russians* (New York, N.Y.: Quadrangle/The New York Times Book Company, 1975), pp. 255, 289.

13. Bryan, C. D. B. *Friendly Fire* (New York, N.Y.: G. P. Putnam's Sons, 1976), pp. 253, 254.

14. *Boston Evening Globe*, August 11, 1976.

15. Patton, Arch. "The Boom in Executive Self-Interest," *Business Week*, May 24, 1976, pp. 16, 20.
16. "Executive's Guide to Living With Stress," *Business Week*, August 23, 1976, pp. 75, 76.
17. "A Home in Business for the Radical Generation," *Business Week*, October 5, 1974, p. 78.
18. "Books," *Business Week*, October 4, 1976, pp. 12–14.
19. Cornuelle, Richard. *De-Managing America* (New York, N.Y.: Random House, 1975).

# 5

# *The Changing World Around Business*

The world around American business is changing—rapidly. The change in American values is only one of a number of momentous developments that will impact with increasing force on the American business leader in the years immediately ahead. In this chapter, we will briefly discuss nine such macro developments:

1. The Velocity of Change (If you don't like the news, come back tomorrow.)
2. Big Government Growing Bigger
3. The New American Political Leadership
4. The Inflation-Cum-Unemployment Fallout
5. The New Challenge from Organized Labor
6. Decay at the Center (American Cities)
7. The Courts' New Reach into Your Pocketbook
8. Income Redistribution in America
9. Evolution of a Global Economic Order

Any one of these subjects could fill volumes. Obviously, we are not going to approach that depth. Here, it will simply be once over lightly on nine fundamental developments that just might determine whether the corporation as we know it will be around for another generation.

## THE VELOCITY OF CHANGE (If You Don't Like the News, Come Back Tomorrow)

> "I don't believe in black majority rule ever in Rhodesia—not in a thousand years."
> —Ian Smith, March 20, 1976

> "Rhodesia agrees to majority rule within two years."
> —Ian Smith, September 24, 1976

Ian Smith is a victim of "future shock," introduced to the world in 1965 by Alvin Toffler and described in his best-selling book of the early 1970s as, "what happens to people when they are overwhelmed by change." Among his many valuable observations, Toffler articulated what many who have lived in the latter half of the twentieth century have felt: Things are changing at a more rapid clip than in the old days. Moreover, this acceleration and the broadening sweep of change can be mighty disorienting.

Many things that were "good" not so long ago are "bad" now.

In the Depression, the Tennessee Valley Authority was a prime example of the physical and social achievement of a free society. Today, environmentalists attack it as a scourge of the Cumberland countryside.

Organized labor in the 1930s was a refuge for "radical" ideology. Today, it is an entrenched part of the establishment.

High-rise public housing projects, which replaced rotting tenements, were once thought of as symbolic of America's refusal to permit its poor to live in filth. Today, the projects are more often than not attacked as dangerous and economically and racially segregated slums.

Smoke coming out of a plant chimney used to be good news—people were working. Today it's pollution.

This is the current surge of water under the bridge—some of it clear, some of it muddy, but virtually all of it presented to Americans through a prism consisting of the nation's wire services, networks, and national magazines, as well as local newspapers and radio and television stations.

If change is becoming increasingly rapid, the American media are a chief stimulant. A candidate's slip of the tongue on national television can cost many points in the public opinion polls. A few weeks later, a well-publicized modest triumph can restore the support. If you don't like the news, come back tomorrow.

In professional athletics, franchises come and go. With the recent contractual changes ("reserve clause" et al.), athletes themselves come and go. Read all about it. See it on the evening news. When I was a boy, it was a near certainty that the Yankees would win the pennant and the World Series. You could count on it. A few years ago, it wasn't even certain that the Yankees would stay in New York.

When I went off to college, I had no doubt that I was beginning a four-year relationship. Today, it is not uncommon for the college undergraduate to change schools at least once and perhaps twice or three times within the four years. If the student feels he has been misled by pre-enrollment promotion, or if the "fit" is not just right, it is easy to make a change.

We all had roles then. Certain things were expected of men. Other things were expected of women. There was no unisex, let alone transsexual surgery. You knew your place, whatever it might be.

All that may sound reactionary. However, I am not calling for the repeal of the last half of the century. *The place of many people a few decades ago was intolerable.* By and large, we have advanced to a much more preferable—certainly a freer—society. I am only saying, with Toffler, that each of us pays a price for such accelerating and widespread change. It is paid in stability and security, both personal and professional.

On the commercial front, special consultancies have evolved to deal with change. For "big think" you go to the Hudson Institute. For "smaller (but still vital) think" on matters such as how changing values will affect product marketing, you can go to a firm like BrainReserve of New York City. This group of marketing communicators will help you deal with questions such as: What do the changing sex roles portend? How should a manufacturer prepare for the increase in supermarket shopping by men who may be less price conscious than women? Should they start thinking about household cleaning products designed for use by men? What about the growing homosexual market? How will increased permissiveness affect TV commercials?

One of the founders of BrainReserve was heard to say in the fall of 1976, "Things are getting nuts. The changes are so fast, it's beginning to freak me out, personally." That from a consultant on change.

## BIG GOVERNMENT GROWING BIGGER

Business leaders have heard a lot of talk recently about government moving "out of your business, out of your lives, out of your pocket books, and out of your hair." Not very likely. "Government" in this discussion will mean the federal government, but much the same can be said for state, county, municipal, and other governing units.

The federal government isn't going to get smaller. It isn't even going to plateau. Its mass and momentum are just too great. First, the mass:

The U.S. Congressional Budget Office reported in mid-1976 that the federal government had in place at that time 84,773 regulators, exclusive of secretarial help or other support positions. These regulators, spread through 33 federal agencies, cost the American taxpayers $2.9 billion a year.

It is estimated that the cost of *all* governmental regulation breaks down to about $2,000 a year per American family. Nobody seems to be able to say whether we are getting our money's worth.

Now, the momentum. Not too long ago, a leading national "think tank" did a study on the life cycle of federal agencies. It reported that in 1932, just before the New Deal, there were 175 government agencies. By 1975, 85 percent of those agencies were still in existence, and there were 246 *new* ones for a total of 394. By 1985, the study predicted, we will have to learn to live with and deal with 700 to 800 federal agencies.

C. Jackson Grayson, head of the Council on Wage and Price Administration in the Nixon administration and the founder of the new American Productivity Center, told the Seventh World Public Relations Congress in Boston in August 1976 that more government intervention in the private sector is certain. Grayson said that the root reason for this growth is that the American public, grouse as it may about bureaucrats and red tape, nevertheless has a number of concerns, frustrations, and insecurities that it feels can be remedied only by big government. These include unmet expectations in life, the sheer complexity of society and most social issues, perceived international tensions, and attitudes such as, "we've-gone-so-far-we-might-as-well-go-further," "the marketplace doesn't work," "income distribution is inequitable," "the environment is befouled," and "social justice has not been achieved."

Also, Grayson suggested, the persistence of inflation will cause the American citizen to look for centralized planning as an antidote.

Once again, the 1976 presidential campaign is relevant. At one point it appeared that the presidential candidates of the two major parties were in a footrace to see who could promise a smaller federal government. But is such a federal government deliverable in the 1970s? Chances are that it isn't, and business leaders had better be prepared for *more*, not less, government regulation.

It is Congress, after all, that passes the enabling legislation for regulatory agencies and maintains oversight, that is, broad supervision, of the agencies. Congress, especially the House, will be responsive to the American public, and if Grayson is right, the American public is a long way from reducing requests for help from Washington, D.C.

Representative John E. Moss (D. Calif.), chairman of a House commerce investigative subcommittee, said as much when the 1976 Congressional Budget Office report was released: "As long as citizens desire regulation of business, the important concerns are going to be not only the size and scope of federal regulation, but also its efficiency and its quality."

It *is* true that the federal government may change some of the ways in which it operates, but whether such changes will be beneficial to business is highly questionable. For example, the government is now supposed to operate "in the sunshine"—that is, with maximum public exposure for a variety of government actions, especially deliberations and decisions. And consolidation or elimination of a few regulatory units or Congressional Committees isn't necessarily significant if there isn't a real reduction in burden of regulation.

Well, what is wrong with government regulation of business? Nothing, if it is really needed, well conceived, and fairly implemented. In retrospect it may well be said that reforms of the trustbusting and New Deal eras saved and improved American capitalism. One of the main reasons business leaders oppose such regulation is the likelihood of surprise. One chief executive officer told me recently: "If the government would only let us know exactly what they will want, we can plan accordingly. But more often than not, the legislation creating or extending a regulatory body is vague or, if it is clear, the regulatory agency disregards much of it and experiments as it goes along. And we have to scurry to adjust. That's contrary to every good business principle I know. . . ."

There is a financial impact as well. The cost of government regulations becomes a cost of doing business and, unless it can be absorbed, is passed on to the consumer.

Finally, there is a more subtle but equally significant effect on business. Make the regulations too costly to business, and you run the risk of major cutbacks in research and development. This is particularly true in research-dependent industries such as the chemical industry. In our economic system (we'll talk about those who want to change the *system* a little later), the corporation still has the prerogative of curtailing operations or withdrawing from a market or industry that is losing its attractiveness. Make regulation too costly, in terms of dollars or reputation, and you drive out some companies. With them may well go the potential for new and advanced products. Government regulation then becomes counterproductive.

## THE NEW AMERICAN POLITICAL LEADERSHIP

There is no better place to begin working together than in the attack on America's social problems. One of the reasons our government has grown so large and unwieldy in recent years is that many of us have left the solution of our problems to the bureaucrats alone. The government should do what it does efficiently and well, but a healthy society requires the efforts of individual citizens and businesses as well.

There is hardly any area—education, the environment, urban improvement, the arts—in which corporations and businessmen cannot make a positive and valuable contribution. There is plenty of work for everyone. . . .

. . . Corporations can do something else, perhaps the most important of all. They can create a climate which encourages their executives and employees to participate in the life of their community, state, and nation. . . .

Some critics say that activities of the sort I have suggested are not proper for a corporation, which exists for the sole purpose of making a profit for its stockholders. This "bottom line" philosophy ignores both the opportunity of the corporation to serve the public in general and the benefits which social action can bring. By working to improve social conditions, the corporation is working to improve its profitability. Social activities may not be immediately translatable into profits on the books. But the well-being of the community will eventually improve the well-being of the corporation. If schools in a community deteriorate, for example, the skills of those entering the local labor market will also suffer. A corporate citizen of that community can only be harmed by having a lower quality work force at its disposal.

. . . I foresee a future in which businessmen come to realize even more fully than they do today the need for corporate action to meet social problems and take an ever expanding and more innovative view of what can be done. The result will be good for business and good for the American people.

Those are the words the new president of the United States, Jimmy Carter, offered in September 1976 in response to one of hundreds of requests for a statement by the presidential candidates. Surely, Stanley G. Karson, Director of The American Council of Life Insurance's Clearinghouse on Corporate Social Responsibility, who issued this request (and printed the candidate's full reply in the Clearinghouse's publication, *Response*) sought a thoughtful summary of the candidates' deepest beliefs on corporate social responsibility. Whether he got that, or the quickly researched and rapidly composed response from one of Carter's many aides is known to only a few. Perhaps it is enough that *Response* exists and drew a response from the man who now occupies the White House. In 1968 there wasn't even the request. (*Response* is only five years old.)

## THE CHANGING WORLD AROUND BUSINESS 59

Carter's opponent expressed similar sentiments in answer to Karson. All in all, the statements read like the rather naïve and simplistic self-testimonials many businessmen were mouthing in the late 1960s. It is not that you could lay a glove on either candidate. What they said was hard to oppose, but corporate social responsibility has advanced much farther than such superficial treatments. Many businessmen have been grappling with the much harder questions for years. If the statements gave no offense, neither did they give much guidance nor shed much light on what political leaders might demand of business in the years immediately ahead.

So we must still ask: Are we in a vestibule of history, on the verge of entering a new era of political organization and economic development? Will the new political leadership—a Democratic President and a Democratically controlled Congress—present a formidable united front more problematic for business than the Ford administration? (Ford's many 1975–1976 vetoes included more than a few on issues of direct concern to business.)

Looking at Carter's positions as stated in 1976, the business leader has to be concerned. Shortly after his nomination, Carter was quoted as saying that he hoped to challenge Ralph Nader "for the title of top consumer advocate in the country." Although at just about the same time he lunched with selected business leaders at New York's posh restaurant "21" and told them they should not fear his administration, his statements at a public citizens forum sponsored by Nader were certainly not reassuring to business. These are some of the things he told the Nader meeting: He endorsed proposed legislation that would enable *state* attorney generals to bring antitrust lawsuits on behalf of all citizens of a state (now law). He also endorsed another bill that would overturn recent Supreme Court decisions limiting the effectiveness of class action lawsuits by citizens. At the same time, he indicated his support for a federal consumer protection agency and legislation against "revolving door" movement of persons from jobs in federal regulatory agencies into industries they had been regulating and vice versa.

Carter's 1976 positions on environment and energy included these published in *Balance*, a newsletter of the National Environmental Development Association:

- Concerning potential conflict between economy and environment: "I would go with environmental quality. That's because it's an irreversible process."

- "When I am President, I am going to get the Corps of Engineers out of the dam building business."
- The independent Government Research Corporation, basing its conclusions on an interview with a key Carter adviser, suggested that Carter would stress environmental health issues including control of mutagens and carcinogens, would seek use of process modification to control air pollutants, and would emphasize economic incentives and disincentives—including penalties—to encourage pollution control. (1)

Significantly, *Balance* reported that the League of Conservation Voters, a coalition of members of organizations such as Friends of the Earth, the Sierra Club, and the Environmental Policy Center, seemed comfortable with the Carter-Mondale ticket. The League of Conservation Voters pointed out early in the campaign that as governor of Georgia, Carter was "consistently ahead of the state legislature on nearly all environmental issues."

The *Balance* analysis also reported that "Industry in Georgia says Carter put environmental regulations 'up front.' They say industry knew what the target was and the target didn't change. Says the Georgia Business and Industry Association: 'He took a very pro-environment stand without being anti-business.'" Discounting the possibility of a bit of chauvinism, the Georgia association statement is nevertheless useful to business leaders casting a wary eye on the new administration.

What remains to be seen is whether such political consistency, which business leaders need for effective planning and which suffered during the presidential campaign, can indeed be maintained at the national level.

The key Carter economic policy of fundamental interest to all business is his announced intention to pursue solutions to social problems in the private sector. Let's examine that in terms of the economic situation in this country.

## THE INFLATION-CUM-UNEMPLOYMENT FALLOUT

I am not an economist.

I understand virtually nothing of various economic theories. For me the dismal science is personally depressing. I read and I simply do not comprehend. I have this terrible inclination to ask "why?" after the few sentences that do get through to me. For all the rest, they seem so highly qualified as to be meaningless. It is my failure, certainly not that of the nation's economists.

So this section is not going to be a learned analysis of various approaches to solving the twin threats to economic stability. We will touch on that out of necessity, but I am more at home with the discussion of public opinion fallout of these issues. And where does most of the fallout land? Right. On the business leader.

Put in its simplest form, the problem seems to be: Can we attack unemployment without self-destructing ourselves with inflation? The traditional wisdom says no. The business cycle is inviolate. Boom and bust. At best, boomlet and bustlet. These economic roller coaster rides are among the prime targets of those who attack the free market system.

People get hurt when either unemployment or inflation is "too high." When they are *both* soaring, you have the makings of revolution. For most of 1976, inflation was somewhat under control—at least the nation was spared the double-digit inflation of a short time earlier. But there was a heavy price for such "stability." (It seems strange to call, say, 6 percent inflation a mark of stability when not too many years ago 3 percent meant the same thing.) The price, of course, was high unemployment, 7 to 8 percent nationally. And the price was paid for the nation largely by the citizens at the bottom of the economic ladder—blacks and other minority groups, the teenager and young adult, the unskilled, the inexperienced.

Then some people, perhaps carried away with campaign rhetoric, started to say, "We don't really have to choose. High employment doesn't necessarily bring increased inflation. We can have our cake and eat it!"

Actually, such discussion started well before the presidential campaign. Arthur F. Burns, chairman of the Board of Governors of the Federal Reserve Board, in March 1976 told the *Reader's Digest*'s millions of readers: "Conventional thinking about economic policies is now inadequate. There is no longer a meaningful trade-off between unemployment and inflation." (2) The article, under a secondary headline which read, "We *can* have full employment and price stability at the same time . . . if we but understand and deal with the roots of inflation," made these points:

- First, we must improve productivity through larger investment in modern plant and equipment. . . .

- Second, full employment and price stability will be promoted by stretching out timetables for achieving environmental and safety goals . . . we must face the fact that environmental and safety regulations have escalated costs and prices and held up industrial construction.

- Third, we must enhance price competition in business. . . .
- Fourth, government labor policies must be reviewed.

For example, the federal minimum wage law is still pricing too many teenagers out of the job market. Unemployment compensation now provides benefits on blunting incentives to work. More realistic manpower-training programs and more effective job banks are needed. . . .

Our ultimate objective should be to eliminate all involuntary unemployment . . . there may be no way of reaching the goal of full employment short of making government the employer of last resort. This could be done by offering public employment—for example, in hospitals, schools, public parks—to anyone willing to work at a rate of pay somewhat below the federal minimum wage.

It is highly important, of course, that such a program should not become a vehicle for expanding public jobs at the expense of private industry.

Well! If the chairman of the Federal Reserve Board in a Republican administration says we can lick both unemployment and inflation in one fell swoop, you have to believe that it may be worth a try.

In the same article, Burns more characteristically admonished: "We need to rethink the appropriate role of government policy with regard to prices and wages. Lasting benefits cannot be expected from mandatory wage and price controls as recent experience indicates."

That "recent experience" is admirably examined in depth in the recently published *Inflation Under Control?* by Jerry E. Pohlman, who contends that "Since World War II, during each business cycle the level of unemployment associated with stable prices creeped ever higher," and "the price system, if left alone, is no longer capable of performing within socially accepted limits." (3)

One of the chief reasons why the economy has moved farther and farther away from the textbook model of perfect competition, Pohlman feels, is "the continued growth of 'power' factors within the economy, a growth that further hampers the self-corrective mechanisms of the market." What "power factors"? Unions and large corporations.

Pohlman concludes:

The severity of both the inflation and unemployment problems leaves little doubt that new policies, including new incomes policies, will be tried . . . we are likely to see different forms of controls adopted from time to time as the search in this country and elsewhere continues for a viable income policy that will allow us to reach a higher level of noninflationary employment while preserving private institutions in the wage and price sphere.

Controls or no, more experts seem to be focusing on the *nature* of unemployment in this country and finding, like Arthur Burns, that maybe the traditional wisdom about unemployment-inflation tradeoffs *is* obsolete.

In this view, the heart of the unemployment problem is the "structural unemployment" generated by an industrial society that has little or no room for the untrained or those who happen to live in a depressed region and have no mobility. Proponents of this view contend that this problem is not one to be solved by fiscal or monetary policy but rather by a precise effort at identifying people's employment deficiencies and remedying them.

Here's how John Cobbs, editor of *Business Week*, has presented this suggestion:

> The answer to the U.S. unemployment problem—and to the plight of the decaying cities—must provide for restructuring the U.S. job market and upgrading the bottom of the U.S. labor force. . . . The starting point should be to look at the people who are now unemployed—who they are, where they are, and what they can do. It might turn out that the kind of jobs the economy creates as it expands are not the jobs the unemployed can fill. . . .
>
> If this analysis is correct, it suggests that a very modest expansion would soak up the available supply of seasoned workers. To push unemployment to still lower levels must mean opening up jobs for the young, the unskilled, the disadvantaged. . . . The lesson for policymakers is clear: The U.S. cannot achieve a significant reduction in its unemployment rate by stimulating the economy into an inflationary frenzy. . . . Instead of trying to choose between two unacceptable alternatives—unemployment and inflation—the nation should see what it can do to change the terms of the trade-off. (5)

In late 1976 *The Business Roundtable* offered this suggestion: The largest employers in the nation could accept quotas of jobless youths to train on the job, with the government paying the training cost and the employer paying for work performed by such trainees.

Why so much attention to this fundamental economic dilemma in this book? Because business leaders, perhaps as much as anyone except for political leaders, bear the brunt of public criticism for the damages caused by high unemployment and inflation. And those damages are not insignificant. Again, Pohlman in *Inflation Under Control?*:

> The entire social structure is shaken by prolonged and high unemployment as crime increases, cities strangle for a lack of

funds, frustrations mount, and disillusionment "with the system" becomes endemic.

The evils of inflation are also myriad. As fixed incomes are continuously eroded, more and more of the population—especially the aged—are pushed into lives of squalor and poverty. Frugality becomes stupidity as speculation becomes responsibility. Again, the social fabric wears thin as inflation breeds increasing discontentment and the stable elements of society become increasingly threatened by forces beyond their control or apprehension. (3)

And where is the business leader in these situations? Right in the middle. For many citizens, the business leader is "heartless" when recession requires layoffs and "greedy for unconscionable profits" when prices must be increased. It's no place to be. In a most interesting analysis of U.S. Department of Labor statistics in which it observed that U.S. employment rose 21 percent from 1966 to 1976 while population grew only 10 percent during the same period, the *Wall Street Journal* observed:

The basic problem lies in the public failure to understand what causes "unemployment." In the popular mind, there is just one cause—people losing their jobs. A given number of unemployed is invariably referred to as so many people being "thrown out of work." But job loss has not been the big cause at all lately. The big cause of current unemployment has been the unprecedented number of new job seekers scrambling to get on the paycheck bandwagon. All the seekers are "unemployed" until they find jobs. (4)

President Carter seems to feel that engaging the unused production capacity in the private sector is a key to breaking the current unemployment-inflation deadlock. Despite his thin electoral mandate, he may well construct a popular mandate enabling him to pursue such policies.

## THE NEW CHALLENGE OF ORGANIZED LABOR

The messianic fervor is gone, but make no mistake, organized labor will continue to have much to say about how business is conducted in the years ahead. Labor is now a mature American institution. The day of bloody organizing is all but over. Membership has leveled off at less than 25 percent of the American work force. To many Americans, labor has become as much a part of the establishment as the corporation. In the process, however, this institution has compiled a record of social reform unequaled in American history.

One of the chief reasons for American labor's sweeping achievements is that to date it has emphatically rejected distraction from its overriding purpose of improving the economic lot of its members. American labor, after an early temptation, rejected alien ideology. Too, instead of focusing on managerial control, it has for the most part demonstrated a much greater interest in a better life for the worker.

There are, however, some disturbing signs that new objectives and affiliations are on the horizon for American labor—objectives and affiliations that will mean new and serious social problems for business leaders.

The new challenge by organized labor, then, is substantial. It involves movement on five fronts:

- A central role for labor in a new sociopolitical alliance involving environmentalists and consumerists.
- A "quantum leap" in bargaining objectives related to job security.
- A sweeping attack on right-to-work legislation.
- A drive for direct participation in management.
- A new potential for genuine international status.

Black Lake, Michigan, early May, 1976: An audience of 300 at the United Automobile Workers' Reuther Educational Center sat in rapt attention as Leonard Woodcock, UAW president, spoke. This was no ordinary labor audience. It was an assemblage of "influentials" from across the country representing environmental organizations, community-action groups, and a good number of unions.

Woodcock's central theme was a call for a new political alliance between labor and activist groups to thwart industries' "environmental blackmail" and hasten full employment. Without such an alliance, Woodcock said, workers will have to continue to fear environmentally induced unemployment and corporate resistance to pollution abatement.

The conference, called "Working for Environmental and Economic Justice and Jobs," heard Barry Commoner, Washington University scientist, suggest that the nation's economy, needed to be reoriented away from "inefficient" use of both energy and capital that were prejudicial to labor. "We face a big debate," he said, "on how we're going to devote resources for the common good rather than for private profit. There's a whole question of inventing a new form of socialism."

Not that there was total agreement between labor and environmentalists. Tom Donohue, Executive Assistant to AFL-CIO President George Meany, cited some key differences of opinion: "We don't see eye to eye with the environmental community in its opposition to nuclear power. On the other hand, we thoroughly supported legislation to regulate strip mining. We haven't agreed with them on banning nonreturnable containers, but we're with them in seeking national land use legislation."

Nevertheless, it was Woodcock who summarized the common cause of labor and the environmental community as the need to fight "the corporate tactic of trying to make workers and communities choose between jobs and ending pollution. . . . It's frequently a false conflict, but to a worker confronted with the loss of wages, health care benefits and pension rights, it can seem very real."

As if that emerging coalition wasn't enough of a challenge for business leaders, I. W. Abel, just before he retired as president of the Steelworkers of America, launched a rocket with a trail long enough to be seen by the entire American industrial-relations community. Abel led his half-million-member union in pursuit of nothing less than "lifetime income security." One labor relations analyst said the Steelworkers' plan represented "a quantum leap beyond the generation-old concept of supplemental unemployment benefits" which in 1976 gave jobless steelworkers about 85 percent of their regular pay for up to a year.

In fact, the union's demand called up visions of the kind of paternalistic system prevalent in Japan where every worker who qualifies for regular employment acquires a passport to full pay, 52 weeks a year, until retirement regardless of whether he or she is actually on the job. The Japanese paternalism was jolted, however, when the recession of the early 1970s produced layoffs.

The concept is, in effect, that every worker has a right to a job. If the corporation fails to provide the job temporarily—or even over an extended period—it must make good on its commitment.

The cost? Obviously, substantial. Just *how* substantial would depend essentially on how the worker eligibility rules are drawn. But whatever the cost, it would become still another cost of doing business to be passed on ultimately to the consumer.

Section 14(b) of the Taft-Hartley Law is 30 years old. Those of us who remember the fight over right-to-work legislation find it hard to believe that it has been in effect for three decades. Of course, it has also been under attack for three decades. But organized labor now has a powerful new ally, the president of the United States.

An AFL-CIO publication of August of 1976 quoted then-candidate Carter as follows: "I think Section 14(b) should be repealed which would permit the abolition of right-to-work laws, and if the Congress passes such legislation, I'd be glad to sign it."

Section 14(b) of the Taft-Hartley Law permits states to enact laws forbidding labor contracts that require a person to be a member of a labor union in order to hold a job. Nineteen states, many of them in the South and West, now have such laws. A mid-1976 survey found that, nationally, 68 percent of Americans wanted to keep 14(b), 16 percent wanted to repeal it, and 16 percent had no opinion on the issue. There is now a distinct possibility that the union shop is coming back. If so, we may all be in for new turbulence in labor relations.

Former Secretary of Labor James D. Hodgson is among those who have raised the fascinating question of how organized labor will meet the challenges of an increasingly global economic system. (6) Will the "international" become truly international? Will the American auto workers seek to affiliate with organized auto workers in various or all parts of the world in order to deal better with auto manufacturers who operate globally? Will we see a world-wide auto workers' federation? And one in steel or other basic industries? Or will American unions demand that multinational corporations accept *them* as the rightful bargaining agents when American corporations establish plants abroad?

Hodgson thinks that the more likely labor response, at least in the short term, will be to exert greater political influence on American international economic policies. But will that be enough influence for organized labor when jobs are being exported? Not at all likely.

Finally, labor's most important recent initiative—nothing less than a role in management.

There are signs that labor's earlier policy of focusing bargaining power on economic gains rather than on managerial control will not be adequate for the labor leaders of the next decade. In addition to the focus on organizing white-collar workers, especially those in lower and middle management—and the increased vulnerability to such advances, according to Arch Patton (see page 47)—we now see labor leaders demanding worker participation in management. Not surprisingly, the United Automobile Workers appear to be in the forefront of this industrial relations struggle as they have been in so many others.

Put quite simply, the union wants seats on the corporation's board of directors. Unlike the requests for worker participation in decision making that affects conditions in the plant (see Chapter 10), this UAW demand is a matter of management's sharing the ultimate responsibility for the welfare of the corporation with union representatives.

Similar systems have been in use in Europe for many years. Workers in West Germany have held half the seats on the boards of coal and steel companies and a third of the seats at other companies since the early 1950s. The practice is also widespread in Sweden. In Great Britain, the government-financed Bullock Report (prepared by a committee tipped in favor of Labor) has recommended that Labor leaders be appointed to the boards of British firms.

Supporters say that such systems can result in increased productivity and labor peace. Opponents ask, "At what price?" When the financially hard-pressed Chrysler Corporation subsidiary in Great Britain sought labor peace by offering its union two seats on its board, Leonard Woodcock lost no time in asking Chrysler in Detroit, "If you're willing to do it in Britain, why aren't you ready to do it in the United States? It's an idea that's never been seriously considered in the United States before."

Chrysler, as the old saying goes, was not amused. However, the corporation gave the matter high-level consideration. Chrysler and other corporations will have to give it a good deal more attention in the years ahead.

Multinationals operating in Europe are well into such consideration because the European Economic Community has evolved a legal structure by which multinationals operating in the nine EEC countries will be regulated. And this model, in addition to specifying transnational standards for accounting, mergers, and taxes, also includes a call for "management boards" responsible to "supervisory boards" composed of shareholders, employees, and public interest representatives.

It is not insignificant, then, that Jimmy Carter has called for voluntary cooperation between business and labor not unlike the "social consensus" West Germany uses to keep its inflation in check.

Will there be such harmony? It's not totally unprecedented. When legislation has threatened an industry—the proposals to apply deposits on nonreturnable beer and soft drink containers provide an example—American union and management representatives have worked successfully for a common end. A stable economy might well be a far greater stimulant to such concord.

### DECAY AT THE CENTER

The United States, like much of the developed world, has become an urbanized society. But unlike older nations, we have not mastered the art of preserving what is old but valuable in our cities. Many European cities, with core areas five hundred or even a thousand years old, seem better able to preserve the venerable while adding to it as needed.

In this country there is hardly a major city without considerable blight. Is it because we do not cherish the old as it is cherished in the Old World? Are we simply too restless and impatient to restore and maintain? Are we hooked on "new"?

The New York City financial crisis was first perceived by the rest of the nation as a local problem brought on by municipal self-indulgence and profligate spending. But before long, mayors and other officials of cities across the country were making it plain that New York's problems, although greater in degree, were their problems as well.

Despite the torturous deliberations that led to federal financial support for New York and grandiose proposals such as a "domestic Marshall Plan," the root problems of our cities remain.

Terry N. Clark, an associate professor of sociology at the University of Chicago, has led a team of researchers that has assembled a highly intricate computerized model of the strains felt by American cities. Studying 51 cities, the University of Chicago team has reached the preliminary conclusion that urban fiscal strain is not necessarily related to size, age, location, population profile, or range of services delivered. The Clark team says it is much more complicated than that. More decisive, according to the study, may be a city's political and governmental structure—the power of the mayor, the health of the local business community, and the strength of municipal unions.

Of the 29 urban strain indicators identified by the Chicago research team, four are particularly significant: per capita long-term debt; per capita short-term debt; per capita spending for such functions as police, fire fighting, courts, highways, and sanitation; and total tax revenue from local sources as a function of the local property values. Not surprisingly, New York was at the upper extreme of most of these indicators, but cities such as Newark, Boston, San Francisco, and Albany were not far behind.

Another recent study has concluded that more than any other single factor, the state of the national economy, including the flow of federal aid, will determine the rate at which cities will improve or deteriorate in the next decade. The study, published by the private Urban Institute in a book entitled "The Urban Predicament," concluded that "national economic prosperity probably is the most important contribution that the Federal Government can make in behalf of the cities." Part of the change in emphasis on direct federal aid to cities, the report suggests, is related to a loss of confidence in the ability to identify the real causes of urban problems: "We now know more than we did, but, deprived of our hubris, are less confident in our ability to shape a future as we will."

Although selective federal intervention—especially assumption of welfare costs—would help, the Urban Institute contends that a booming economy, more jobs, and increased urban revenue from taxes provide the best long-range hope for cities.

There have been many business-generated programs to improve our cities. In the late 1960s, with unlimited hubris, some business leaders plunged into the urban morass confident that business know-how and can-do would set things straight. For the most part, these were well-motivated attempts to help improve the communities in which the companies did business. Many achieved only modest success. The massive problem of urban decay was hardly touched. Its complexity and pervasiveness was just too much for the kind of piecemeal and uncoordinated efforts most corporations were able to undertake.

One of the most ambitious programs of this sort was undertaken by the life insurance industry. Coordinated by The Institute of Life Insurance, the industry's trade association, the program poured $2 billion of life insurance company money into urban mortgages, some of which would not have been granted under normal lending standards. In 1973 the Institute issued a comprehensive report on the program's achievements. To be sure, $2 billion *had* made possible many new structures in a number of cities across the country. However, the report noted that "the problems of America's troubled cities defy ready solutions, and remedies of any worth must go far beyond the capacity and resources of one business or one program, no matter how well designed and intended." (7)

Parenthetically, a later study of the participating companies' experience with the loans they granted was also revealing. Of the 100 companies surveyed, 81 replied. They reported that 18.4 percent of the amount invested in the Urban Investment Program loans represented foreclosed and delinquent mortgages as of June 30, 1975. There was quite a range of individual company experience. About 30 percent of the companies responding had no foreclosed or delinquent loans at the time they responded (despite a period of record-high mortgage delinquency rates). For most of the participating companies the foreclosed and delinquent loans represented somewhere between 1 percent and 50 percent of the amount disbursed.

Total loan losses in the program were estimated at about 1.5 percent of the amount disbursed—higher than a few of the reporting companies had expected but considerably lower than what *most* of the reporting companies had expected. (7)

Why include this brief commentary of such a complex subject? Because the experience of business leaders in the urban affairs area during the past eight or nine years has taught them a very valuable lesson. That lesson is if you bite off more than you can chew in the social responsibility area, you are going to create additional problems for yourself.

We have paid a price for the overly ambitious business programs of a few years back. The price is credibility among the general public and within the American business community as well. Most business leaders are now concentrating first on meeting social standards in running the corporation—how they manufacture and market, how they relate to the members of the corporate family of shareholders, employees, and customers. There is plenty to be done right there.

As for the problem of America's cities, these companies will surely play a part—but only a part—in helping to improve the communities in which they operate. Most of them seem to have learned that even a little hubris is a dangerous thing.

## THE COURTS' NEW REACH INTO YOUR POCKETBOOK

Americans root for the underdog, but what has been going on in some of our courts in recent years is enough to make many an underdog top dog—at the expense of business first and then ultimately the consumer. And when the consumer wakes up to this new assault on the pocketbook, there's going to be hell to pay. For business, the trick will be to stay out of the line of the consumer's fire.

Basically, here is what has been happening in recent years. Consumerism, for all of its needed reform, has generated in some consumers a hunger for instant wealth through hefty awards given them as victims of product or professional liability. All the elements for courtroom drama are there. Mr. Underdog seeking redress from the powerful. Judge and jury intent on justice. Perhaps a trial attorney working on a contingency fee—a piece of the award. Increasingly, the net result has been substantially larger awards to plaintiffs.

Liability insurance experts call the process "social inflation." Normal price inflation is, of course, also a factor in currently escalating insurance premiums, but it pales next to "social inflation." This relatively new phenomenon consists of two main elements. In the first place, courts, regulators, and legislatures are *extending* liability into many new areas. Second, the *value* of liability is skyrocketing. Awards have been soaring. This social inflation is now considered a threat to the viability of the American private insurance industry. It exposes insurance companies to enormous and unpredictable risks. Malpractice rates are an example. In 1976 the American public was scandalized to learn that a group of doctors would not perform operations because their medical malpractice premiums had become prohibitive. The national swine flu vaccination program was almost aborted because vaccine manufacturers feared the cost of potential malpractice awards. Today, product liability represents an open-ended risk because the courts have extended it to a wide range of cases in which the product was not the cause of the accident.

Judges and legislatures have been moving toward the position that injury—virtually any injury and almost regardless of the circumstances—requires recompense. And sympathetic juries have been putting much higher values on plaintiffs' pain, suffering, and loss of income.

*Business Week*'s editorial opinion is that the new social inflation is "a sign of something dangerously wrong with the way the nation's legal system is creating huge new liabilities and laying them off on insurers." Warning that whole categories of risk are going to be uninsurable by private carriers, the magazine predicts that unless the trend is checked, either government will have to get into this part of the insurance field or major hazards of living and doing business in this country will go uncovered. "If outsize awards drive the costs out of sight, the pro rata share of each policyholder (his premium) becomes more than he can afford. It is time for policyholders in each state to start reminding the legislature that they are the ones who pay the bill. . . ." (8)

You may well ask why liability insurance companies are not telling this story effectively to consumers. After all, isn't this anticonsumer consumerism? Isn't this the best example extant of the consumer paying the price of reform?

There are two answers. The first lies in the nature of the liability insurance company. It is a major pool of financial resources. Its profits depend largely on how it manages that pool, how prudently it invests its assets. And the larger the assets (i.e., the more premium income generated by increased rates), the more there is to invest. Nevertheless, relief from social inflation through increased premiums cannot be a perpetual solution in so regulated an industry, and so the social inflation story is beginning to be told. However, telling it *effectively* is not easy. There are about 2,000 liability insurance companies in this country fragmented not only regionally but by nature (stock, mutual, or reciprocals). Then there is the sprawl of the target—legislatures in 50 states and the federal regulatory maze. Nevertheless, the industry's trade associations are pushing for change. Their objectives are new limitations on awards and lawyers fees, and a time limit on product liability.

Until such changes are made, corporations of all types will continue to incur high premiums for product liability, heavy commitment of staff and retained counsel for defense, and, perhaps most significant of all, the periodic ignominy of page-one headlines heralding another award for thousands and even millions of dollars.

## INCOME REDISTRIBUTION IN AMERICA

The tax reform law of 1976 was about 1,500 pages long. That is what it took to encapsulate the many opinions and interests now at work on income redistribution in this country. That is what tax legislation is all about these days. It is part of a trend toward economic egalitarianism, a matter of taking from the rich and giving to the poor. Proponents say that this process is what this country is all about: "Equal opportunity is a farce if one person starts out in life with a lot more money than someone else." Critics say that such redistribution is a sure way to limit investment and kill ambition: "It's the very opposite of what this country is all about."

Whichever way you look at it, the process of income redistribution in this country is a fact. And reformers have a large target at which to take aim because income distribution here is undeniably unequal. Census Bureau statistics for 1974 indicate that the lowest-income 20 percent of American families received 5.4 percent of total income (benefits in kind, such as food stamps, not included), whereas the highest-income 20 percent received 41 percent (capital gains not included). Furthermore, the income pattern has not changed significantly since 1968 when the lowest-income fifth of American families received 5.6 percent of the national income. This, of course, was the period when affirmative action, minority business support, and other new national income leveling programs came into their own. Perhaps even more revealing are recent statistics showing that the number of Americans living below the poverty line decreased from 19 percent in 1964 to 11.2 in 1974, but jumped in 1975 to 12.3 percent. The 1975 "poverty line" was considered to be an annual income of $5,469 for a family of four. The number of poor persons in the United States increased by 2.5 million in 1975, the largest increase in a single year since the government began compiling such statistics in 1959. Moreover, the largest proportional increases in the American poor in 1975 occurred among those who do not ordinarily dominate poverty statistics—whites, families with a male head, and those who are not elderly.

To be sure, the overall income structure in this country has been moving upward steadily. In other words, all Americans are sharing in an expanding "pie," the growing American economy. But the real growth of income at the lower levels has been through massive government transfer payments—welfare, social security, veterans programs, and the like.

Affirmative action, already under attack as "reverse discrimination," is a potentially effective leveler. However, its effect will be felt only over a good number of years, after minority workers have had sufficient time to progress from various entry level positions to more responsible and higher-income jobs. That process is indeed underway, but it is taking time and we are paying its necessary price—social conflict.

There is really only one other way to produce a more regular national income "profile"—increased taxes on higher-income earners and increased transfer of such revenue to the lower brackets. Passage of the federal minimum tax in 1971, which precluded sheltering of *all* taxable income, was the beginning of a tax pattern that includes reduced exemptions and shelters, a higher tax rate in the higher brackets, and, some day, capital gains treated as ordinary income. And how long will it be before the United States adopts the kind of taxes that have virtually leveled the old British class structure—stiff estate and gift taxes? Only as long as American voters continue to believe that a breadwinner, having worked hard to amass assets, should be able to hand them down to the children virtually intact.

The federal government transfers from higher to lower tax brackets are sizable and growing rapidly. In 1975 such transfers were estimated to have reached $150 billion or 42 percent of federal spending as compared with only $78.6 billion, or 33 percent of federal spending just three years earlier. The handwriting is on the wall.

The income disparity between rich and poor is a subject for increasing discussion in many parts of the world. Americans, many of whom believe that we invented egalitarianism, may be surprised to learn that among the developed nations we have close to the highest disparity between low-income and high-income families.

A recent study by the Organization for Economic Cooperation and Development concluded that France had the greatest after-tax income disparity, with the United States not far behind. Japan and Australia, the study concluded, have the lowest degree of after-tax income disparity. Some say that income disparity is one index of a nation's potential for social turmoil.

What effect *did* the 1976 tax reform bill have on income redistribution in this country? If we put aside the problem of the complexity of the law (shortly after its passage, the *Wall Street Journal* said it couldn't understand the tax package), a few relevant provisions jump out:

- The minimum federal tax was increased from 10 percent to 15 percent for higher-income families. Also, an estimated additional $1.6 billion annually was generated by adding some 270,000 taxpayers to the 30,000 who earlier "qualified" for such payment.

- Tax shelters in real estate, farming, oil and gas, and other enterprises were restricted.
- The $60,000 estate exemption and the $30,000 gift tax exemption were changed to tax credits that after five years will be changed to a $175,000 exemption. If an estate is willed to a spouse, half the value, or $250,000, whichever is larger, is tax free.
- The holding period required to gain lower capital gains tax treatment on certain assets was increased from six months to a year.

Capital formation, so vital to economic expansion, will undoubtedly suffer from these changes.

Nevertheless, tax reformers were not satisfied. Robert Brandon, director of the Tax Reform Group, expressed dissatisfaction with the extent of the changes on shelters and termed the new estate provisions a giveaway. These are clearly areas that reformers will hammer away at in the years immediately ahead.

A short diversion from the specifics of the 1976 Tax Reform package. A few pages ago, I said that I understood very little of what I have read in the field of economics. One economist who *has* gotten through to me, with a simple and forceful argument on increased government spending as it relates to both income redistribution and the inflation-unemployment tradeoffs, is Henry Hazlitt. Back 30 years ago, in *Economics in One Lesson,"* he wrote:

> Here we shall have to say simply that all government expenditures must eventually be paid out of the proceeds of taxation . . . every dollar of government spending must be raised through a dollar of taxation. . . .
> 
> With public works necessary for their own sake, and defended on that ground alone, I am not here concerned. I am here concerned with public works considered as a means of "providing employment" or of adding wealth to the community that it would not otherwise have had. A bridge is built . . . the bridge has to be paid out of taxes. For every dollar that is spent on the bridge, a dollar will be taken away from taxpayers. If the bridge costs $1 million, the taxpayers will lose $1 million. They will have that much taken away from them which they would otherwise have spent on the things they needed most. Therefore for every public job created by the bridge project, a private job has been destroyed somewhere else. . . . Taxes inevitably affect the actions and incentives of those from whom they are taken. . . .
> 
> In brief, capital to provide new private jobs is first prevented

from coming into existence and the part that does come into existence is then discouraged from starting new enterprises. The government spenders create the very problem of unemployment they profess to solve. . . . The larger the percentage of the national income taken by taxes, the greater the deterrent of private production and employment. (9)

Hazlitt is equally unsympathetic with government "bailouts" for business:

When the government makes loans or subsidies to business, what it does is to tax successful business in order to support unsuccessful private business. Under certain emergency circumstances, there may be a plausible argument for this. . . . But in the long run it does not sound like a paying proposition from the standpoint of the country as a whole. And experience has shown that it isn't. (9)

Hazlitt, as a professional economist, need not be concerned with the human cost implicit in the dislocations when say, a Lockheed, denied federal financial support, fails and lays off a few hundred thousand employees. Eventually, some or all of those employees may find work in another industry or another part of the country. It's the "eventually" that hurts. And what has happened in this country in the 30 years since Hazlitt wrote his *Economics in One Lesson* is that power blocs have evolved or grown stronger and are able to prevent Hazlitt-type solutions, that is, "paying propositions for the country as a whole." Whether it is a labor union, an effective corporate lobbying effort, or a well-organized consumer group, politicians listen carefully to blocs and very often act accordingly.

Hazlitt's message about government growth crowding out investment in production and therefore limiting private employment is not simply a time-worn bit of economic philosophy. As recently as October 1976, a study by the Hudson Institute Europe indicated that overall growth is lowest in those countries where the government sector is largest. The study raised once again the strong suspicion that growing public spending actually causes slower economic growth.

One final aspect of the 1976 tax law, the first major federal tax legislation in seven years, should be noted. In keeping with the "government in sunshine" philosophy now in ascendancy, the final provisions of the tax bill were hammered out *in public*. In an unprecedented congressional procedure, a Senate-House conference committee offered arguments and reached compromises on some 250 disputed provisions in the presence of lobbyists, the press, and other interested representatives of the public. It seems doubtful that congressional tax conferences will ever return to the old system of settling such issues behind closed doors. Consider the ramifications of *that* change.

## THE EVOLUTION OF A GLOBAL ECONOMIC ORDER

Global natural resources, like beauty, lie in the eye of the beholder. Sometimes the beholder's eye can grow more perceptive over the years.

Only a few years ago, the prestigious Club of Rome generated world-wide discussion in business and academic circles by publishing "The Limits To Growth," an ambitious Massachusetts Institute of Technology study that projected disaster if mankind did not mend its ways. The Club of Rome is a group of scholars and businessmen from many countries who are concerned with global problems affecting the prospects for human survival. The club's "Limits to Growth" study predicted that mankind would face catastrophe within a century if current growth trends continued. The report sold more than 2 million copies around the world and precipitated many a great debate on growth versus no-growth economic policy.

In 1976 the Club of Rome met in an international conference called "The New Horizons for Mankind" at the University of Pennsylvania where its leaders said, in effect, "Hold it, boys and girls, we're not against growth, only *unplanned* growth." In fact, Aurelio Peccei, founder of the Club and a former managing director of Olivetti, was quoted as saying that the purpose of "The Limits to Growth" had been to get the world's attention focused on the ecological dangers of unplanned and uncontrolled population and industrial expansion. That it had.

Peccei also said that although the study had "punctured the myth of exponential growth," solving the world's resource and economic problems would require "puncturing a second myth—the myth of national competence." (10)

The thrust of the Club's warning had shifted, then, from emphasis on the physical limits to growth (i.e., the finitude of earth's resources) to something very different—the willingness and ability of mankind to evolve new systems for resource allocation.

Ervin Laszlo, a fellow at the United Nations Institute for Training and Research, put it this way:

> . . . The real issue is not whether to grow or not to grow. Rather it is how to grow: with which technologies and in what sectors of the economy. . . . A no-growth economy could easily lead to stagnation and weaken incentives to work. Economic growth is also needed to assure basic minimum standards of need

fulfillment to hundreds of millions in poor countries and in poor sectors of rich countries. (11)

Growth must continue, Laszlo concluded, but it must be "sustainable without harmful short- and long-range consequences."

The reconciliation between the Club of Rome's 1973 warning against "exponential" (unplanned) growth and its new, more optimistic projection is its plan for "organic growth"—growth that takes due account of the necessity of avoiding pollution, of conserving nonrenewable resources, and of meeting basic needs that enhance the quality of human life.

John R. Bunting, chairman of the First Pennsylvania Corporation, which sponsored the 1976 Club of Rome meeting, agreed with the need for long-range planning for the United States as well as for the world economy: "The market, essential as it is, is myopic; it is good for dealing with problems that lie only five or seven or possibly ten years ahead, but our most serious problems are long-range problems," he said.

Herman Kahn, a pioneer futurist, agrees with the Club's new, less pessimistic assessment of what lies in store for the planet. In *The Next 200 Years*, written with William Brown and William Martel, Kahn states that among other projected crises the "population bomb" will most likely never go off. (12) The authors contend that birth rates fall when, under new economic and cultural circumstances, parents want fewer children. The developed nations are certainly in that stage, and the masses of Asia, the authors write, will surely enter it through economic growth.

Kahn and his Hudson Institute associates are even more sanguine than the Club of Rome concerning the world's technological ability to solve its energy problems and other resource needs. But they warn against sociological brakes on such advances. Among such retardants are "ritualist and pseudo rationality" and "ideological polarization."

Robert Bartley, commenting on *The Next 200 Years* in the *Wall Street Journal* summed up the issue this way:

> Persuade yourself you can't grow and thus have to redistribute income, and you will destroy the capital that fuels the growth that can conquer poverty at home and abroad. . . .
> 
> Precisely such policies obviously have wide appeal, especially among the most affluent classes of the most affluent nations. Is the source of this appeal merely mistaken information, or is it something deeper? Can neurosis be cured by rational refutation? That is the ultimate issue and one is entitled to some doubts. . . . Growth remains the answer above all to the problems of the developing world. (13)

The "developing world," however, has some ideas of its own on how to solve its most pressing problems.

The world's rich and poor countries have been involved in discussions on the possibilities of redistributing the world's wealth for some time. At one time, it seemed like a one-sided discussion. The "have" nations (i.e., the developed, or "rich" nations) seemed to have all the cards; but that changed dramatically in 1973 when the Organization of Petroleum Exporting Countries—with several members in the "third-world," "non-aligned," "developing," or just plain "poor" category—showed what a resource cartel could accomplish through boycott or other economic pressures.

From that point forward, "have not" nations with needed natural resources became "haves" in their own right.

Recognition of this fact of global life and the planned or actual formation of other producer-nation cartels have stimulated a troubled global dialogue (essentially a North-South dialog). A prime vehicle for this dialogue, the Conference on International Economic Cooperation, has frequently been in recess because of one disagreement or another. Nevertheless, the CIEC exists and has functioned as a bargaining exchange for some nineteen developing countries on one hand and eight major industrialized countries on the other.

Equally enlightening are the statements made when the developing nations caucus. The mid-1976 meeting of non-aligned nations at Sri Lanka heard insistent demands for a "new economic international order," that is, a narrowing of the gap between the rich and poor nations of the world. The leaders of these nations envisage a world in which people in the richest nations cut back their consumption to leave more for everybody else. Not long ago, such hopes would have been diplomatically rebuffed in public and privately scoffed at by leaders of the industrial nations. Now it is abundantly clear that the developing world's mineral resources provide it with important leverage. Very few Americans realize that in addition to becoming increasingly dependent on foreign oil, the United States also imports virtually all of its columbium, mica sheet, strontium, manganese, cobalt, tantalum, and chromium. Third World countries are important sources of such minerals.

The poorer nations, if they can build and sustain economic unity, could very well attempt to make decisions now made by Western managers concerning trading patterns and currency values. Moreover, Prime Minister Sirimavo Bandaranaike of Sri Lanka reportedly foresees "The developing world . . . strong enough to think in terms of a merchant shipping fleet to carry its import and export cargo," and the ability "to regulate freight rates, insurance and banking, and thereby redress the imbalances to some extent." (14)

More producer-nation cartels, a Bank of the Third World (backed by its wealth of natural resources), and even a regional currency to lessen dependence on the franc, the dollar and the pound are all under consideration.

Perhaps the most pressing problem, however, is the crushing burden these nations now bear in terms of debt to the industrialized nations. The developing nations seek some form of moratorium or stretch-out of such debt, which in 1976 had topped $100 billion and was growing fast. A pricing mechanism that might protect developing nations from the gyrations of world-wide market demands for their resources is also high on their list of priorities.

With such abrasive issues still separating the industrialized and developing nations—the North and South of the planet as it were—what kind of international economic order is feasible?

The Club of Rome has produced a blueprint. "Reviewing the International Order" (or RIO, as headline writers will often put it) is the club's latest major effort. Largely the work of Nobel Laureate Jan Tinbergen of the Netherlands, it does indeed suggest the framework for global economic cooperation. Its chief recommendations include:

- Creation of additional monetary reserves for financing more rapid development of Third World countries.

- International income redistribution through transfer payments to Third World countries with particular attention to use of these resources for directly addressing the poverty problem.

- Closer collaboration among regional blocs with more "multilaterality" rather than bilateral trade relations as well as reduction of import impediments on products shipped by Third World nations.

- Implementation of the World Food Conference recommendation for adequate international food production distribution and stockpiling.

- A World Energy Research Authority to coordinate increased research on fusion, and nuclear, solar, and geothermal energy.

- A federation of international organizations to develop and coordinate environmental programs and ocean management.

- Internationalization of multinational corporations, that is, separation of such organizations from the national governments of their home countries.

- A system of subsidizing the prices at which technological expertise is made available to Third World countries.
- Arms reduction.
- Increasing the efficiency of the United Nations. (15)

The thrust of the Tinbergen report, then, is to urge substitution of international economic planning for the uncontrolled play of market forces.

If the RIO framework—or anything like it—evolves, American corporate leaders will within the next decade be operating in a vastly changed global arena. What these changes will mean in terms of operating pressures and opportunities, it is much too early to say.

Yet as a communicator, I am tremendously impressed with the *nature* of the challenge as it is now perceived. We are no longer talking in terms of *can* we work things out (technological progress) but *will* we do so (with sociological advances).

Here, *Will the Corporation Survive?* takes on a different context, a different dimension. And no one can answer the question with certainty because no one knows whether mankind is smart enough to resolve the *social* problems inherent in the proposal.

As if to confirm the key conclusions of the new Club of Rome deliberations, a blue-ribbon United Nations study issued in the fall of 1976 concluded that the limits to growth on the planet are not physical but rather the political and institutional deficiencies in the developing countries. Entitled "The Future of the World Economy" and issued by the U.N.'s Department of Economic and Social Affairs, the report is the work of a team of 15 international economists headed by Nobel Prize winner Wassily Leontief. "To insure accelerated development," the report states, "two conditions are necessary: first, far-reaching internal changes of a social, political and institutional character in the developing countries, and second, significant changes in the world economic order."

Finally, in a paper with cosmic ramifications, G. J. V. Nossal, director of the Walter and Elizabeth Hall Institute of Medical Research, Melbourne, Australia, told the "New Horizons for Mankind" conference that man, despite his tremendous symbolic and scientific achievements, remains "the prisoner also of other evolutionary forces—of the greed and selfishness and aggressiveness acquired during the dark struggle out of the jungle." Man's biological fitness, he said, is not yet a perfect match for the global problems confronting him. He needs to learn to think "not as a hungry hunter-food gatherer but as a citizen of a single, tiny, fragile, finite, crowded planet." (16)

## REFERENCES

1. *Balance*, No. 38, August, 1976, p. 1.
2. Burns, Arthur F. "The Inflation-Unemployment Web," *Readers Digest*, March, 1976, pp. 103–107.
3. Pohlman, Jerry E. *Inflation Under Control?* (Reston, Va.: Reston Publishing Company, Inc., a Prentice-Hall Company, 1976), pp. 6–11, 230.
4. "The Outlook," *Wall Street Journal*, January 17, 1977.
5. Cobbs, John. "Two Wrong Choices and a Way Out," *Business Week*, September 20, 1976, p. 21.
6. *Newsday*, September 5, 1976.
7. "Response," Institute of Life Insurance, September, 1976.
8. "Uninsurable Risks," *Business Week*, September 6, 1976, p. 88.
9. Hazlitt, Henry. *Economics in One Lesson* (New York, N.Y.: Manor Books, Inc., 1962), pp. 21–33. (First published by Harper Brothers in 1946.)
10. *New York Times*, April 13, 1976.
11. *New York Times*, April 14, 1976.
12. Kahn, Herman; William Martel; and William Brown. *The Next 200 Years* (New York, N.Y.: William Morrow & Company, 1976).
13. *Wall Street Journal*, May 25, 1976.
14. *New York Times*, September 5, 1976.
15. *New York Times*, April 13, 1976.
16. *New York Times*, April 14, 1976.

# 6

# *Attacks On the System*

> "We have concluded that social demands that business be accountable for a wider range of its impacts than has been traditional is part of a very general social trend which will occupy our attention for many decades."
>
> —Robert Ackerman and Raymond Bauer, in Corporate Social Responsiveness: The Modern Dilemma (1)

There is a temptation to think that the anticorporation activist movement has crested and is receding. Don't believe it. Public interest groups are having more *substantive* success in their attacks on the corporation than ever before.

It is true that the *number* of public interest organizations confronting corporations is undoubtedly reduced from, say, five years ago, but we are witnessing an organizational "natural selection." The public interest groups that have survived are indeed the fittest. They are strong and they are committed for the long pull. Furthermore, new well-based public interest groups are still coming into being.

Perhaps the most telling point here is that this movement is integral, not peripheral, to the way society is moving. Robert Ackerman and Raymond Bauer, experts on corporate social responsibility well before the term was popularized and virtually beaten to death, tell us:

> At this stage of the movement for the humanizing of society, one needs to look at the relative strength of the underlying forces. The strength of the movement lies in part in the moral basis for many entitlements that have come to be generally accepted and, in part, in better understanding of environmental and ecological issues, as well as many health issues. . . . It is difficult indeed to envision the circumstances which would reverse certain trends of the recent past: the recognition of equality of rights for minorities and women; our understanding of com-

plex ecological processes and of the factors that have a long-term and subtle impact on health; the rights of consumers to be informed and to get safe and reliable products. (2)

In a comprehensive analysis of the current corporate dilemma (included in a *Context* magazine article authored by Harvard University Professor Louis Banks), David Vogel of the University of California, Berkeley, argues that we are in the midst of a "publication" of all United States institutions, and most notably the corporation. This, as he sees it, is a process in which public pressures directly influence corporate operations:

> Each of the corporation's constituencies—government, the public, institutional and private investors, employees, neighbors, consumers, and suppliers—defines its power as well as its vulnerability. The diversity of tactics—consumer boycotts, picketing, disruption of business meetings, occupation of company headquarters, strikes, harassment of recruiters, class action suits, press conferences, research studies—should suggest the extent to which any corporation, even the largest and most powerful, is vulnerable to persistent and imaginative pressure tactics. (3)

"He might have added," Louis Banks comments, "that institutions dedicated to the pursuit of these tactics are by now well staffed and established and not likely to fade away."

Just as important are the *roots* of the current generation of activist organizations. One of the earliest effective organizers of such activity was the late Saul Alinsky who gathered the poor in the Back Yards of Chicago in the 1930s and kept applying pressure to corporations and other establishment institutions until his death. It is instructive to consider some of Alinsky's philosophy and tactics because much of each has been adopted by the current generation of activists.

Philosophically, Alinsky's basic assumption was simplicity itself: Society is divided into three parts: the "Have Nots" (those with poor housing, disease, ignorance, inadequate nutrition, and despair); the "Haves" (those with power, money, food, security, and luxury); and the "Have-a-Little, Want-Mores" (the middle class torn between upholding the *status quo* to protect what they have, yet wanting change so they can get more). It is this middle class, Alinsky contended, who not only represent the prize for the revolutionary conflict (broad-based support) but, ironically enough, also produce many of the leaders of such conflict.

In *Rules for Radicals,* Alinsky wrote that, "Organization for action will now and in the decade ahead center upon America's white middle class. That is where the power is. . . . Large parts of the middle class, 'the silent majority,' must be activated; action and articulation are one, as are silence and surrender." (4)

In the same book, Alinsky listed the attributes of a good radical organizer: curiosity, irreverence, imagination, a sense of humor (which he seemed to find lacking in many current activists), an organized personality, ego, a free and open mind (tactical flexibility), political schizophrenia ("the organizer must be able to split himself into two parts— one part in the arena of action where he polarizes the issue 100 to nothing . . . while the other part knows that when the time comes for negotiations that it really is only a 10 percent difference"), and "a bit of a blurred vision of a better world." As to the organizer's method of operation, Alinsky was unequivocal:

> The organizer's job is to inseminate an invitation for himself, to agitate, introduce ideas, get people pregnant with hope and a desire for change and to identify you as the person most qualified for this purpose. Here the tool of the organizer in the agitation leading to the invitation as well as actual organization and education of local leadership, is the use of the question, the Socratic method. (4)

In other words, the activist does not need to have answers, only embarrassing questions. Many of *today's* public interest groups go considerably beyond mere questioning. As we will see shortly, many such organizations have a list of specific demands. Before examining those demands, however, a few more rules for radicals from Alinsky:

> Tactics means doing what you can with what you have. . . . Here our concern is with the tactic of taking; how the Have Nots can take power away from the Haves. . . . Always remember the first rule of power tactics: *Power is not only what you have but what the enemy thinks you have.* The second rule is: *Never go outside the experience of your people.* . . . The third rule is: *Whenever possible go outside the experience of the enemy.* (4)

And:

> Once the battle is joined and a tactic is employed, it is important that the conflict not be carried on over too long a time. . . . I cannot repeat too often that *a conflict that drags on too long becomes a drag.* . . . There is a way to keep the action going and to prevent it from being a drag, but this means constantly cutting new issues as the action continues, so that by the time the enthusiasm and the emotions for one issue have started to de-escalate, a new issue has come into the scene with a consequent revival. With a constant introduction of new issues, it will go on and on. (4)

And:

> Organizations must be based on many issues. Organizations need action as an individual needs oxygen. The cessation of action brings death to the organization through factionalism and inaction, through dialogues and conferences that are actually a form of rigor mortis rather than life [a position not unlike Mao's "perpetuation" of the Chinese Communist Revolution]. It is impossible to maintain constant action on a single issue . . . a single issue drastically limits your appeal, where multiple issues would draw in the many potential members essential to the building of a broad, mass-based organization. . . . Many issues mean many members. (4)

If you doubt the vigor or effectiveness of the current public-interest, anticorporation activities, take a look at (1) some recent organizational developments among activists, (2) the recent *accomplishments* of these groups, and (3) what they and others are demanding of the corporation in the years immediately ahead.

## RECENT ACTIVIST ORGANIZATIONAL DEVELOPMENTS

First, let us take a look at a few, selected newer activist groups.

In the fall of 1976, New Directions, an international citizens' action organization burst upon the American scene attended by generous national media coverage. New Directions, characterized as a global counterpart of Common Cause, the seven-year-old United States citizens' lobby, has some ambitious objectives. Its president, Russell Petersen, formerly chairman of the U.S. Council of Environmental Quality, outlined those objectives to Gladwin Hill of the *New York Times* in this way:

> We'll have four main areas of concern. One is helping the poorest of the world's poor to help themselves through such avenues as reducing population growth, producing more food and improving housing and other community facilities—and through reduction of waste in the affluent societies.
>
> We will also be concerned with protection and enhancement of the environment, reduction of risks of war and violence throughout the world, and the safeguarding of basic human rights. (5)

Significantly, Petersen indicated that New Directions will work for change by concentrating on informing and mobilizing public opinion to obtain action through political processes "or any other channels open to us."

Corporate leaders, who could scarcely quarrel with the general aims of the new organization, nevertheless had to be concerned about the many value judgments that would have to be made en route to forming the organization's policies. Would everyone who paid annual dues (in the $15–$25 area) be entitled to a voice in policy formation? Just what does "reduction of waste in affluent societies" include? *Whose* standards of "enhanced" environment would guide New Directions? Would economic fallout weigh in such deliberations?

Petersen's record as a federal environmental administrator did not encourage many business leaders to think that New Directions would pay much attention to cost/benefit or risk/benefit ratios. Still, some decided to join in the hope that they could provide useful perspective for progress without painful dislocation—or just to keep informed on the organization's plans.

The Bicentennial year also provided a perfect setting for another more strident organization, the Peoples Bicentennial Commission, to get in some good licks on the imperfections of American capitalism. PBC, the "alternative" Bicentennial organization, first attracted national attention by demonstrating at the April 1975 ceremonies marking the opening of the American Revolution at Concord, Massachusetts. By early 1976, according to *Washingtonian Magazine,* "PBC had a paid membership approaching 25,000 with PBC affiliates—nearly 70 of them —located in almost every state. They have written six paperbacks— published by Simon & Schuster and by Bantam—one of which is going into its third printing. They have produced historical literature on the American Revolution that has been purchased by 70,000 religious institutions, 2,000 library systems and 5,000 public and private schools." (6)

The PBC "product" is "economic democracy," meaning worker ownership and control of industry and purchase of the assets of large United States corporations by the federal government in order to lease the companies back to the employees.

With a less than impressive turnout at its 1976 Fourth of July alternative celebration, PBC changed its name to something a bit more permanent—the People's *Business* Commission. Before long, PBC had a new approach to attacking the American business system. It sought equal time and space from various media to counter the national "economic education" campaign prepared by the nonprofit, establishment-oriented Advertising Council. Although PBC was unsuccessful in matching the free public service air time and print space given to the Advertising Council campaign, PBC did succeed in limiting the exposure for that campaign. The CBS and ABC networks, apparently concerned that they might indeed have to give PBC equal time, decided not to broadcast the Advertising Council spots.

Hard on the heels of the PBC campaign came alternative economic advertising produced by other public interest groups, the Public Media Center and Americans for a Working Economy. Here is a sample of ad copy from AWE:

> (Headline): If You Think The System Is Working, Ask Someone Who Isn't
> 
> Even if you've got a job, chances are you know someone who is out of work. . . . These people know first hand that our economy is not working the way it should. . . .
> 
> High levels of unemployment seem to have become part of business as usual, even in good times. The giant corporations that control our economy don't seem to mind having lots of people competing for a few jobs. . . .
> 
> SPEAK UP, AMERICA!
> 
> . . . We understand that we're not going to have an economy that puts *people* back to work until we have some basic changes in the way our economy works. . . .
> 
> We want to get Americans talking about economic change. It's the first step toward a democratic economy, one that works for all of us.

Notice the equation. Big = Bad. Randall Meyer, president of the Exxon Company, USA, has offered an interesting interpretation of that equation:

> Americans equate size with power, whether economic or political, and have always viewed the growth of large institutions with apprehension. When people think of business, they like to think of the corner grocer, the town druggist, or the service station at the neighborhood shopping center. *Small* business, which is perceived as being accessible, personalized and understandable, has been the national ideal. (7)

But all the philosophical attacks aren't the works of *organized groups*. For example, there is also a growing number of *individual* radical economists who have taken root on the nation's campuses and are imparting a whole new vision to undergraduates. One recently wrote:

> Many radical economists entered graduate school in the 1960s. If our professors ever deigned to mention Marx at all, they typically dismissed him, in Samuelson's words, as a "minor post-Ricardian." Growing more and more critical through our political experiences and our studies of the economy, most of us eventually decided that the Marxian perspective provided a more penetrating view of the world than the conventional analyses. While we are still "first fired, last hired," in economics depart-

ments around the country, we have begun to claim some professional turf. As the economy continues to deteriorate and mainstream economists have not yet come up with a cure, more and more people have begun to listen to other kinds of explanations. . . .

Emboldened, we dare more and more openly to struggle for a socialist America, a society promoting both rational planning and democratic control of our working and political lives. Arguing the possibility of that transition, none of us can yet provide a "model" of the specific social relations that might eventually unfold, so some call us "utopian" for dreaming about the future. We think it is the mainstream economists who are "utopian" for dreaming that our present economic system could possibly work. (8)

## RECENT ACTIVIST ACCOMPLISHMENTS

Have the *established* public interest organizations been effective? Common Cause's then-chairman, John Gardner, in a mid-September 1976 advertisement seeking new members wrote: "I don't think it would be an exaggeration to say that some of the most promising developments that have taken place in the country lately would not have taken place if it weren't for the battles fought—and won—by the 260,000 members of Common Cause and their allies." (9)

Among the "Battle Ribbons of Common Cause" cited in the ad:

- The five-year battle to take big money out of politics.
- The battle to let citizens see what's going on in their government.
- The battle to close the oil-depletion loophole.

Gardner signed off with, "Look what we have accomplished in a few short years with 260,000 members. Can you imagine what we could do for our country if we were 500,000 strong?"

"The battle to close the oil-depletion loophole" is related to another fast-developing war between corporate interests and their critics—divestiture, or dismemberment, of the major oil companies. The significance of this fight would be great if it were limited only to the future structure of the oil industry, but many business leaders see the dispute as the leading edge of a much broader confrontation: break up the oil companies today, attack the concentrations in the food, auto, or any other industry tomorrow.

Divestiture of oil companies vertically (by separating functions such as exploration, production, processing, transportation, or marketing) or horizontally (by prohibiting a company's involvement in more than one source of energy) seemed far-fetched just a few years ago. Yet in the fall of 1975 a divestiture amendment was offered on a Senate natural gas deregulation bill and but for a swing of five votes the U.S. Senate would have been recorded officially as favoring a revolutionary control of such bigness. In the spring of the following year, the Senate Judiciary Committee voted in favor of reporting a similar measure out for floor debate. Congress adjourned without such debate.

My purpose here is not to delve into the complex pros and cons of the divestiture argument but rather to note a few revealing, if rather bizarre, media developments when the issue really warmed up in mid-1976.

Here is one: *Business Week*'s "Economics" section ran a story on divestiture headlined:

> THE FLAKY ARGUMENTS OVER BREAKING UP BIG OIL
> "Independent economists see little or nothing to be gained—or lost—by it." (10)

Well, so much for that little problem.

Or how about some candid remarks by Robert Sherrill, the Washington correspondent for *The Nation*, writing in the *New York Times Magazine*:

> There is one thing that can be said categorically about the opposing sides: they do not lack for authoritative opinions. Indeed, if the general public must depend on experts for advice, there is absolutely no way for it to know, or even to guess, what the effects of divestiture would be. . . .
> As a paying spectator, I'm entitled to say that I find it very easy to side with the divestiture crowd, although, in part, for the wrong reasons. It gives me considerable pleasure to see Big Oil quaking at the thought that the worm—the public—has turned. Smug arrogant, Big Oil has always had its way with us. (11)

Once again, Big = Bad.

The activist concern for size and concentration in industry was instrumental in the passage of significant new federal antitrust legislation in 1976:

- The federal government has been given new powers to compel the production of documents and testimony to aid its investigations of possible civil violations of the antitrust laws.

- The government's ability to attack mergers has been bolstered by requiring companies above a certain size to notify the government in advance of contemplated mergers.

- The attorneys general of the 50 states now have the power to bring suits for damages against violators of the antitrust laws on behalf of all the citizens of a state. These damages, which could amount to as much as three times the actual overcharges that resulted from the illegal behavior, could run to millions of dollars.

A late-1976 antitrust "milestone" occurred when fifteen executives of cardboard box manufacturing companies were sentenced to jail (for periods ranging from several days to two months) and fines after pleading no contest to price-fixing charges. Thirty-two other executives charged in the case were fined.

Another key *systemic* attack on the corporation by public interest organizations is what Saul Alinsky identified as "the proxy tactic." In *Rules for Radicals* he explained how this tactic evolved in 1967 as an outgrowth of his confrontation with Eastman Kodak on behalf of the black ghetto organization called FIGHT:

> The proxy idea first came up as a way to gain entrance to the annual stockholders' meeting for harassment and publicity . . . it began with nothing specific in mind except to ask Eastman Kodak stockholders to assign their proxies to the Rochester black organization or come to the stockholders' meeting and vote in favor of FIGHT.
> . . . The first real breakthrough followed my address to the National Unitarian Convention . . . in which I asked for and received the passage of a resolution that the proxies of their organization would be given to FIGHT. The reactions of the local politicians made me realize that senators and congressmen up for re-election would turn to their research directors and ask, "How many Unitarians have I got in my district?" The proxy tactic now began to look like a possible political bank shot.
> . . . The church organizations had mass members—*voters!* It meant publicity and publicity meant pressure on political candidates and incumbents. We hoisted a banner with our slogan, "Keep your sermons; give us your proxies." (12)

A few years later, Alinsky saw the proxy tactic as "a key to participation of the middle class" and planned a nationwide organization of individual and institutional stockholders to impact on corporation—and national—policy. Alinsky died before he could bring it off, but there were others, many others, quite prepared to use the proxy to exert pressure on the corporation.

By 1976 the proxy tactic had become institutionalized. Nonprofit institutions—religious groups, foundations and universities among them—led the charge. According to the Investor Responsibility Research Center, in the spring of 1976, 174 significant proxy resolutions on social issues had been raised by stockholders of 140 companies. A year earlier, according to IRRC, 76 such resolutions were voted on at 50 annual meetings.

The resolutions rarely pass, but they do have effect. Some companies have considered or even changed policies when social resolutions have been introduced. According to IRRC, in 1976 at least 79 resolutions were withdrawn before being presented to shareholders because management and the activist sponsors of such resolutions had reached agreement. At a bare minimum, even an unsuccessful resolution will generate unfavorable corporate publicity, sometimes widespread and sustained.

The proxy tactic is a radical departure from the traditional Wall Street rule: "Vote for management or sell your holdings." The socially oriented investors—individuals and organizations alike—are not very much concerned about tradition.

Still another instrument for attack on the corporation—the class action suit—is experiencing a rebirth. Such suits, which until recently were filed primarily in the areas of environmental control and consumer redress, seek to enlarge the grievance of a single client into a wide-ranging, multimillion-dollar attack on the corporation. Although a 1974 U.S. Supreme Court ruling reduced the number of certain kinds of class action suits brought in federal courts, class actions are now being brought in fast-increasing numbers in state courts.

*Business Week* reported in mid-1975 that "most who work in the class action specialty think that the general consumerist trend in the U.S. is adding so much fuel to class action litigation that they will continue to flood the courts." (13) Typically, plaintiffs now include mortgage holders, automobile owners, motel franchisees, telephone answering service subscribers, and service station dealers. And in October 1976, a new stimulant for anticorporation suits came into existence: Defendants found guilty must pay plaintiffs' legal costs.

This kind of litigation is leading to the development of legal institutions undreamed of just a few years ago. Public interest law firms now abound, not only in Washington, D.C., but in state capitals across the country. And an "anticorporation corporation," the Public Equity Corporation—perhaps the ultimate in such institutions—announced in mid-1975 that in order to raise money to launch an ongoing program of such suits, it was making a public offering of shares!

On the other hand, the Pacific Legal Foundation, a nonprofit law firm specializing in defending private enterprise in a wide variety of courtroom and regulatory agency disputes, recently announced that it was expanding its operations to provide coast-to-coast service.

The Pacific Legal Foundation expansion is reflective of another key aspect of current public interest organization development—increasing reliance on the courtroom and the legislature. Whether class action or any of a number of other legal stratagems, it is judicial and legislative redress (with attendant publicity, of course) that seems to attract the more mature public interest organization these days.

An expert in activist strategy whom I greatly respect made this interesting distinction to me in a conversation about the many environmental and public health referenda appearing on state ballots in November 1976:

> Corporate people often make the mistake of thinking of the public interest organizations as some kind of monolithic, or homogenized, unit. Nothing could be further from the truth.
> We have our "pros" and our "amateurs" too. Those of us who are into this for some time and have made long-term "career" commitments realize that it's going to take time to change the system. After all, some of the corporations we've been attacking just a few years ago practically owned some statehouses and legislatures. We know they are beginning to adjust. Of course, we're going to keep the media and other pressures on them to see to it that they *do* adjust.
> The amateurs—the zealots—want instant change and if it doesn't occur after a particularly dramatic demonstration of say, lying down in the middle of the highway, they say "the hell with this system of trying to influence public opinion, we need a revolution."

## THE REMAINING DEMANDS

Attacks on American-style capitalism have been coming thick and fast during the past few years. The economy's sustained high unemployment, coupled with the ever present threat of double-digit inflation, seems to have released a lot of pent-up intellectual energy concerned with the shortcomings of the corporation and the American business system in general.

A rash of well-publicized books appearing in 1975 and 1976 attacked contemporary American business with a force unseen since the original muckrakers. (Are our publishers onto something in terms of the taste and temper of the American reader?) Within one year, a number of powerful minds—Daniel Bell, Robert Heilbroner, Michael Harrington, Barry Commoner, and Christopher Stone among them—offered severe criticism of the system and prophesied radical change in it.

In *The Cultural Contradictions of Capitalism*, Daniel Bell contends that "the principles of the economic realm and those of the culture now lead people in contrary directions." (14) Bell, the father of the concept of the "post-industrial society," is certainly not an anticorporate activist. A renowned academician and author, his opinions are not taken lightly. He sees the current cultural changes as evolving directly from the long-term American commitment to mass consumption. Equally important, he feels, is the political contradiction of capitalism —the inability of the state to cope with demands and problems that call out for solution. Bell suggests that we consider a philosophy of a "public household" to build agreement on social needs to be addressed before appetites are satisfied, to use the national budget to satisfy those social needs, and to recognize the new limits of our resources.

Robert Heilbroner, Norman Thomas Professor of Economics at the New School for Social Research, is sure that capitalism is dying. In his *Business Civilization in Decline* he suggests that capitalism is in decline not because of its failures but because of its successes—creation of affluence which generates anticapitalistic sentiment among intellectuals and children of the well-to-do; increased economic power for workers which breeds inflation; a hierarchical organization of work easily transferred to hierarchical control; and depletion of resources and pollution of the envelope of human life. (15)

Economic growth, on which capitalism has fed, must cease, according to Heilbroner. Capitalist entrepreneurs will be succeeded by state planners. Private property and the free market will wither and die. And, most significant of all, with the death of capitalism, Heilbroner laments, will come a time when liberty itself is severely restricted and people long for the day when "artistic statements, social or sexual habits and political utterances" were a birthright.

Michael Harrington, on the other hand, *looks forward* to *The Twilight of Capitalism*, which he has used as the title of his 446-page blockbuster attack on the business system. (16) This attack, one must remember, is presented by the chairman of the Democratic Socialist Organizing Committee. Like Bell, Harrington has a list of contradictions of capitalism in our modern setting. They center on the tendency of business executives to urge, according to Harrington, what is most destructive of capitalism and to resist what might save it. He includes as an example of this alleged subconscious death-wish business leaders' opposition to effective redistribution of wealth.

Harrington, who popularized the tragedy of American poverty in the early 1960s with his *The Other America*, has apparently decided to take on the role of chief prophet of the death of capitalism in the 1970s. He has recently written that:

> During the past seven years, America has been taken on a sickening roller coaster ride plunging from boom to bust, stagnating and inflating at the same time. In addition, we have casually allowed most of our great cities to disintegrate, ruined the rail system, polluted the earth, air and water so even in "good times" we are a manifestly unhappy people.
> . . . Our economic problems are, I suggest, systemic, not accidental. . . .
> Capitalism then is on the way out, sometimes with capitalists in the lead. It is forced to collectivize itself in order to cope with the ruinous consequences of its own spontaneous tendencies.
> In the name of protecting a market-based system, it has to destroy the rule of the market. It cannot turn back to a simpler age since it has created a world economy of such complexity that it cannot be run by the "invisible hand" of Adam Smith. The real question for the future, then, is whose visible hand will run the post-capitalist society? That of the people, asserting their priorities in a free democratic process? I call that socialism. Or will it be the invisible hand of a new class, the technological grandchildren of today's sophisticated corporate planners? (17)

Enter Barry Commoner. A biologist by training, Commoner in recent years has become a commentator on an increasingly broad spectrum of business-in-society issues. In his latest book, *The Poverty of Power*, Commoner, in the opinion of one reviewer, attempts to weave the ecosystem, the production system, and the economic system into a pattern that, in Commoner's view, should signal a shift to socialism. (18)

Commoner is undaunted by the "scientist-go-home" reaction he has received from some economists. He says *somebody* has to make the bridging effort. One of the main struts of his bridge is a discussion of how understanding and proper interpretation of the Second Law of Thermodynamics can lead us all to socioeconomic salvation. (At the risk of oversimplification, that interpretation might well be stated as "use the right kind of energy for the right kind of job.")

Having misread or ignored the Second Law because of their preoccupation with profits, American corporate leaders have created great havoc in the environment and economy and had better be stopped, according to Commoner. He concludes that "there are grounds to at least consider the possibility that the pervasive and seemingly insoluble faults now exhibited by the U.S. economic system can best be remedied by reorganizing it along socialist lines."

*Where the Law Ends: The Social Control of Corporate Behavior,* by Christopher Stone, is an attorney's approach to the broad changes he feels necessary to bring the corporation into "sync" with the rest of American society. (19) Naturally, Stone focuses on the legal aspects of the problem. He believes that new laws and new series of intracorporate "configurations of authority and information flow" are necessary. New laws or amendments to existing statutes are needed, he contends, to set minimum experience requirements for high-level corporate office, to require that corporate safety directors and environmental directors be placed at high management levels, and to impose "public representation" on management as well as boards of directors.

Stone suggests director systems that would not only be tolerant of "intrusions" but would also engage in active cooperation with agents of society, "even if doing so involves a sacrifice of profits in some cases." Nevertheless, he fully expects the corporation of the future to remain fundamentally oriented toward "profit, expansion and prestige."

The market system (for which read free enterprise, private enterprise, or any of a half-dozen other labels for the current American economic system) has also been taking its lumps in periodicals, brochures, leaflets, flyers, mimeographed memos, and every other process of bonding ink to paper. We cannot possibly present the full potpourri of such attacks, but a selected few are especially interesting in terms of authorship and/or grace of expression.

First, excerpts from a recent article by Gar Alperovitz and Jeff Faux, codirectors of the Exploratory Project for Economic Alternatives, a group reportedly *established by 25 foundations to define practical approaches to economic restructuring:*

> We Americans must begin to consider how we will replace the large corporation as the central institution of our economy. . . .
> . . . The corporation is a device for perpetuating the maldistribution of income and wealth. . . . The corporation is a source of constant upheaval and instability in the lives of people who do not belong to it and many who do. . . .
> As we move deeper into the economic difficulties of the final quarter of the century, we will accordingly have to evolve new institutions that emphasize greater equality, stability, conservation, and community. We need to support *small-scale* [emphasis added] community-centered businesses that can prosper without explosive growth. We need public control over capital and natural resources so both can be allocated according to

public priorities. . . . In connection with some larger economic functions, we will need to replace the large corporation with new institutions directly accountable to public priorities. (20)

Similarly, Hazel Henderson, a brilliant economist who is codirector of the Princeton Center for Alternative Futures, recently called for decentralization of economic institutions:

> I believe that private enterprise does have a future, both in this country and elsewhere in the world. But it is likely to be very different from what we see today. . . .
>
> We must continually check the tendencies in human societies for knowledge and power and wealth to cluster. This clustering produces centralized and exploitable surpluses; these in turn excite greed and envy and create opportunities for despotism. Human history can be seen as an endless replay of the abuse of power and of surplus, and the struggle to check and balance the destabilizations thus caused.
>
> Perhaps there is no possibility of ordered human societies without such instabilities. Perhaps all we can hope for is the continual redress of imbalances by periodic redistribution. What may distinguish our current instabilities are their unprecedented size and concentration.
>
> As we Americans cross the frontier into our third century, the stakes have never been higher. We have exhausted the limits of empty technique. From our efforts to retool the world around us, we must now turn to retooling ourselves. We must change our values and our ways of seeing things. For the first time in human history, morality has become pragmatic. (21)

Still another straw in the wind: When the 1976 Democratic national platform committee held hearings, a strong pitch was made for inclusion in the platform of a plank on corporate accountability. It came from Democracy '76, an advocacy group that includes numerous members of Congress; Governor Michael Dukakis of Massachusetts; Victor Gotbaum and Jerry Wurf of the State, County and Municipal Employees Union; Floyd Smith of the Machinists; and such noted public figures as Robert Lekachman, the economist; Julian Bond, the black leader; and Betty Friedan, the feminist.

The Democracy '76 proposals included such ideas as the licensing of plant location to promote maximum investment in areas that need jobs most desperately; the submission by the Federal Reserve of an annual report to Congress on the employment effects of its policies; the acquisition by government of equity in corporations it bails out or props up, with the equity then being used to put public representatives on the corporations' boards; and the establishment of "yardstick" corporations in various fields, with labor, community, and consumer representation on their boards.

Finally, what may turn out to be the most important of all the recent anticorporation books and articles: Ralph Nader's attempt at a haymaker, *Taming the Giant Corporation*. (22) Cowritten with colleagues Mark Green and Joel Seligman, the new treatise is said to have taken five years to research and compose. The book attacks giant corporations as "private governments" that have "direct and decisive impact on the social, economic and political life of the nation."

In *Taming the Giant Corporation* and in many other articles and speeches, Nader has been pushing for federal chartering of corporations; that is, federal controls much stricter than those currently imposed by the relatively "lax" standards of states such as Delaware and New Jersey. *Taming the Giant Corporation* is the bill of particulars that Naderites used in their lobbying of the 1976 session of Congress. Those particulars, of course, have long been on the public record.

How significant is the federal chartering proposal? Put it this way: If it, or any of the variants proposed to achieve the same purpose, becomes the law of the land, corporate managers will be operating in a totally different economic institution.

In the late spring of 1976, when congressional hearings began to take testimony on federal chartering and other proposed limitations on corporate power, *Business Week* was moved to observe that "out of the hearings will emerge—within two to four years—a law or set of laws that may turn out to have as much impact on the conduct of business in the United States as the New Deal reforms did in the 1930s." (23)

So let's take a close look at the federal chartering proposal advanced by Nader and his Corporate Accountability Research Group. First, the law would apply to about 700 "giant" corporations—those corporations with shares listed on a national securities exchange or held by 2,000 or more United States shareholders and with more than $250 million in annual sales or more than 10,000 employees. These companies, Nader's group contends, constitute America's "executive oligarchy" which thwarts corporate democracy.

In general terms, Nader's CARG federal chartering proposal would alter the way companies are governed, increase what they must disclose to the public, decrease their size, and change the way they deal with employees. More specifically, here are key provisions of the CARG proposal:

> 1. Management autonomy would be greatly restricted. Federally chartered companies would have to establish boards that would review many actions currently mandated to manage-

ment, including hiring and firing of top executives. In addition, each board member would be responsible for a key area of the company's "public" operation—legal compliance, disclosure, consumer protection, and so on. Shareholder selection of directors would be liberalized, and management would be subject to harsh penalties for violating laws relating to corporate operation.

2. Corporate disclosure would be greatly increased. As originally drafted, the CARG federal chartering bill required each regulated corporation to publish a vast list of data on economic and social performance, all this data to be published in a new government publication, the *Corporate Register*. Publication of the names of the 100 largest beneficial owners of the company's stock, government contracts, holdings in other companies, profit by product line, and executive compensation would also have to be divulged.

3. Employees would be granted a "bill of rights" that would provide for protection of employees who reported corporate lawbreaking or other misbehavior. And it would ensure employee privacy by prohibiting corporate use of devices and equipment deemed to represent an invasion of such privacy.

4. Industrial deconcentration would be stimulated. The mere existence of a highly concentrated industry would trigger antitrust action to split the industry into smaller companies.

There are many people in the corporate world who think that CARG's federal chartering proposal does not stand a chance of enactment in 1977—or ever. They may take comfort in a mid-1976 editorial in the *New York Daily News* (the nation's largest-circulation newspaper) which, under a headline, "Unwise In Any Form," stated, "Nader's scheme is based on his conviction that doing business is a privilege which Big Brother should have the right to grant, refuse or take away." (24)

There is one other attack on American business leadership that belongs in this discussion. This attack, less direct and certainly not organized, is nevertheless potentially just as damaging. I am referring to the portrayal of the business leader by influential American writers.

Robert F. Lucid, chairman of the graduate group in the University of Pennsylvania's department of English, recently addressed the subject in an article entitled "Post-War Literature and the American Businessman" published in the university's *Wharton Quarterly*. Lucid wrote:

> From one point of view, talking about the figure of the business man in the annals of American literature is as idle and merely predictable an activity as talking about the figure of the Negro in pre-bellum Southern fiction. One figure is as much a stereotype as the other, and a reasonable reaction, at least from the point of view of the businessman and the Negro, is that most of the time the writers don't know what the hell they're talking about. . . .
>
> When one turns to the American literature which has appeared since the Second World War and examines the work of our major writers, it is to discover that the figure of the institutional manager has undergone a change. If we accept the anthropological hypothesis that the major literature of a society reflects the working of that society's imagination, then we must conclude that the postwar American imagination began to envision the businessman as either a villain or a weakling, and sometimes both.
>
> . . . We must of course conclude that the figure of the businessman seems to our imagination to have changed. But further investigation would quickly show that all "figures" and all significant institutional activities seem to our postwar imagination to have changed. The fact is that there is something arbitrary about our focusing in on the figure of the businessman—present though he frequently is in our fiction—and what we need centrally to focus upon is the distress and anger and alarm of the individual in our postwar American society.
>
> Our artists would seem to be telling us that something happened to us in the fairly recent past and that we have come now to believe ourselves capable of stooping to things we would never have imagined ourselves sinking to before. If that is the burden of what postwar American literature is saying, and a strong case can be made to prove that it is, then we should not be surprised that the figure of the businessman, when he happens to appear, is represented in grim and unsympathetic terms. (25)

Then there is television. Question its artistic credentials but not its reach and hold on the American public. Here is Benjamin Stein recently appraising TV's portrayal of American business executives:

> What do businessmen look like on TV? They look like thugs and murderers, psychopaths peering furtively out from their ledgers, pillars of society who secretly destroy from within. . . .
>
> In conversation after conversation with TV writers, the same points come up. To the TV creative community, businessmen really are dangerous people. The businessman's hazardousness comes under a number of headings as far as the Hollywood writer is concerned. First of all, to writers in show business, the

business types are the enemy. The producers and agents and studio people are the ones who mess around with their product and ruin it for the sake of money. Not only that, but the businessmen don't pay them enough for their creative juices. The scripts are, in a sense, the writer's revenge. . . .

But there is some innocent ignorance mixed in here too. For the Hollywood writer, the word "business" means illegal campaign contributions . . . and CIA connections. . . . This is so consistently the image of business that one finds in Hollywood that it obviously is the definitive word on the subject. Free of any contact with the larger world of business, the writer free-associates from the stories he has seen on the evening news of businessmen who are really criminals. (26)

In the fall of 1976, CBS presented an interesting case in point, a new weekly prime time series called "Executive Suite." Described by one reviewer as a series struggling with its reality quotient, "Executive Suite" concentrated on its characters' personal relationships. Boardroom soap opera, "Executive Suite" entertained Americans at business's expense. It stressed executive venality and greed while projecting corporate social responsiveness as all but impossible.

Stein puts this kind of TV programming in perspective:

> This view of the world given out into living rooms across the land does not, by itself, change many minds, I suspect. But for those who are already inclined to view business and businessmen with a jaundiced eye, the TV show sends a legitimating message. It says, "Yes. You're right. That guy behind the desk dictating letters to his secretary is a dangerous character. You had him pegged." (27)

## REFERENCES

1. Ackerman, Robert, and Bauer, Raymond. *Corporate Social Responsiveness: The Modern Dilemma* (Reston, Va.: Reston Publishing Company, Inc., a Prentice-Hall Company, 1976), p. 17.

2. *Ibid.*, p. 26.

3. Vogel, David, as quoted by Louis Banks in "Business and the Rise of Individualism," *Context* magazine, No. 1-76, p. 4.

4. Alinsky, Saul. *Rules for Radicals* (New York, N.Y.: Random House, 1971), p. 184.

5. *New York Times*, September 8, 1976.

6. Makower, Joel W. "Power on the Potomac: Revolution 1976 Style," *Washingtonian Magazine*, April, 1976, pp. 65-75.

7. Meyer, Randall, in a speech delivered at the President's Lecture Series, Florida State University, Tallahassee, Florida, November 22, 1974.
8. Gordon, David M. "Recession is Capitalism As Usual," *New York Times Magazine*, April 27, 1975, pp. 60–63.
9. Advertisement in the *New York Times*, "The Week in Review," September 19, 1976.
10. "The Flaky Arguments Over Breaking Up Big Oil," *Business Week*, August 16, 1976, pp. 93–96.
11. Sherrill, Robert. "Breaking Up Big Oil," *New York Times Magazine*, October 3, 1976, pp. 15, 86–98.
12. Alinsky, Saul. *Rules for Radicals*, pp. 172–173.
13. "Class Actions Refuse to Die," *Business Week*, June 9, 1975.
14. Bell, Daniel. *The Cultural Contradictions of Capitalism* (New York N.Y.: Basic Books, 1976).
15. Heilbroner, Robert L. *Business Civilization in Decline* (New York, N.Y.: W. W. Norton & Company, 1976).
16. Harrington, Michael. *The Twilight of Capitalism* (New York, N.Y.: Simon and Schuster, 1976).
17. *Newsday*, May 30, 1976, pp. 1, 7, 10.
18. Commoner, Barry. *The Poverty of Power* (New York, N.Y.: Knopf & Company, 1976).
19. Stone, Christopher D. *Where the Law Ends: The Social Control of Corporate Behavior* (New York, N.Y.: Harper & Row, 1975).
20. Alperovitz, Gar, and Faux, Jeff. "After the Corporation," *New York Times*, June 28, 1976.
21. Henderson, Hazel. "A Farewell to the Corporate State," *Business and Society Review*, Spring, 1976, pp. 49–56.
22. Nader, Ralph; Green, Mark; and Seligman, Joel. *Taming the Giant Corporation* (New York, N.Y.: W. W. Norton & Company, 1976).
23. "A Step Toward the Federal Corporate Charter," *Business Week*, June 21, 1976, pp. 80–84.
24. "Unwise In Any Form," *New York Daily News*, August 4, 1976.
25. Lucid, Robert F. "Post-War Literature and the American Businessman," *Wharton Quarterly*, Spring, 1975, pp. 6–9.
26. Stein, Benjamin. "Draculas in the Executive Suite," *Wall Street Journal*, May 28, 1976.
27. *Ibid.*

# 7

# One-on-One: The Issue Attacks

Even if the current assault on the private enterprise system somehow fails to wreak havoc on the American corporation, there is another powerful force for change being brought to bear on the corporation. That force, represented by the dozens of attacks on *specific* corporate activities and policies, if more diffused than the broad-scale attacks on the economic system, is no less potent.

In fact, the single-issue attacks have already proven *more potent*, more capable of producing change. It is, after all, rather ambitious to suggest a complete upheaval of the economic order, especially when no one knows exactly how it will all turn out. It is more reasonable to attack one issue at a time.

Virtually every major segment of corporate operations has come under scrutiny and criticism in recent years. In this chapter we will select a few of the key issues that have surfaced, examine the attack in each case, and measure the impact of these attacks.

### EQUAL EMPLOYMENT OPPORTUNITY

It has become rather chic in some circles to bad-mouth equal employment opportunity in industry. Representatives of some minority organizations and women's groups love to hyperbolize about "tokenism." I still attend meetings where speakers rail against the practice of hiring a *black* community relations director or a *woman* consumer relations specialist. "We never get the jobs with real responsibility," say these spokespersons. They also point out correctly that during economic cutbacks minority and women employees with low seniority are very often the first to be laid off. The hallowed seniority system stands firm.

Interestingly, EEO and affirmative action programs have also fallen into disfavor among many of the nation's intellectuals, especially at some of our leading academic institutions. It was not ever thus. When such programs were imposed on or voluntarily introduced in industry, many an academic watched gleefully as corporation after corporation struggled, and sometimes floundered, in this new, deep water. Then the federal government did a terrible thing. It decided to enforce equal employment opportunity among teachers and administrators on the nation's campuses. It wasn't long before a string of academicians were out with published opinions on the injustice of "reverse discrimination" or the reasons why the university should be exempted from such well-intentioned but onerous programs.

Let's say it clearly: Providing equal employment opportunity, given the history of this country and our current economic problems, is a hellish problem. For generations this society tolerated a basically white, male, hierarchical structure in business. Millions of minds were wasted. Some of these minds tried to buck the system; it never occurred to others to try.

When public opinion finally coalesced in favor of a fundamental revision in the makeup of the American workforce, the corporation was tagged both as scapegoat for society's past errors and the vehicle for nothing less than a revolution in 200-year-old work patterns.

When, in similar fashion, the nation awoke to inequities in our schools because of long-standing racial segregation, it evolved an artificial, controversial solution—busing of school children to equalize educational opportunity. (We didn't do very well at solving the nub of the problem, which is the fact that in most communities, blacks and whites don't live side by side.)

In equal employment opportunity, we came up with another artificial, controversial solution—the affirmative action program. Many of the early affirmative action programs were conceived by the federal government. The Labor Department Office of Contract Compliance developed employment standards for all companies doing business with the government. Before long, such standards, with variations as necessary, constituted the model for affirmative action programs now in place in most American companies.

Affirmative action is unfair as life is unfair.

It seeks to protect several selected minorities—endangered species, as it were—but not *all* minorities. It seeks to establish timetables for upward career mobility, but such moves *do* take time. It potentially sets black against white and man against woman in the competition for promotion and growth, where only ability should count. And, yes, when there are layoffs, "last hired, first fired" is still generally the rule despite affirmative action programs.

But it is all we have and all we are likely to get. It is what young minority and women students can bank on as they plan their careers in business. It is the only vehicle that ensures the chance that for many did not exist at all 20 years ago. It is the worst possible idea—except all the rest.

And the corporation is the laboratory in which this impossible experiment is taking place. Whether they came willingly or were dragged kicking and screaming into affirmative action, American corporations are in it now. Some have realized the opportunity that exists in tapping new sources of bright human beings. They have undertaken extensions well beyond what is mandated, because in their judgment, there are good business reasons to lead in such activity. And perhaps most important of all, many corporations are institutionalizing affirmative action (and other social responsibility) objectives. Increasingly, at companies such as the Bendix Corporation and Standard Oil Co. (Indiana) middle-level managers are being evaluated not only on traditional standards such as meeting production targets but also on how well they attain the newer, socially oriented goals.

Clearly, some corporations are into affirmative action only because the price of not being in it is so high. Payments to settle equal employment opportunity cases are no longer insignificant. In June 1976 Merrill Lynch Pierce Fenner & Smith, Inc. settled two such cases by agreeing to pay $1.9 million to individuals it had failed to hire or promote and to adopt a $1.3 million, five-year affirmative action plan to employ more women and minority-member workers. In early 1977, NBC settled a similar EEO complaint at an estimated cost of $2 million.

In mid-1976, Labor's Office of Federal Contract Compliance Programs moved with new verve into the white-collar financial-and-service industries, specifically banks and insurance companies. The intent was clear. Since these are the fastest growing sectors of the private economy, OFCCP was looking for the biggest impact in terms of numbers of jobs being opened to minorities and women. OFCCP has EEO jurisdiction over some 250,000 companies that hold government contracts, and it is seeking to make an impression on all of them by concentrating on the government's most visible suppliers. OFCCP's very large club is the ability to declare a company ineligible for government contracts if its affirmative action program is not what OFCCP thinks it should be.

One of the more troublesome aspects of OFCCP regulation has

been the incredible red tape spawned by the early affirmative action regulatory structure. In effect, 17 federal agencies had EEO compliance responsibility with OFCCP operating as a kind of coordinating advocate. Under controversial new rules, much of this red tape will be eliminated and enforcement will be simpler and more uniform. However, critics of the new rules say they represent relaxation of enforcement procedures. Some feel that only a Cabinet-level agency can work.

For the most part, the government-mandated affirmative action programs seek to eliminate job discrimination based on national origin, race, and sex. Targets—let's not argue over whether they are "quotas" or "goals"—are set for the number of minority and women employees to be in place at various pay levels or job classifications within six months, a year, or several years of the projection. Critics call this reverse discrimination because it tends to reserve jobs for certain types of individuals, thereby closing off these opportunities to "unprotected" job seekers.

Nathan Glazer, a professor of education and sociology at Harvard University and author of *Affirmative Discrimination*, is one of the more vociferous critics. He has written:

> There are at least four things wrong with this ill-conceived policy. It operates in defiance of its parent Civil Rights Act of 1964 and the Constitution; it divides the nation by trying to draw a line, which is necessarily arbitrary, between groups that deserve the protection of the law and those that do not; it does not reach the major problems or those most in need of help; and it is based on the unrealistic picture of what is good for a multiethnic society. (1)

To be sure, the courts have begun to give comfort to those who claim that affirmative action really means reverse discrimination. A few years ago, the issue was sharply drawn in the DeFunis case, wherein a young law student charged that he had been denied admission to a law school because the school's affirmative action commitments had made it necessary to favor members of "protected" groups. By the time the case came to the Supreme Court, the issue had been resolved for DeFunis personally and the court declared the case moot. However, other cases are quite alive and represent a great potential for harassment to the many corporations that have undertaken affirmative action programs.

For example, in June 1976 a court ruled that AT&T, by administering an affirmative action program in which a woman was promoted ahead of a man who had a higher promotion rating, discriminated against the man. AT&T a few years earlier had entered into a consent decree obligating it to accelerate promotion of women and minority-member employees. The court ruled that the plaintiff "stands as an innocent employee who had earned promotion but was disadvantaged when AT&T rejected his application in order to rectify its past discrimination against women." The court awarded the man a sizable settlement which the court described as constituting "an added cost which the stockholders of AT&T must bear."

If decisions such as this stand, corporations actively seeking to promote women and minority employees are in danger of being entrapped in a massive EEO Catch-22: they must set acceptable goals for relatively rapid promotion of minority and women employees; if the companies favor "protected" employees over higher rated "nonprotected" employees, the AT&T case ruling can be applied against them. But if the companies rely strictly on seniority and experience, minority and women employees will, for the most part, have to put in their time thereby making attainment of affirmative action goals all the more difficult.

To add to the affirmative-action morass, suits have also been adjudicated on the issue of who gets laid off when times get tough. In March 1976 the Supreme Court decided that blacks who were denied jobs in violation of the Civil Rights Act of 1964 must be awarded retroactive seniority once they succeed in getting those jobs. In such cases, the court ruled, blacks must be given the same seniority they would have had if they had been hired initially. In one fell swoop, the court in effect reduced the seniority of many white workers—those who were hired after the blacks' initial job applications but before the blacks were put on the job. Legal experts have said that the decision extends to women as well.

All these aspects of affirmative action relate to eliminating discrimination based on race, national origin, or sex. Corporate managers will also have to be alert to the EEO demands of other types of employees or potential employees as well. Although not covered by the Civil Rights Act of 1964, older citizens, the handicapped, and armed services veterans are all marshaling strength to see to it that their employment potential is protected or enhanced in the years ahead. Although OFCCP is not likely to set hiring goals or request annual reviews in these areas, it will act when it receives complaints.

Despite all the affirmative action activity, complaints from women, minority-member employees, and many others exist by the thousands. The federal agency charged with the responsibility of adjudicating them, the Equal Employment Opportunities Commission, has been swamped for years with no real relief in sight. As a matter of fact, 1976 was the tenth consecutive year that EEOC recorded a sizable increase in its backlog of job discrimination complaints. The backlog on June 30 1976 was in the area of 130,000 complaints.

A rapid succession of commission administrators, increased budgets, and more complaints actually handled has made no difference. The complaints keep piling up. In 1966 there were about 8,700 such complaints received at EEOC. By fiscal 1975, with the commission processing complaints based on sex as well as race, the number received totaled 71,000.

The purpose of this little trip through the land of EEO is not to decide whether affirmative action programs are just or unjust, effective or ineffective. It is merely to explore the seriousness of just one of many attacks on the corporation. Fines or settlements totaling hundreds of thousands, or millions, of dollars are certainly significant. Even more significant in this day and age—when the attacks are coming with increasing rapidity from many directions—are the page-one headlines and the nightly news commentaries that once again, in society's judgment, the corporation has been found wanting.

## OTHER EMPLOYEE-RELATED PROBLEMS

EEO is only one of a number of employee-related changes coming to the corporate way of life. Corporate managers are also going to have to deal increasingly with employee demands for privacy as well as protection from firing for "blowing the whistle." And the new personal liabilities facing management itself, board members, and the professions in general represent still more problems. Admittedly, the employee privacy and job protection issues have barely surfaced. They are horizon issues that corporations would do well to anticipate.

The national Privacy Act of 1974 was a multifaceted attempt to put some order into the record-collecting procedures of the federal government, establish some standards for maintenance of records about individuals, and regulate disclosure of such records. One of the chief collectors of information on an individual is, of course, that individual's employer. There is now an embryonic movement among employees to control the amount of information an employer can accumulate and the availability of that information once it is collected. Employees are beginning to formalize demands that employers furnish information on an individual's employment record only upon receiving written authorization from the employee. Some employees are also beginning to demand that less information be gathered on them and that they have the right to inspect their personnel files in order to ask that corrections be made and outdated material deleted. At IBM, a wide-ranging program on employee privacy is already in place (see Chapter 12).

The challenge of job protection for employees who "blow the whistle" is also a gleam in a few critics' eyes. Ralph L. Stavins, director of the Institute for Policy Studies' Project on Official Illegality, has sketched the way the challenge may well evolve:

> Employees are caught in a moral dilemma. Increasingly, they are being asked to carry out illegal and improper acts, and they will go to jail if they do, and lose their job if they don't. . . . You do not have the legal right to stay at your job if you refuse to carry out illegal or improper orders. How can employees protect themselves against unfair commands of their bosses? . . .
>
> The Employees Legal Society would be the place where employees could speak with each other freely and openly about moral and legal problems they face at work. They could share their experiences with each other and offer practical advice. They could begin to codify their experiences in the form of an Employee Bill of Rights.
>
> Among those rights would be the right to refuse illegal or improper orders; the right to treble damages, court costs and attorney's fees in the event a court certifies that the employee had challenged an illegal order and was subsequently discharged; and the right to collectively debate the public policies of the firm. (2)

Those who are outraged by Stavins' assertion that employees are "increasingly asked to carry out illegal and improper acts," must nevertheless resist the temptation to scoff at the potential for an Employees Legal Society. Ralph Nader, among others, has urged protection of employees who "blow the whistle." The operational quagmire that could result from employees' making individual judgments about whether their activity on the job is "right" is a nightmare. But if the Nuremberg Rule is indeed becoming widely accepted, if everyone is more conscious of ultimate responsibility, then "blowing the whistle"—rightly or wrongly—becomes an increasing possibility.

Another very serious threat to corporate stability is the personal peril managers now face in conducting their business. I'm not referring to the possibility of abduction that threatens in less-than-stable societies. I mean the erosion of the imaginary shield that has protected managers from individual accountability for corporate acts of negligence or lawlessness. New regulations being enforced by federal agencies are intimidating partly because of their very vagueness. In many cases, although the penalties for transgression are considerably greater than before, there is not yet a clear definition of just what constitutes such transgression.

One alarming recent court decision holds that an executive's liability for criminal conduct can extend far below the level of his direct supervision. New Food and Drug Administration regulations require drug companies to pinpoint individuals responsible for quality control. And it doesn't stop there. A revolutionary concept called "reckless default," now under legislative consideration, would subject a corporate officer to prosecution for failure properly to supervise employees who violate federal regulations. Much of this trend toward increased executive liability is patterned after European legal tradition.

To many corporate executives, this new muscle in federal regulatory agencies goes much further than Congress intended when it established Environmental Protection Agency (EPA), Food and Drug Administration (FDA), Occupational Safety & Health Act (OSHA), Securities and Exchange Commission (SEC), Consumer Product Safety Commission (CPSC), Equal Employment Opportunity Commission (EEOC), and other agencies. They would like to see Congress rein in these agencies by reviewing the need for, and the operation of, a given agency at regular intervals.

Many of these same pressures are afflicting members of boards of directors. "The growing threat of financial liability and of public censorship for directors of errant companies," *Business Week* has reported, "makes potential outside board members increasingly leery." (3)

Many corporations have tried to shield both their management and board members from the direct effects of liability by indemnifying them against expenses generated by litigation. Liability insurance is one way to provide such protection, but with the increasing frequency of suits against corporations and the steady rise in the amounts awarded plaintiffs, such insurance is much more expensive than just a few years ago (see Chapter 5).

Corporations who contract for professional services of accountants, architects, engineers, scientists, lawyers, or doctors are also finding that these professionals are similarly sensitive to public attack. Opinion polls show that the public is increasingly skeptical of professionals' claims of probity and competence. Moreover, society is now charging professionals with the job of *preventing* harm, of keeeping their clients on the straight and narrow.

This challenge goes much deeper than superficial arguments such as whether lawyers can advertise their services. It really relates to, once again, ultimate responsibility. Who is the professional's client, the corporation that hired him or her, or society as a whole? True, in many professional relationships with clients, this is not an issue; but there are also many gray areas in such relationships, and in these areas, don't be surprised if the professional increasingly resolves doubts on the side of the public rather than on the side of the client.

## THE ENVIRONMENT

Herman Kahn writes in *Things to Come—Thinking About the '70s and '80s:*

> The widespread adoption of the environmental issue is an interesting and important development. Society as a whole seems to be embracing an issue that has been in the past part of a broad anti-bourgeois, anti-industrial platform. The rise of a strong concern about pollution does not mean that everyone is rejecting industrialism; but everyone is not accepting it as automatically as before. This is not necessarily bad, but it does represent a big change.
> 
> . . . our handling of the pollution issue represents an important change, or at least modification, of our traditional attitude toward material progress and technology and perhaps toward modern society itself. (4)

A big change? In terms of effect on the corporation, Kahn was putting it mildly. Within the four weeks from early September to early October 1976, two major corporations experienced just how such change may be measured in dollars and cents. Just after Labor Day, the General Electric Company agreed to a negotiated settlement of its longstanding environmental dispute with New York State over the company's discharge of PCBs (polychlorinated biphenyls) into the Hudson River. The cost to GE was $4 million—$3 million to be paid to help clean up the river and $1 million earmarked for research. Although under the agreement GE was neither exonerated nor blamed for the PCB problem, environmentalists hailed it as a precedent for holding polluters responsible for discharge of toxic substances.

The ink was hardly dry on the GE settlement when on October 5, the Allied Chemical Company was fined $13.3 million for polluting the James River with the pesticide Kepone. The fine is thought to be the largest ever imposed on a corporation in a pollution case.

Lest anyone think that such fines do not have financial reverberations ("a company that size can afford a few million dollars"), it is interesting to note the effect on Allied's quarterly earnings announced a few days later. The company's earnings for the third quarter of 1976 were $10,320,000, or 55.8 percent lower than a year earlier. And in announcing the quarterly earnings, Allied commented ominously, "A further evaluation of costs relating to this [Kepone] matter will be made in the fourth quarter as additional factors become known." None of the fine could be recovered by insurance. On the day of the earnings announcement Allied stock fell 1¾ points.

The fine was stiff but so were some admonitions delivered by the court, admonitions not only directed at Allied but at corporations everywhere: "I hope, after this sentence," Judge Robert R. Merhige, Jr., said, "that every corporate employee who has any reason to believe that pollution is going on will say to himself, 'I'd better do something about this if I want to keep my company, if I want to keep my job.'" (5)

Can the Employees Legal Society be far behind?

Some critics were not mollified. *Newsday* commented editorially:

> Money talks to American business and industry in a language they understand. The $13 million fine assessed this week against Allied Chemical for dumping the pesticide Kepone into Virginia's waterways is likely to be a stronger deterrent than any amount of federal regulation or outcry from environmentalists . . . it serves notice that polluters can no longer expect a mere slap on the corporate wrist . . . no amount of help to workers directly affected can make up for the overall damage to the environment itself, and through it to the public at large. (6)

Nor was that the end of it. The Justice Department expects Allied to pay for cleaning up Kepone contamination of the James River as well as to reimburse the $2 million spent by EPA on the Kepone problem. The river cleanup could cost many millions of dollars. And Allied volunteered to provide $8 million to fund a totally independent Virginia Environmental Endowment to alleviate the effects of Kepone on the environment and on those whose lives were impaired by the insecticide. Judge Merhige then reduced the original fine from $13.3 million to $5 million. Critics contended that the $8 million Allied endowment had generated a $4 million tax break. The Judge said, in effect, "Enough."

The GE and Allied cases offer clear statements to corporate managers, but the corporate environmental case that is the granddaddy of them all—the one that has lessons and morals for all—is that which has engulfed Reserve Mining Company, of Silver Bay, Minnesota, for the last nine years. It all began with a US Interior Department study of Lake Superior that produced charges that the Reserve's plant effluent, iron "tailings," was polluting the lake.

The Reserve Mining case is the national environmental controversy in microcosm. It ranges from the 1950s when Reserve Mining was thought of as an economic blessing to Minnesota and a good corporate citizen in its community, to the late 1960s when the company was charged with a variety of damnable environmental crimes, to the mid-1970s, when Reserve stands condemned as guilty of having created a serious public health hazard.

We cannot detail the Reserve's nine-year metamorphosis from hero to villain in these pages, but in a seminal book on this subject,

*Judgment Reserved*, Frank D. Schaumburg does just that. Thorough but readable, it makes a good claim for the Reserve case as a "landmark environmental case." Schaumburg, head of the department of civil engineering at Oregon State University, offers thoughtful analysis applicable to many environmental controversies now enveloping corporations:

> Reserve's opponents in the case had charged that any risk regardless of magnitude was totally unacceptable and superseded any consideration of economics, jobs, and/or ecological impact of tailings disposal on the terrestial environment. Such demands for absolute elimination rather than minimization of risk can be defended only on narrow, albeit appealing, humanitarian grounds.
>
> Most citizens would agree that the elimination of carcinogens from the environment would be a desirable goal. When more facts are gathered and more experience gained, however, it may be that this goal is tantamount to the physically impossible goal of zero environmental pollution. . . .
>
> Surely man's quest for a high standard of living has resulted in the production of literally thousands of synthetic substances that ostensibly enhance the well-being of society. Unfortunately, many of these non-natural substances, including fibers, pesticides, cosmetics, drugs, detergents, and countless others, generally are resistant to rapid assimilation in natural sinks or repositories of residue. Some are, in fact, deleterious to ecological systems and public health. But before these chemicals are condemned and removed from the marketplace, and hence the environment, their relative benefits should be weighed against associated risks. . . .
>
> The President's Science Advisory Committee pointed out in 1973 . . . that the absence of quantitative information is likely to bias regulation toward the *overprotection of health and ecology*. . . . The committee concluded: *"We must always live with some risks both because nature forever confronts us with hazards and also because the contributions of chemicals to human welfare are so vital."* (7)

Schaumburg also provides a very useful discussion of the "guilty until proven innocent" position of many industries under environmental attack:

> Proving that a substance *is* a health hazard is less difficult by several orders of magnitude than *proving* that a substance constitutes *no* health hazard, i.e., proving a negative. In the first instance, an elaboration of toxicity or other deleterious response to a test organism in a carefully controlled laboratory experiment can be accepted as evidence of a possible health hazard. Failure

to observe toxicity, i.e., a negative finding, cannot be interpreted as proof of no health hazard because it could be argued that the test conditions were not proper, or different test organisms should have been used, or different responses should have been observed, or the effect is likely chronic rather than acute and would be observable only after years rather than hours of exposure. (7)

And, as a bottom line concerning risk of the unknown Schaumburg concludes:

> But while life is revealed to be growing more dangerous with each passing day, the average life span of Americans has increased nearly 20 years since 1900. Perhaps the benefits of our industrialized society—in health effects—outweigh some of the inherent concomitant risks. Before these benefits are wiped out by poorly conceived legislation and overly conservative court rulings, we had better develop effective tools for assessing cost-risk-benefit so that they may be used for rational decision making. (7)

The Toxic Substances Control Act of 1976 is a classic example of how the strong environmental tide that is still running in this country, given an unexpected boost by a celebrated case of industrial pollution, can result in a completely new dimension of environmental regulation.

Toxic substance legislation had been discussed in Congress for years with the many pros and cons debated as thoroughly as an issue of such importance can be. Then, in late 1975 came Kepone. The well-publicized tragedy in Virginia seemed to pump new life into environmentalist lobbyists. Chemical industry representatives were put on the defensive. It became obvious early that a major piece of new regulatory legislation was going to pass the Congress. In a presidential election year, a veto seemed improbable. Who was going to vote against "fighting cancer"?

The act requires manufacturers to notify the Environmental Protection Agency 90 days before a chemical is produced or put to a significant new use. The agency can delay the proposal and require testing if it believes that the chemical is potentially hazardous. At the time of passage, it was estimated that the act will require EPA review of notification forms for 500 to 1,500 newly developed chemicals a year to decide which will require full testing.

A national business publication reporting on the legislation said that as a result of its passage:

> . . . the chemical industry faces a new era of stepped up research and testing of thousands, perhaps tens of thousands, of compounds to determine which of them is toxic or contain cancer-producing substances. Chemical companies, anticipating en-

actment of a toxic substances law, have already increased their toxicology research and substantially expanded their facilities to carry out intensive testing of chemical compounds. (8)

And that additional testing came on top of some rather intensive testing already in place. For example, in the pesticide industry, chemical companies in 1973 had to screen an average of 10,231 compounds to achieve a single commercial pesticide compound. In that year, it cost an average of $6.1 million to bring a pesticide compound from discovery through commercialization, and it took an average of 80 months of development to do it. Costs have certainly risen appreciably since then.

But such figures meant little in two other key environmental confrontations for the chemical industry as 1976 came to an end. First, the New Jersey Cancer Commission, a special task force of the state legislature, proposed a ban on *any* plant emission of what it called 16 cancer-causing substances. The proposal, according to the Chemical Industry Council of New Jersey, "would have a devastating effect on the chemical industry."

Clear across the country a few weeks later, Dow Chemical Company abandoned plans to build a $500 million petrochemical complex near Collinsville, California. Dow withdrew after spending two years and an estimated $4 million trying to deal with environmentalist objections.

A very different environmental problem—the problem of power—has enmeshed corporate giants in a net of suits and countersuits, claims and counterclaims, and seemingly unending controversy. William Houseman, editor of the respected *The Environment Monthly*, which ceased publication with its December 1976 issue, told me in mid-1976 that in his opinion, "one of the towering [emerging] issues will be that of who owns, manages and controls the power—literally the power—of the nation."

The power controversy, a longstanding environmental issue, has been made all the more critical in recent years by the increasing urgency of the nation's energy crisis. Today, electricity accounts for about 28 percent of our primary energy consumption. But by the year 2000 it may well represent 50 percent of such consumption. How to build the added electrical generating capacity is now a national problem.

First, there is the matter of raising the money needed to build this new capacity, regardless of what fuels it consumes. Equally basic is the issue of whether nuclear energy—ironically, the "cleanest" energy source now available to this industry—is adequately safe. The financial problem is to increase the attractiveness of electric utility stocks and bonds as compared with other equity and debt investments. A discussion of the many proposals to do this, including tax credits, accelerated depreciation, and revision of regulatory provisions to facilitate rate relief, would take us far beyond the scope of this book. Suffice it to say that the electric utility industry is in a financial bind.

The industry's environmental problem, however, is worth a good deal more attention. Until the more exotic energy sources such as solar power, fusion power, and geothermal power are harnessed—perhaps 20 years from now—the electric utilities must work with hydropower, natural gas, oil, coal, or nuclear power. However, there are only a few remaining sites in which to place new hydroelectric generating plants. Natural gas and oil are fuels in tight supply. Coal represents twin environmental challenges: emission standards and land restoration after mining. Environmentalist pressure was instrumental in the April 1976 withdrawal of a plan by southwestern utilities to build the nation's largest coal-fired power facility, the Kaiparowits Power Plant, in Southern Utah. So the utilities turn increasingly to the prospect of nuclear power only to find that here, too, they are cast by some as environmental villains.

The issue was fought fiercely in California in preparation for the June 1976 initiative measure, Proposition 15, which sought to establish stringent conditions for construction of nuclear power plants. Basically, the proposition called for public demonstration that all aspects of atomic power production have been made safe and a guarantee of full compensation for harm from accidents. Californians struggled as only they can on such an environmental issue and when it was all over, the environmentalist-backed Proposition 15 was defeated rather handily.

Interestingly, before the vote was taken, the California State Assembly Committee on Resources, Land Use, and Energy held 15 days of hearings on the measure, took 4,000 pages of testimony from 120 of the most imposing witnesses the opposing sides could produce, and issued a report that said, in part:

> After listening to 120 learned witnesses who could not agree on the merits of the initiative or the safety of nuclear power, it is clear that no objective conclusions can be drawn.
> The issues are not solely resolvable through application of scientific expertise. The debate is more the result of differing views on human abilities, human fallibility and human behavior than anything else.
> The questions involved require value judgments and the voter is no less equipped to make such judgments than the most brilliant Nobel Laureate. (9)

*Value* judgments, not *scientific* judgments. And public opinion reigning supreme. How often, as we examine environmental controversy, we run into that ultimate expression of democracy.

Not surprisingly then, the California vote was by no means the end of the nuclear power fight. In November, voters in Oregon, Montana, Ohio, Washington, Arizona, and Colorado were presented with proposals to limit nuclear energy development. Before they could vote, decibels were added to the national debate on the safety of nuclear energy when the matter became a subject of discussion in the 1976 presidential campaign. Nuclear engineer Jimmy Carter expressed strong concern about the safety of nuclear power. And that fall a 27-year-old reaction engineer resigned from the federal Nuclear Regulatory Commission alleging that the NRC had "covered up or brushed aside nuclear safety problems of far-reaching significance." (Earlier in 1976 a middle-management official of the NRC had resigned on somewhat the same grounds, and in November columnist Jack Anderson reported widespread concern on safety among NRC personnel.)

As if to punctuate the discussion, in early September, an explosion occurred at the government-owned Hanford, Washington, nuclear reprocessing facility. Although damage was slight, no one was seriously injured, and the explosion had nothing to do with the plant's nuclear reactor, the well-publicized accident raised many eyebrows across the country. The *New York Times* opined:

> Since the dawn of the nuclear era more than three decades ago, not a single accident has occurred from either civilian or military uses of atomic energy that resulted in heavy loss of human life or large-scale environmental damage. . . . Yet the fear of such a catastrophe—and the understandable, visceral anguish most people feel about exposure to radioactivity—has kept the possibility of accidents a matter of deep concern. It is that concern, rather than what actually occurred, that underlies the importance of the Hanford explosion. . . . If a small accident can occur at Hanford, could not a larger one occur elsewhere? There is something about the nuclear danger that cannot be answered by statistical evidence of the unlikelihood of catastrophe. . . . These special psychological factors justify all the investment already made in special precautions to avoid nuclear accidents— and more. For the rapid expansion of nuclear power in the United States and abroad is multiplying whatever risks do exist. (10)

Two earlier events had provided special problems for the nuclear power industry. Again, amid much media attention, two nuclear engineers had resigned from General Electric claiming that the installations they were working on were unsafe. And a study from a respected scientist conducted for the federal Energy Research and Development Administration concluded that radioactive waste stored at nine scattered locations across the country represented a major health hazard and would continue to do so "for hundreds of thousands, perhaps millions of years." The credibility of those environmentalists who had been claiming much the same thing jumped like a startled rabbit.

Environmentalist credibility had *already* been given a big boost in mid-1976 with the tragic collapse of the Teton Dam on Idaho's Snake River. During construction of the $60 million dam, environmental groups had opposed it vociferously, claiming that it was being built on porous rock and soil subject to earth tremors. An official of the U.S. Bureau of Reclamation, responsible for the project, was quoted after the collapse as saying, "We were warned of an unstable foundation and took extreme care. Theoretically, what happened could not happen. But it did."

In September, the national semi-monthly, *Conservation News*, reprinted an editorial from the June 18th issue of *High Country News*, of Lander, Wyoming, which said in part:

> Teton Dam should stand as a monument to the demise of a timeworn, outmoded philosophy. That philosophy is one of damn-the-environment, progress-at-any-price. Such a philosophy rode roughshod over every opposition to the Teton Dam project. It rejected rational, reasonable argument of the long-term worth of such a project in comparison to natural values that were there at no cost to society. And finally it rejected sound scientific evidence that the site was no place to put such a dam. It was wrong—and all who backed it were told so. (11)

Hanford and the Teton Dam should not be written off as merely occasions for environmentalists to say "I told you so." They represent serious, perhaps long-term, damage to establishment credibility coming at a time when that credibility is near an all-time low. The average citizen wants assurance. Environmentalists and other public interest groups have the best of the argument. They say, in effect, "Don't take the risk. Don't bend to the 'vested interests' who speak with forked tongues about benefit-risk ratios. Remember Hanford. Remember Teton Dam."

In the November balloting, Oregonians, many of whom consider their state to be the nation's environmental laboratory, nevertheless resoundingly defeated the nuclear-limitation proposal. Voters in Montana, Ohio, Washington, Arizona, and Colorado defeated similar proposals. Clearly, voters seemed to be saying that they were willing to accept what they perceived to be low risk of danger in the face of high likelihood of escalating utility bills.

In contrast with their defeats on the nuclear referenda, public interest organizations achieved a meaningful breakthrough on another referenda issue—deposits on beverage containers. Why are throwaway beer and soda cans and bottles of special significance? Because they have been chosen by environmentalists as symbols of the profligate, throwaway psychology of this society, a psychology that, according to the environmentalists, must be reversed. For several years, environmentalists have been attacking nonrefillable beverage containers as significant to the litter problem in various parts of the country and wasteful of energy and other resources.

Beverage marketers, labor unions, and others countered such attacks by pointing out, among other things, that serious job dislocations could take place should deposits be imposed on beverage containers. Furthermore, defenders of the nonrefillables contended that there were better solutions to the problems raised by environmentalists, solutions including voluntary and municipal recycling programs.

Over 1,000 deposit-related pieces of legislation had been introduced at state and local levels through mid-1976. In all but a few locations, particularly Oregon and Vermont, such legislation was defeated. Furthermore, in eight referenda held on the issue through early 1976, proposed deposits on beverage containers were always voted down by consumers. In November 1976, however, such proposals were put to direct citizen vote in Maine, Massachusetts, Michigan, and Colorado. Many knowledgeable observers called these initiative votes a significant test of the impetus of the environment movement. If that is so, the result of the voting should give corporate executives reason to pause. Michigan became the first highly industrialized state to approve such a container deposit referendum. Maine did likewise. The measure was defeated narrowly in Massachusetts, and lost by a comfortable margin in Colorado. But clearly, the dam had burst.

The *Wall Street Journal*, commenting on the 1976 nuclear and container deposit referenda, summarized the situation this way: "Conservation is still a political force . . . but voters aren't going to let it interfere excessively with economic growth." (12)

Incidentally, the beverage container deposit issue illustrates that environmental issues, like politics in general, can indeed create strange bedfellows. Business by no means presented a united front on this issue. It was not a monolith opposing such measures. Labor, on the other hand—which so often opposes industry on environmental matters, especially in the area of occupational safety—was an ally of those business interests opposing the container deposits. Another anomaly is that the recently formed Environmental Industry Council, composed of companies that make pollution control products, sometimes supports environmental groups in their battles with companies resisting new pollution standards.

No less strange to the scientific and economics professionals who wrestle with the complexities of environmental issues is the emergence of a new kind of environmental expert—the celebrity. In recent years an increasing number of public-spirited actors, authors, and playwrights have asserted their right to speak out publicly on issues that concern them. Look! It's Paul Newman, speaking for the Energy Action Committee in its attempt to "break up big oil." Or check that out, over there, folks, it's Robert Redford fighting a proposed new power facility. The media, of course, love it. Quotations and pictures move on networks and wire services reaching Americans across the country.

It's a free country. If a star chooses to debate complex environmental issues, who's to prevent it? But the light shed by the star ought to be examined very closely. Is it starlight or the light of an informed intellect? Let's hope that most Americans are discerning enough to recognize the difference.

## A SAFER PLACE TO WORK

Few federal agencies have gotten off to a more troubled—and troubling—start than the federal Occupational Safety and Health Administration (OSHA). Troubled, because of the sheer size of its task. Troubling, because of the sheer weight of new procedures imposed on the corporation.

Ten years ago, job safety was a matter of interest mainly to the plant manager. Essentially, it boiled down to keeping plant accidents to a minimum. Now, senior vice presidents and even presidents must be concerned with precautions and performance on what used to be a MEGO ("My Eyes Glaze Over") issue for many an executive. The change came with the passage in late 1970 of the OSHA enabling legislation aimed at assuring "so far as possible every working man and woman in the nation safe and healthful working conditions."

OSHA has five basic goals: inspections of the workplace; development of safety standards, especially relating to health; training of employers and employees to develop self-inspection programs; approval of state plans to provide job safety and health; and administration of programs for federal employees. A companion regulatory agency, the National Institute of Occupational Safety and Health, which is a part of the Department of Health, Education and Welfare, conducts research and recommends criteria which OSHA converts to enforceable standards.

How big a job is occupational safety? It is estimated that four million businesses—ranging from mom-and-pop grocery stores to giant corporations—are currently affected by OSHA regulations. A McGraw-Hill survey concluded that in 1976 American industry invested about $3.2 billion for employee safety and health, up a healthy 17 percent over 1975. The survey was able to identify $3.6 billion in *preliminary* plans for such spending in 1979. About 2.5 percent of total planned capital investment between 1976 and 1979 is expected to be spent for worker protection. Nevertheless, corporate critics often say that isn't enough.

A 1976 Ford Foundation study, "Crisis in the Work Place: Occupational Disease and Injury," dramatized the most significant difference between the old plant-safety concern and today's chief occupational safety concern—job-related disease. The study concluded that the problem is so widespread that the federal government alone cannot cope with it. The study recommends the involvement of workers individually and through organized labor (see Chapter 5).

Nicholas A. Ashford, author of "Crisis in the Work Place," is a lawyer with a Ph.D. in chemistry. At the time of the study's publication, he commented:

> The task is monumental. It involves redesigning technology in some cases, redesigning jobs in others. . . . I don't think OSHA can do the job alone. . . . There are limitations on how successful the improvement of occupational safety and health can be without participation by the workers in the monitoring or surveillance of conditions in the work place. It may mean a reorientation of our institutions. It may mean management's relinquishing some prerogatives. (13)

The fear of job-related disease, especially cancer, is at the heart of many of the new occupational safety regulations. But there are also demands relating to the shifting standards of industrial workers. An example is factory noise. For decades, many factory workers put up with the ear-splitting din of 100-decibel noise levels. Not any more. Federal interim regulations set the acceptable noise level at 90 decibels, and major unions, supported by the Environmental Protection Agency, have pressed for an 85-decibel level. Peter Bommarito, president of the United Rubber Workers, has said: "The notion that deafness is a fair exchange for a job is no longer acceptable to a vast majority of workers."

The troubled early history of OSHA is reflected by the fact that the agency had three administrators in the first five years of its existence. Morton Corn, a professor in the field of industrial hygiene, administrator from late 1975 until early 1976, launched a multifaceted effort to define "serious" and "nonserious" hazards, hoping to revise and standardize the system of penalties for each category. But the main OSHA problem is overload. As one industrial relations expert who studied OSHA has said, "The typical business establishment will see an OSHA inspector every 77 years, as often as we see Haley's comet."

Nevertheless, the OSHA standards exist and even when inspections don't take place, employee protection equipment must still be installed and the heavy load of paperwork must be maintained. When the existing standards are not adhered to, there is the possibility, critics claim, of serious illness and perhaps death. In those few cases where such tragedy strikes, the drama is likely to be played out in the full glare of national media attention, as in the Kepone case.

## SAFER PRODUCTS MORE HONESTLY SOLD

Consumerist organizations have come a long way since Ralph Nader's classic confrontation with General Motors in the mid-1960s. The congressional hearings of that confrontation were a public spectacle that catapulted Nader to national notoriety and permanently etched consumerism into the public consciousness.

Since then consumer protection groups, like a lot of the public interest movements, have been absorbed into the American mainstream. By now, it is almost commonplace to read about a national product recall involving millions of units. We sometimes forget that just a few short years ago, the threat of such recalls produced shudders not only in corporate sales departments but also among those executives who were concerned with the effect of such action on the public's opinion of the company in question. Since then we have seen unit pricing introduced in many supermarkets, rewriting of hard-to-understand warranties and guarantees, revitalization of service organizations for appliances and other big-ticket items, and the resolution of a host of other justifiable consumer demands. The temptation might be to conclude that the consumerist attack on corporate operations is behind us, which would be a serious mistake.

For one thing, the federal Consumer Product Safety Commission, activated in 1973, is now approaching what might be called agency maturity. It is clearly here to stay and likely to grow in power. It already has the authority to set and enforce safety standards for more than 10,000 products—including their design, construction, content, performance, packaging, and labeling. Manufacturers must monitor the safety of their products and report defects immediately to the CPSC. The agency has the authority not only to ban hazardous products but also to seek severe civil and criminal penalties for violations.

In the spring of 1976, the muscle of the CPSC was increased by new legislation expanding the commission's authority by permitting it to issue preliminary injunctions prohibiting distribution of *potentially* hazardous products. Also on the horizon is the possibility that the CPSC will be authorized to file its own criminal cases rather than turning them over to the Justice Department.

Interestingly, some CPSC officials feel that the commission's most important long-term role is to educate the consumer, and it is expending some considerable resources in this effort. Among the CPSC educational programs are a toll-free telephone number to answer consumer questions on the safety of various products and "blacklist" booklets containing the names of banned products.

The CPSC, of course, is not the only federal agency monitoring products and the way they are marketed. Although legislative proposals for a cabinet level Agency for Consumer Advocacy have not gathered sufficient support for passage (a new effort is underway in the 95th Congress), consumer interests continue to be protected in more and more places in the federal bureaucracy. In September of 1976, for example, the Ford administration unveiled a plan to establish consumer affairs offices in every major federal agency.

There's now a threat of a quantum leap in federal involvement in private product development and marketing. That threat stems from proposed legislation that would revolutionize the century-old system of establishing acceptable product standards. Senator James Abourezk (D. S. Dak.) introduced legislation to this effect and presided at 1976 hearings on the subject held by the Senate Antitrust and Monopoly subcommittee of the Judiciary Committee. Abourezk, who plans to leave the Senate after his current term expires in 1978, has told the Senate that "voluntary standards and certifications, in their present form, must be challenged because they are a basic component of industry attempts to restrain trade by price-fixing, boycotting, controlling supply and foreclosing new technology from the market."

It is estimated that about 20,000 product standards have been established by various private, nonprofit organizations coordinated by the American National Standards Institute. The system, all but invisible to the American public, is in effect the funnel for all new products coming to market. The Abourezk bill would establish a new set of government ground rules for the product standards system. For example, an aggrieved individual could appeal to the federal government and quite possibly get a standard modified or replaced. There would also be a new system of accreditation of private testing and certification laboratories. The ANSI contends that there are already adequate grievance procedures in the existing system. Underwriters Laboratories, also opposing the Abourezk bill, has stated that the legislation would retard new product innovation. And the American Society for Testing Materials has called the present system "one of the most efficient means of technology transfer ever developed."

There is another arena in which consumer complaints against the corporation are heard—the courts. Here, too, things are getting warmer. Consumer disenchantment with products and services as expressed in court cases has grown sufficiently in recent years to prompt the U.S. Chamber of Commerce to offer a plan for overhauling the nation's small claims courts in order to give consumers a fairer hearing.

The Chamber of Commerce has offered a "model consumer justice act" calling for the establishment of locally run small claims courts with branch courts open evenings and Saturdays. The courts would deal with cases involving claims up to $1,000, would not allow lawyers to act as principals, would not allow collection agencies to use the courts to sue for bad debts, would require speedy processing of all claims, and would provide a follow-up mechanism to ensure that judgments are paid. Appeals with the use of lawyers would be allowed.

The courts may soon be jammed with many additional consumer suits. Under the Federal Trade Commission Act, only the FTC has been empowered to file federal suits on alleged deceptive practices, but that may be changing. The courts are now looking at the possibility of allowing individuals to file suit in certain "deceptive marketing" cases. The potential for new litigation against the corporation may be substantial; the FTC reportedly investigates only about 15 percent of the thousands of complaints it gets each year.

The FTC used to be called "the little old lady of Pennsylvania Avenue." In recent years, however, "the little old lady" seems to be undergoing a Virginia Slims kind of transformation. "You've come a long way, baby" is not inappropriate.

Among the statutes administered by the FTC are the Fair Packaging and Labeling Act, the Truth in Lending Act, the Fair Credit Reporting Act, the Equal Credit Opportunity Act, and the Federal Energy Administration Act, as well as a number of acts relating primarily to single industries.

The FTC has been increasingly active on a number of fronts troublesome to the corporation. One of the most expensive and counterproductive in terms of corporate objectives is the controversial FTC "corrective advertising" campaign. Since 1970 the commission has compelled some very large national advertisers to retract "misleading" claims. The FTC has not only enjoined such claims but has been successful in forcing companies to buy advertising to "confess" prior "misstatements" and to "clarify" such matters. In choosing its targets for corrective advertising, FTC looks for evidence that an ad led to erroneous beliefs "about the core function of the product" leading to customer injury or heavy expense.

The practice is in litigation with the Warner-Lambert Company, which has refused to honor such directives. Nevertheless, the FTC, which relies heavily on market research data to show what consumers believe as a result of the suspect ads, intends to extend its application of corrective advertising. Some corporations, increasingly sensitive to the threat, have taken the precaution of naming an individual—in the company or in its advertising agency—to assume the responsibility for meticulous checking of the supportability of questionable ad claims.

Other important recent corporate actions relating to consumer advertising include stronger efforts at advertising-industry self-policing on ad accuracy and a growing reluctance to sponsor television programs which tend to glorify violence.

## ATTACK ON THE MULTINATIONALS

How is one to assess the persistent criticism of the multinational corporation? It comes from many sources, condemns many alleged abuses, and prescribes a host of solutions. The multinational company is questioned in the movie *Rollerball* and condemned in the book *Global Reach*. Some accuse it of "milking" the developing countries whereas others challenge it as harmful to United States employment and our economy. It is attacked as too big, too powerful, and too bad.

Some Americans seem to see all kinds of intrinsic evils in the international trade carried on by American multinational companies (although these critics undoubtedly consume and presumably enjoy products of *foreign-owned* multinationals such as Good Humor ice cream, Schweppes beverages, Nestlé chocolate, Shell oil products, and Lever Brothers detergents). George McGhee, the former State Department diplomat, has offered a perceptive summary of the attacks on multinationals. In part, McGhee has written:

> A disturbing change has occurred in recent years in the American attitude towards United States corporations doing business overseas. There appears to be an increasing divergence between the views of Americans toward our economic system at home and its operations abroad. . . .
> Criticism of the multinational companies originated in the developing countries. . . . The loss of our oil concessions in Mexico in 1934, like the expropriation of the United Fruit Company in Central America, was not wholly undeserved. It is curious, however, that as the multinational companies moved to correct the evils of the past, the attack against them only increased. . . . But when one comes to consider the alternatives one faces reality. The plain fact is that the business of the world today, both national and international, is conducted by a market economy through the corporate structure. . . .

It becomes self-evident, therefore, that the future economic progress of the world hinges not on the elimination but the perpetuation of something like our present multinational corporations *adapted to the changed conditions of our times.* Many countries which have sought to decrease their dependence on the companies have already discovered this and desperately seek to get them back [emphasis added]. (14)

In recent years, some host countries have indeed made it tougher for the multinationals to operate successfully. These countries have been demanding a bigger share of the profits, jobs, markets, and technical and managerial skill that multinational companies create or control.

Apparently some of the multinationals have had enough harassment, especially in some of the Third World countries. In October 1976 the *New York Times* Paris Bureau reported that "a wave of disenchantment over investments in the third world is spreading in board rooms of multinational corporations and is already leading to a cutback in private capital flow." (15)

The disenchantment, the *Times* reported, was owing mainly to "political and financial risks in developing countries, poorer business conditions the world over and the shortage of capital." The article quoted an unnamed European corporate executive describing his company's recent Third World experiences: "In Indonesia, they gave us a contract and after three years changed the rules of the game. In Brazil, we have a majority interest in a company but because we have that majority stake we are not allowed to repatriate our royalties. In India, it has become difficult because of administrative controls."

What can be said of the charge that American multinationals export jobs? Some recent studies seem to seriously undermine this position. A 1974 project by Robert B. Stobaugh and associates at the Harvard School of Business, "US Multinational Enterprises and the US Economy," concluded that multinational operations of American corporations have created 600,000 additional jobs in this country. A 1975 US Department of Commerce study estimated that more than 500,000 United States jobs have been created by such commerce. And in 1976 the Business International Corporation, a research firm that primarily serves multinational companies, completed a survey that indicated that American-based multinational companies showed a greater increase in employment between 1970 and 1973 than did manufacturing companies in general.

The hairier questions arise when politicians, especially in well-publicized congressional hearings, question multinational company executives on policies and actions that seem to be inimical to American national interest or to be in conflict with American moral standards. The implication of much of such questioning is often, "Are you an American company or aren't you? Well, if you are, we expect you to act abroad in the American national interest and in concert with American traditions." (However, Good Humor, Schweppes, Nestlé, Shell, Lever, and all other foreign-owned companies operating here had better live by *our* rules.)

The Conference Board of New York recently surveyed 73 executives of multinational firms asking them, among other things, if American companies abroad should "adopt the commercial modes and moral standards of countries in which they do business or if they should adhere to U.S. standards?" A slight majority—52 percent—believed that United States ethical standards should control overseas behavior, whereas 48 percent held that United States companies should adopt the customs and practices of the countries in which they are domiciled.

As to the second fundamental criticism, that multinationals operate beyond the control of any single government and can therefore exploit a host nation as they see fit, a study sponsored by the socially active United Church of Christ concluded:

> As a sovereign nation, the host country is ultimately more powerful than the MNC, no matter how large the latter's world sales are. It follows that the government is increasingly sure to find ways to insure that transnational business will only invest in those industries that the rulers want. The rulers are now able, if they wish to do so, to direct companies into channels that they think will help the country in the long run. (16)

Similarly, Ross R. Millhiser, President of Philip Morris Incorporated, in a lecture at Duke University's School of Business Administration, said that "the multinational corporation maintains its welcome only if it can contribute to the economic well-being of the host country, and it demonstrably does so in several ways." (15) Millhiser contended that "investment capital, knowledge, products at reasonable prices, and tax income, all of which the multinational corporation delivers in the host country, are indeed demonstrable contributions."

To be sure, Millhiser admits, the corporate motivation in such situations, as in most corporate operations, is anticipated profit. And, he says, proposals to increase United States taxes of "repatriated" profits or to tax profits earned abroad and temporarily or permanently left there could seriously impair American multinationals' ability to compete abroad.

There is much at stake in such attacks on American multinationals. A Commerce Department study in March 1975 indicated that in the prior year the net cash inflow from the international operations of United States multinational corporations (i.e., the difference between the amount sent abroad for investment and the amount brought back into the country as earnings) was about $14.6 billion, which represents not only a major contribution to the United States balance of payments but a lot of jobs for American workers.

As for behavior in the host country, Millhiser said to his Duke University audience:

> Contrary to the charge that multinational corporations seek to impose American tastes and values on other people, we use our technology and skill to meet local preferences. Otherwise we would be ignoring large and profitable segments of the potential market. In their home countries, the local managers of Philip Morris affiliates are successful to the degree that they keep our company attuned to national and regional consumer tastes, national laws, national customs and national values. . . .
>
> What seems to confound some people is that the growth of multinational companies has coincided precisely with the rising tide of nationalism. The confusion disappears when it is understood that the corporation is an instrument used by and within all political and economic systems, with no sacrifice to the national character or culture. (17)

As we noted in Chapter 3, socioeconomic history was made in June 1976 when the 24 member countries of the Organization for Economic Cooperation and Development (OECD) ratified a voluntary code of conduct for multinational corporations. Although the code agreement was sparked by the international furor over corporate payments and therefore included specific provisions relating to that problem, it also presents general ground rules for the multinationals and their host countries.

Among the key provisions of the code (beyond those listed in Chapter 3 relating to payments, improper political activities, and disclosure) there is a "general policy" that enterprises "should take fully into account established general policy objectives of the member countries in which they operate; in particular, give due consideration to those countries' aims and priorities with regard to economic and social progress, including industrial and regional development, the protection of the environment, the creation of employment opportunities, the promotion of innovation and the transfer of technology."

In a section titled "Financing," the code says that "enterprises should, in managing the financial and commercial operations of their activities and especially their liquid foreign assets and liabilities, take into consideration the established objectives of the countries in which they operate regarding balance of payments and credit policies."

In return, the 24 OECD member nations (in Western Europe, North America, and developed Asia) agree that treatment of the multinationals should be "no less favorable than that accorded in like situations to domestic enterprises."

## ACCOUNTABILITY/DISCLOSURE

Ralph Nader has made a rather telling point: "There is often little difference between the text of a failing corporation's annual report and a healthy corporation's report." (18)

Accountability—to shareholders, employees, customers, the government, and the public at large—is now the corporation's Number One social challenge. In recent years, the American corporation has been besieged by new demands for information about its policies and the implementation of those policies. For the most part, these demands have focused on issues relating to the corporation's impact on society.

Public interest groups such as the Council on Economic Priorities have insisted on having these data in order to publish, on an industry-by-industry basis, studies of the way corporations have been performing in areas such as pollution control, equal employment opportunity, and occupational safety. Other groups, mainly large private investors such as churches, foundations, and universities, have used their shareholder rights to demand information on these issues and others such as defense contracts and corporate operations in nations they deem worthy of condemnation, the Republic of South Africa being their best example. (In early 1977, twelve major U.S. firms said they would end segregation and increase fair employment practices in their South African plants.)

Some corporations have considered it inappropriate to provide much of the data requested by public interest and shareholder groups. This was especially true several years ago when corporate social action was still very much in a start-up phase. Release of some of the requested data probably would have caused embarrassment to these corporations. Today, with more corporate self-confidence—based on more action—the information flows somewhat more freely. But the key disclosure question remains: what to tell, when, and to whom.

The Securities and Exchange Commission (SEC) provides theoretical guidance with its "materiality" concept, but for many public interest groups the concept is inadequate. Others call it obsolete. And the SEC's recent abortive move toward extracting environmental data from corporations seemed half-hearted at best.

The entire matter of corporate disclosure is going to have to be rethought in the light of new social realities. The people who run corporations will have to begin to think in these terms because some influential voices on the "outside" are already doing so. For example, the accounting profession seems to be stirring. Abraham J. Briloff is one of a number of accounting academicians who is unhappy with the profession's role in the current corporate disclosure system. In *More Debits Than Credits*, he proposes that Congress establish a Corporation Accountability Commission "to assume the responsibility for studying, determining, and promulgating standards pertaining to corporate morality, antitrust and monopoly aspects, accounting and accountability, and corporate tax policy—all this on a national and multinational scale." (19)

Perhaps more ominous, in 1976 the SEC formed a 13-member advisory committee, headed by former SEC commissioner A. A. Sommer, to study and define the purposes of the corporate disclosure system. And the Financial Accounting Standards Board is instituting far-reaching changes in American accounting systems to give investors much more financial information on which to judge the performance of American corporations. Similarly, the American Institute of Certified Public Accountants in early 1977 published a draft of a new set of guidelines for auditors to be applied "when client acts that appear . . . to be illegal come to . . . attention during the examination of financial statements in accordance with generally accepted auditing standards." (20)

We said at the outset of this chapter that we would examine only a selection of the current single-issue attacks on the corporation. The list is arbitrary. The reader may well have favorite issues that have not been covered. There are dozens. Their existence in the real world, if not in this book, only reaffirms the seriousness of the current assault on the corporation.

There is one more thing to be said before we finish with this brief catalogue of current threats to the corporation: even as these new threats become increasingly focused, the traditional problems of running a corporation—the problems that only 20 years ago were the *only* challenges executives had to face—these, of course, remain. The corporate executive, as always, must still produce a product or service, provide jobs, and generate a profit. These challenges have not faded, not a bit. They are only being seen in a very different perspective.

### REFERENCES

1. Glazer, Nathan. "Not the Way to Right the Wrongs of Racism," *Newsday*, "Ideas" section, April 4, 1976, p. 5.
2. *New York Times*, October 11, 1976.

3. "Why Lawyers and Bankers Desert the Board," *Business Week*, March 29, 1976, pp. 100, 104.
4. Kahn, Herman. *Things to Come—Thinking About the '70s and '80s* (New York, N.Y.: Macmillan Company, 1976), p. 219.
5. *New York Times*, October 6, 1976.
6. "Raising the Ante for Pollution," *Newsday*, October 9, 1976.
7. Schaumburg, Frank D. *Judgment Reserved: A Landmark Environmental Case* (Reston, Va.: Reston Publishing Company, Inc., a Prentice-Hall Company, 1976), pp. 227–234.
8. "Toxic Substances Law Will Usher In New Era," *Journal of Commerce*, September 17, 1976, p. 1.
9. *New York Times*, June 2, 1976.
10. "The Hanford Explosion," *New York Times*, September 3, 1976.
11. *Conservation News*, September 1, 1976, p. 5.
12. "Environmental Voting," *Wall Street Journal*, November 5, 1976.
13. "Health Problems Traced to Jobs," *New York Times*, March 17, 1976.
14. McGhee, George C. "The Attack on the Multinationals," *Wall Street Journal*, March 16, 1976.
15. "Multinational Corporations Turning Away From Third World," *New York Times*, October 16, 1976.
16. Hill and Knowlton Executives. *Critical Issues in Public Relations* (Englewood Cliffs, N.J.: Prentice-Hall, Inc., 1975), p. 214.
17. Millhiser, Ross R., President, Philip Morris Incorporated. "The Multinational Corporation: The Economic Bridge," a lecture at the Graduate School of Business Administration, Duke University, November 14, 1975.
18. Nader, Ralph. "Who Rules the Corporation?" *Business and Society Review*, Summer, 1976, p. 43.
19. Briloff, Abraham J. *More Debits Than Credits* (New York, N.Y.: Harper & Row, 1976).
20. "Illegal Acts by Clients," New York: American Institute of Certified Public Accountants, Inc., 1211 Avenue of the Americas, 1977.

# *The Response*

# 8

# The Emerging Corporate Model

## as Revealed in the 1975 American Management Association Survey

> "We are witnessing the development of a responsive corporation, which—if it is in fact learning—should be increasingly capable of handling new issues whether they be 'business' or 'social.'"
>
> —Robert Ackerman and Raymond Bauer, Corporate Social Responsiveness, The Modern Dilemma (1)

After analyzing the data generated by our 1975 American Management Associations survey of 644 chief executives on the future of the corporation, we stated the study's central conclusion this way:

> The corporation will either transform itself, or be transformed by the agents of the American public, into a unit that formally and continuously considers the desires, needs and concerns of the individual (be he or she worker, customer, neighbor or shareholder) and forms and executes its policies accordingly. (2)

A bit wordy, perhaps, but every bit as valid today as the day it was written. In fact, after cataloging the major attacks on the American economic system and some of the key individual-issue assaults on various corporations, I am even more convinced that corporate survival is going to have to mean corporate change—and significant change at that.

In this and the following chapters, we will examine some of the more important changes already taking place in corporate thinking and corporate action, changes related to the social milieu of the 1970s. However, let's first briefly consider the prospects for fundamental change in the American *economic system*. Although there is still strong debate on the subject, it appears that some form of additional economic planning is on the way. That's national economic *planning, not a planned economy*.

As noted in Chapter 4, there are a number of reasons to expect that the individual will look increasingly to government to solve problems. Although some of the more comprehensive demands for overturning the system are not likely to win widespread support, there is a certain attraction—perceived order, stability, and minimized dislocation—in the call for national economic planning.

There have been many suggestions on how to accomplish such macrocoordination. However, a central proposition seems to be the one advanced in 1975 by several liberal thinkers, including economist Wassily Leontief and United Auto Workers President Leonard Woodcock, together with such business leaders as investment banker Robert V. Roosa, W. Michael Blumenthal (then chairman of Bendix, now Secretary of the Treasury), and Irwin Miller, chairman of Cummins Engine. This unusual combination called for the establishment of a United States office of national economic planning. The planners in this office would be several hundred forward-looking scientists and technicians and a few economists, who would study the United States economy and try to estimate the economy's future needs for developing domestic supplies, expanding industries, and raising capital. They would also attempt to project how many cars, houses, and basic materials the economy would demand. Then they would propose guidelines such as tax and investment incentives, as well as broader monetary and fiscal policies to meet these goals. In a way, the Carter energy program is an example.

A surprising number of American business executives—although decidedly a minority—seem to support the idea. Henry Ford II, in testimony before the Joint Congressional Economic Committee, acknowledged that although planning could lead to socialism, it was worth the risk. "In my 30 years as a businessman," Ford said, "I have never before felt so uncertain about the future of both my country and my company." Thomas A. Murphy, chairman of the board of General Motors Corporation, has been one of the leading business executives against such planning.

Interestingly, national economic planning has opponents on the left as well as among businessmen. Some anticapitalist critics contend that, given the power of business, planning will simply be used to guide government policy in the interests of the capitalist class.

Some business observers say that there are programs bordering on national economic planning already in place. Such business-government programs rely essentially on *voluntary* participation by industry and sometimes even industry *initiative*. One case in point would appear to be the national energy conservation program that evolved out of the 1973 energy crisis. Some industries, faced with the realization that industrial energy consumption would have to be reduced, voluntarily negotiated with the Federal Energy Administration a pattern of reduced consumption. The aluminum industry, for example, agreed to cut its use of energy by 10 percent during the 1972–1980 period and is now well on its way to achieving the goal. Its energy conservation program involves production efficiencies, "housekeeping" conservation in plants and offices, product redesign, and increased recycling. (It takes only 5 percent of the original energy expended to bring an aluminum product back to molten metal.)

Despite some very strong arguments to the contrary—such as Robert Nozick's marvelous caution that we should not discourage "capitalist transactions between consenting adults"—the chances are that the corporation is going to operate in an environment of increased national planning of some sort. If that is true, then prudent corporate managers will anticipate how best to position their companies to minimize the pain of participation and maximize its effectiveness.

At the beginning of this chapter we proposed that the corporation, if it is to survive, will have to be increasingly responsive to social demands. Before we get on with characterizing the emerging profile of such increasingly responsive corporations, it may be useful to present two brief opinions on *why* corporations should accept this model. The opinions are from spokesmen sympathetic to the nature and operation of the corporation.

First, Ian H. Wilson, the General Electric Company corporate planner:

> The events of the past two decades demonstrate, beyond any reasonable doubt, that—without proper business response— today's expectations become the political issues of tomorrow, the legislated requirements of the next day, and the litigated penalties of the day after. . . . For business, the major significance of this sequence is that at each stage the range of business options becomes narrower until we reach the "no-option" stage of paying penalties for failure to comply with new legislated requirements. In graphic terms, there is an inverted pyramid of business freedom of action. (3)

And, once again, Ackerman and Bauer, who contend that there are some very positive *business* reasons for moving in this direction:

> . . . grappling with social issues sometimes forces, and often encourages, reexamination of regular business practices. There is

no business function on which the handling of social issues does not impinge. . . . In tackling some new social issue, the corporation often discovers that the business function which is relevant is deficient in the handling of its more traditional tasks. The social issues put the existing functions under stress and suggest ways in which their efficiency and effectiveness may be improved. . . . we are building social values into the production of goods and services. (4)

Just what *did* we learn from the AMA survey?

Perhaps the significance of the survey findings rests in the high degree of acceptance that business itself now seems to give the socially responsive corporate model and the amount of planning and execution already underway in many corporate structures to bring it about.

## STATE OF THE ART

First, let us burst the myth of corporate altruism. We asked, "Why do companies plan and evaluate social responsibility programs?" Respondents were asked to list first most important, second most important, and third most important reasons.

Totaling all three, we found these to be the most important motivations: (1) to integrate social programs into the organizational planning process (59 percent); (2) to identify areas in which the organization is vulnerable to social criticism (51 percent); and (3) to protect long-term profitability (50 percent).

Those who reside outside of the corporation may be surprised by the survey findings on the state of the art of social responsibility in American corporations. For example, the respondents recognize that social responsibility programs cannot be limited to those areas where government, through legislation or regulation, demands it. Eighty-six percent of the respondents said that their companies' position was to undertake social responsibility programs in areas mandated by government as well as to initiate voluntary and anticipatory programs. Fourteen percent said that their companies' programs were limited to government-mandated areas and activities.

Equally significant, 63 percent of the respondents agreed that many social responsibility programs introduced during the past few years have now become integral, rather than peripheral, to basic corporate operations. Eleven percent disagreed, and 26 percent were uncertain. Corporate contributions are one example. The question, "Has your corporate contributions program been integrated with overall corporate objectives?" drew affirmative replies from 58 percent of the respondents.

Some important gains appear to have been made in the administration of such programs in recent years, but management of social responsibility programs still appears to be in its formative stage. Although most respondents (70 percent) reported that there was no centralized responsibility in their companies, the individual ultimately held responsible for such programs is usually at a high level, or at least reports at a high level.

It is difficult to measure the corporate resources being applied to these programs. People and funds assigned to such programs often have other corporate functions as well. Nevertheless, survey respondents provide the following picture of people and dollars being applied to coordinating social responsibility programs: In 90 percent of the companies covered in the survey, staff size ranged from only one to 10, not surprising in light of the high percentage of smaller companies responding to the questionnaire. Budgets also appear modest—less than 1 percent of total corporate (or staff) budget in 63 percent of the companies and only a little more, 1 percent to 3 percent, in another 28 percent of the companies surveyed.

## EFFECT OF ECONOMIC DOWNTURN

One controversial issue explored by the AMA survey is that of how corporate responsibility fares when business is bad. The survey asked: "What effect has inflation/recession had on your organization's social responsibility programs?" The response will surprise many. Fifty-seven percent of the respondents answered that inflation and recession had no effect on such programs, and an additional 8 percent said they had only a small effect.

A possible explanation is the survey finding that a significant number of social responsibility programs have become integral to basic corporate operations. If, indeed, this is the case, the vulnerability of such programs during a time of budget reductions would be decreased.

The results of a 1975 study of corporate contributions conducted by The Conference Board, New York, seem to support these findings. According to the study, 1975 contributions budgets increased about 10 percent over 1974. A key reason for the increase, the study said, was the conviction that corporate good citizenship must be maintained in bad times as well as good. One of the key growth areas in corporate philanthropy is support to the arts through national organizations such as the Business Committtee for the Arts and local groups such as New York's Arts and Business Council.

Nevertheless, a substantial proportion of the AMA survey respondents (35 percent) admitted to "various" effects caused by a business downturn. Some of their comments are quite revealing:

- Target dates for completion extended.
- Have to abandon some programs and lessen efforts in others.
- Contributions are related to profits.
- We have had to devote longer hours to assure that displaced employees relocate properly.
- Severely curtailed the *expansion* of such programs.
- Sharpen priorities.
- Greatly reduced involvement.
- Caused deferral of initiation of new programs, but current programs are continuing.
- Slowed expansion into fringe areas, but still maintain the "core" of social responsibility programs because we think it is good business and the right thing to do.

## SOURCES OF HELP

Respondents to the AMA survey also provided some insights into sources of aid in planning and executing their social responsibility programs. Trade associations, with 143 mentions, led the "most helpful" list. This finding should not be surprising. Trade associations, with their tradition of coordinating areas of common interest within industries, are likely vehicles for coordination of progress in social responsibility as well.

The life insurance industry has provided a model for such coordination. The Institute of Life Insurance, now called the American Council of Life Insurance, several years ago established a Clearinghouse on Corporate Social Responsibility. Through an industrywide social reporting program, member companies have reported to the Clearinghouse management policies, expenditures, and results of programs in community service, contributions, investments, equal employment opportunity, individual involvement, and environment.

Several trade associations representing industries producing and marketing consumer durables have established consumer arbitration panels to resolve disputes over product quality, warranties, service, and related issues. Among such industries are manufacturers of major household appliances and automobile tires.

Next most helpful were the national business associations such as the National Association of Manufacturers and the U.S. Chamber of Commerce (102 responses), the business press (54), and the general press (47). It may be significant that the fifth most effective means was the contact with public interest groups (41); one wonders whether a poll five years ago would have produced a *single* response listing such groups as helpful to business in any way. This designation seems to say something about the maturity of the American corporation, the public interest groups themselves, or both.

## A ROAD MAP FOR FUTURE CORPORATE SOCIAL RESPONSIVENESS

The respondents' opinions on the emerging social responsibilities in their organizations (Table 8-1) tell us a great deal about where the corporation is heading. The inescapable conclusion from these responses is that American corporate managers expect to do much more in terms of their *direct* social responsibilities—in relationships with employees, customers, shareholders, plant communities—and perhaps not much else, unless society's demands change.

Ackerman and Bauer seem to have reached the same conclusion: "The trend toward concentration on matters which are more directly associated with the firm's operations and perceivable self-interest will continue at the expense of corporate philanthropy and efforts to address social problems not directly related to the firm." (5)

By contrast, several years ago some business and social observers were claiming the legitimacy of an amorphous "outer circle" of corporate social responsibility—this "circle" encompassing efforts to improve the general social environment. Clearly, corporate managers are now saying that they are not going to attempt to work out of their classification. Furthermore, they seem to recognize that there is a vast amount of social improvement to be accomplished in terms of how they run their businesses.

In the "Expect Increased Activity" column of Table 8-1, the most heavily supported entries are:

- Response to changing aspirations of minority groups and female employees (59 percent).
- Improvement of physical working environments (55 percent).
- Job enrichment programs (53 percent).
- Better consumer relations (52 percent).
- Increased employee participation in decision making (43 percent).

Table 8-1

The Future of Corporate Social Responsibility

What are the emerging priorities among your organization's social responsibility programs?

| | Expect Increased Activity | Expect Decreased Activity | Expect to Remain about the Same | Does Not Apply |
|---|---|---|---|---|
| Reduction of damaging environmental effects | 39% | 4% | 26% | 32% |
| Improvement of physical working environments (OSHA, etc.) | 55 | 2 | 36 | 7 |
| Response to changing aspirations of minority groups and female employees | 59 | 2 | 35 | 4 |
| Increased employee participation in decision making | 43 | 1 | 51 | 5 |
| Employee "voluntarism programs" (sabbaticals, etc.) | 21 | 2 | 48 | 29 |
| Job enrichment programs | 53 | 3 | 38 | 6 |
| Product safety improvement | 42 | — | 25 | 33 |
| Better consumer relations | 52 | — | 31 | 16 |
| Truth in advertising/marketing | 29 | — | 49 | 22 |
| More purchasing from "minority vendors" | 16 | 2 | 54 | 29 |
| Improved relations with socially oriented investors (churches, universities, foundations, etc.) | 16 | 1 | 47 | 36 |
| Contributions to urban or community improvement | 41 | 2 | 51 | 6 |
| Support to education | 37 | 2 | 55 | 6 |
| Support to the arts | 19 | 4 | 63 | 14 |
| Support to other philanthropies | 14 | 5 | 68 | 13 |
| Other | 76 | — | 24 | — |

In addition, it seems clear that but for the nature of the companies responding (which had a distinct effect on the "Does Not Apply" column), two other social responsibility activities also would have ranked high among the priorities: reduction of damaging environmental effects (of manufacturing processes or products) and product safety improvement. Finally, the category "Contributions to urban or community improvement" also ranks high in the "Expect Increased Activity" column, perhaps an expression of agreement with a leading urban affairs expert who commented that "the inner city is our new frontier and the people living there are our real pioneers."

Significantly, the entire "Expect Decreased Activity" column had a minimum of entries.

Interestingly enough, all respondents who classified themselves as multinational companies—191—had these same seven issues at the top of their priorities list. One-third of the multinational respondents felt that their international status made for special social responsibility problems. The main problems, according to these executives, are conflicting legislation/regulations in countries in which plants and offices are maintained (37 percent).

## A COMPARISON OF AMERICAN, BRITISH, AND EUROPEAN ECONOMIC COMMUNITY (EEC) COMPANIES

In late 1974 Management Centre Europe (MCE) conducted corporate social responsibility surveys of executives of British companies and companies headquartered in the European Economic Community (EEC) countries. A number of interesting comparisons can be made of some of the results of these surveys with the AMA survey of American firms.

Assuming that the rather modest returns on the MCE surveys (28 British companies and 68 EEC companies) are as valid as the 644 AMA replies in reflecting the situations in the respective survey areas, the following differences are readily apparent: British and EEC companies seem to have given greater emphasis to centralization of responsibility and coordination of corporate social responsibility (Table 8-2). In the United States, 30 percent of the respondents indicated that such centralization existed in their companies, whereas in Great Britain the figure was 50 percent and in the EEC countries it was 52 percent.

Similarly, the social audit/social performance review seems to have been attempted in a higher percentage of companies abroad. In the United States only 19 percent of the companies represented in the survey reported undertaking such a comprehensive evaluation. In Great

Table 8-2

A Comparison of American, British, and EEC Companies' Policies and Programs on Corporate Social Responsibility

| | American Companies | British Companies | EEC Companies |
|---|---|---|---|
| Percentage of companies with centralized responsibility for CSR | 30% | 50% | 52% |
| Social audit/performance review status | | | |
| Percentage of companies that have conducted such studies | 19% | 39% | 44% |
| Motivations for conducting studies (in order of priority) | 1. To integrate social programs into the organizational process<br>2. To protect long-term profitability<br>3. To improve employee relations | 1. To identify areas in company that are vulnerable to criticism<br>2. To protect long-term profitability<br>3. To anticipate new social legislation | 1. To protect long-term profitability<br>2. To identify areas in company that are vulnerable to criticism<br>3. To formally integrate social issues into planning |

| | | | | |
|---|---|---|---|---|
| Chief difficulties in conducting studies | 1. Establishing acceptable measures of performance<br>2. Separating social issues from others | 1. Establishing acceptable measures of performance<br>2. Separating social issues from others | 1. Establishing acceptable measures of performance<br>2. Separating social issues from others | 1. Establishing acceptable measures of performance<br>2. Separating social issues from others |
| Top social pressures or priorities | 1. Responding to changing aspirations of minority groups and female employees<br>2. Improving physical working environment<br>3. Installing job enrichment programs | 1. Responding to demands of organized labor<br>2. Providing wide opportunities for employees to participate in decisions that affect them<br>3. Complying with new social legislation | 1. Responding to demands of organized labor<br>2. Providing wide opportunities for employees to participate in decisions that affect them<br>3. Complying with new social legislation | 1. Responding to demands of organized labor<br>2. Providing wide opportunities for employees to participate in decisions that affect them<br>3. Complying with new social legislation |
| Status on a key issue: Equal Employment Opportunity | Government-mandated "affirmative action plans" near universal | (Not available) | | 22% have written policies; 9% have developed plans |
| Percentage of companies that have conducted employee attitude surveys | 11% | 54% | | 57% |

Britain and in the EEC countries, the percentages were 39 and 44 percent, respectively. There is, however, a great similarity among the three surveys both on motivation for such surveys and on the chief obstacles in conducting them.

The differences that show up in the "Top social pressures or priorities" category seem to be essentially related to the role of organized labor abroad. In both the British and EEC surveys, response to the demands of organized labor topped the list of pressures. In the United States survey, it was not even on the priorities list.

Conversely, a key social issue in the United States—equal employment opportunity—was not discussed in the British survey. In the EEC countries, only 22 percent of respondents' companies have written policies in this area, and a meager 9 percent have actually developed plans. This difference reflects the deep concern over the rights of women and minorities that has evolved in the United States.

Finally, in the area of surveys of employees' attitudes and opinions on corporate social responsibility, American companies again seem to be lagging. Only 11 percent of the United States firms reported conducting such surveys, considerably fewer than the 54 percent and 57 percent for British and EEC countries, respectively.

In sketching this basic model for the corporation of the future I have chosen not to examine the alternative corporate structures already with us or on the horizon. Some say that the public-private corporate forms like COMSAT, AMTRAK, and the Corporation for Public Broadcasting may well be the wave of the future. Too, imaginative quasi-corporate forms like the "sweat equity" housing cooperatives springing up in urban areas have promise for specific situations. There are, after all, instances in which profit is virtually impossible but the social cost of allowing an enterprise to fail is prohibitive. Examinations of such alternative forms have already filled many volumes. We mention them only to acknowledge that productive enterprise can take many forms.

Finally, in this opening chapter on the current and anticipated response to new social forces, there are a few thoughts on the emerging corporate *leader*. Although observations on the people who will run successful corporations will surface throughout the rest of this book, let us conclude this chapter with a few brief generalizations.

First, the matter of ethics among business leaders: Robert Cushman, the aforementioned (Chapter 3) president of the Norton Company, recently wrote in *Business and Society Review*:

> It is all very well for us to proclaim that free enterprise and the profit principle are the most productive and efficient devices

ever conceived on this earth, but that is not enough. The new opinion-shapers—in the universities, in government, in media— are demanding more. They want society to move toward what they see as more justice, more equality, more meaningfulness in human terms. These are not unworthy or mean goals. To a large extent, we in business should share them, not resist them. . . . Somehow we must find a way to rethink the business ethic in human terms that make sense and appeal to the deeper side of man. (6)

Similarly, as if to emphasize that ethics are "in," a recent book called *The Ethical Basis of Economic Freedom* has achieved wide readership. (7) A compilation of essays and commentaries edited by Ivan Hill, it is particularly relevant to the current social challenge facing the American corporate leader. One high point of the book is a passage from an address by former Secretary of the Treasury William E. Simon:

Nothing is more efficient than honesty; those who break the law or abuse the basic moral code in the name of profit are doing more to make "profit" a dirty word than all of the critics of the free-enterprise system put together. . . . In the last analysis, good ethics actually do make good business because a vital free market, like any other voluntary association of individuals, can thrive only on mutual trust and voluntary cooperation. (7)

As to the matter of breadth of the corporate executive's experience and sociopolitical involvement, a quotation from *Ethics and Profits* by Leonard Silk and David Vogel follows: ". . . the survival of business institutions and the values of independence of liberty that businessmen cherish depend not just on profits, but on a broader and deeper conception of the public good." (8)

Having offered in this chapter a general profile of the corporation that can survive in the current and emerging social environment, we will next get specific on several key aspects of the current process of corporate adaptation: corporate futurism, a new approach to the structure of the workplace, and the erection of an "environmental bridge,"— these and other significant shifts in policy form the heart of the new corporate evolution.

## REFERENCES

1. Ackerman, Robert, and Bauer, Raymond. *Corporate Social Responsiveness, The Modern Dilemma* (Reston, Va.: Reston Publishing Company, Inc., a Prentice-Hall Company, 1976), p. 13.

2. Paluszek, John L. *Business and Society, 1976–2000* (New York, N.Y.: Amacom Division of American Management Associations, 1976), p. 4.

3. Wilson, Ian H. *Corporate Environments of the Future: Planning for Major Change* (New York, N.Y.: The Presidents' Association of the American Management Associations, 1976), p. 38.

4. Ackerman and Bauer. *Corporate Social Responsiveness*, pp. 27, 29.

5. *Ibid.*, p. 27.

6. Cushman, Robert. "Let's Put Our House in Order: A Businessman's Plea," *Business and Society Review*, Spring, 1976, Number 17, © 1976, Warren, Gorham, and Lamont, Inc., 210 South Street, Boston, Mass., pp. 49–52. All rights reserved.

7. Hill, Ivan, ed. *The Ethical Basis of Economic Freedom* (Chapel Hill, N.C.: American Viewpoint, Inc., 1976).

8. Silk, Leonard, and Vogel, David. *Ethics and Profits* (New York, N.Y.: Simon and Schuster, 1976), p. 238.

# 9

# The Corporate Futurists

Mort Darrow is tall, trim, fiftyish, and professional. Judging by his looks, you might expect to encounter him behind a desk at an Ivy League school (where, in fact, he has put in a few years). In the fall of 1976, however, more often than not, he could be found in a handsomely appointed office in an incongruously placed skyscraper in downtown Newark. Mort Darrow is a corporate futurist. Vice President of Planning and Analysis for the Prudential Insurance Company of America, he is one of a growing number of business executives monitoring the social environment. The corporate futurist is at the center of the corporation's response to the changing world about it. So I visited Darrow in late October 1976 to make a firsthand appraisal of corporate futurism.

I asked Darrow, "How did you become a corporate futurist?"

> "I did my graduate work at Columbia after World War II, in history, public law, and government. When I finished that I went to Princeton University on a post-doctorate fellowship, and then taught at Princeton. After some work in state government, I came to Prudential as a research person in 1956.
> "In 1965 or 1966, the head of our company was the head of a life insurance trade association, then called the Institute of Life Insurance, which was involved in a project to take a look at the life insurance industry ten years down the pike. His involvement in the project led to my being selected as a member of an eight-man task force of insurance company executives. I

headed up one part, the marketing study. We came out with a report that received wide attention in the insurance industry.

"The prime stimulant for this study was the fact that Medicare had been enacted despite a great deal of opposition from insurance companies, a sort of mindless rear-dragging because it had pretty well been established that this was a sector of the economy that could not be handled by private business.

"It soon became apparent that the time span of the report was really too short, a ten-year projection. That was just sort of looking around the corner. So the company relieved me of operational and administrative responsibilities so that I could set up a futures group, to take a look at the longer range perspective and to set up my own timetable of what ought to be looked at. I decided to operate with a time span out to the year 2000.

"Subsequently, I was asked to take on administrative responsibility for maybe 20 percent or 30 percent of my time, which included being in charge of long-range planning and being in charge of a small department.

"The essential reporting mechanism was to our Executive Office when I had findings that warranted discussion or working directly with various staff departments and line operations. But it was a kind of 'off the chart' relationship."

"What is the reporting mechanism now?" I then asked Darrow.

"Well, now we've evolved into a more sophisticated arrangement. Now I'm in a Public Affairs Department. One of the major functions we have defined for the department is to monitor the environment—technological, economic, social, and political—in order to make some judgments about where we are going, short term and long term. I spend perhaps a little more than 50 percent of my time dealing with short-range implications of these outside factors, and perhaps a little less than half the time exploring long-range implications."

"What else does the Public Affairs Department do?" I asked.

"When we set up the Public Affairs Department, we postulated that over the years, apart from executive speeches, little had changed within the corporation regarding its role as a social institution, as distinct from an economic one. The department was set up to try to put greater thrust behind this idea of greater social responsiveness. To make it most effective, we selected its several functional elements rather deliberately. We started with the public relations and advertising groups, brought them in bodily so that we would have the communication mechanism. We added the community relations department, which included contributions as well as urban affairs. I was brought in, the consumer affairs area was brought in, as well as an investment representative; and the governmental affairs at the federal level was brought in. We also set up a number of specialists in order to be more self-contained in what we call a general staff, so that we have our own lawyer and we have our own actuary.

"We also set up a public attitude study unit that conducts surveys and utilizes surveys available from other sources. One of its main functions is to alert various parts of the corporation to attitude changes among the public in general and among specific publics.

"I tend to get involved in either large-scale enterprises which have political and economic and social implications, or in projects that deal with academia and foundations."

"What would be a typical long-term concern?" was my next question to Darrow.

"The University of Southern California in Los Angeles has a future study sector, and we are a partial sponsor, working with them on a 20-year study of world food problems," he replied.

"Why is an insurance company looking at the food problem 20 years down the road?" I then asked.

"There are a number of disaster scenarios that are floating around, including some that are based upon possible climatic changes, in which we are talking about hundreds of millions of people dying—scenarios which would mean quite a change in our value structures in regard to life and death and which would have an impact upon mortality and morbidity within this country as well as elsewhere in the world.

"Even more directly than that, we have $42 billion in assets invested throughout this economy and ultimately therefore in the world economy, and if we enter into very severe food shortages there are going to be tremendous disruptions and changes in investment patterns, not least of all in terms of investments in food industries."

"What would be a short-term issue for your futurist activity?" I inquired.

"A group of businessmen in New York sponsored a rally on the need for federalization of welfare and welfare reform, and I was sent as one of several company representatives. I have been preparing an analysis of what the implications are for us, with recommendations as to what we might do on that issue. Now there you have a short-term sociopolitical issue because the action discussed was signing a petition to the incoming president, and Congress calling for welfare reform and federalization of funding of welfare."

"Your operation is part of the Public Affairs Department. How does it plug into top management?" I wanted to know from Darrow.

"We report directly to the Chief Executive Officer," he replied.

"Is most of your work anticipatory or is it reflective of requests made by different people within the Prudential organization?"

Darrow answered, "I would say now more of it is responsive, largely because the Public Affairs Department is getting into so many different areas of activity where judgments are requested. I think this is a function of the newness of the set-up and at some stage we've got to get back to being more creative."

"Is it possible, though," I asked, "that more managers within the company are aware of the sociopolitical problems that exist and the impact on their operations and therefore come to you with problems that 10 or 20 years ago weren't even perceived?"

"I agree that there's a greater awareness of the need for being socially responsive and I think there is a growing realization that it's perhaps better to get involved now—rather than later in a less friendly atmosphere," he answered.

"Are you sometimes confronted with the challenge to justify your existence in commercial terms or profitability? What's the bottom line on all of this?"

"More the other way—surprisingly the other way," Darrow responded. "I do not publish my results. It is felt by my superiors that the concepts or specifics have competitive *value* that ought to be retained within the corporation. The people I've had as superiors over the last 12 years feel that it does have bottom-line applicability to a greater degree than I do."

"Do you accept the description of being a company futurist?" I asked.

"The title was self-given. The in-company title, despite all the different assignments I've had, since I became a senior officer of the company, has been Vice President, Planning & Analysis. I've left that alone, but I am the assigned person who is responsible for future study, and so early in the game I called myself Company Futurist. When the World Future Society was first formed about eight years ago, they sent out application forms. I remember when I applied there was a blank asking for 'profession.' I replied 'Futurist.' They wrote back and said—mine was about the 800th reply—'you are the first person who has said he is a futurist.'"

"What are the main instruments that a company futurist has at his disposal? How do you do your job?" I asked.

"It has changed as circumstances have changed. For most of the time I reported directly to the Executive Office. Let's say I have a 'great inspiration,' and I feel that as a result of the way I'm reading the future, certain policy action needs to be taken. I would ask for a session with the Executive Office.

"A specific example: Some time ago I felt that because of

changes in values relating to work, specifically among the youth but also in other parts of the working population, we should embark on a large-scale job enrichment or job redesign program. I talked with the executive officers about changes in institutions and work out to the year 2000. I indicated that there was a high probability that under a number of different alternative futures we would still be finding it more difficult to get people to do dumb jobs, that we had to change the nature of the job. My proposal was approved. We began by setting up a pilot program to redesign jobs in 10 areas of the company. I was counselor and adviser to that project. Now when you get into a continuing operation of this nature, when do you pull out? Because of its sensitivity I stayed with this one for five years, while doing other things, of course.

"First I got involved in analyzing the results of its pilot phase. Three of the experiments worked very well, four of them failed, and three never got off the ground. In analyzing the individual cases we were able to come to some operational hypotheses—why some things worked and why others didn't. Then we got to the next stage of implementation. Here I got into an even more active role. We had all the major units laying plans for the next five years as to how they would redesign their jobs. I then went around the country assisting them in setting up the five-year plan, counseling with them and helping secure budgetary approvals for what amounted to a massive program.

"Presently we have, I would say, the largest, most complex job redesign program as far as I know, anywhere in the world. Other companies have had more employees affected because they change a single job that affects 120,000 workers, but we've changed *hundreds of jobs* affecting several thousand people. We've done it on a basis of tailoring each redesign to individual units' situations.

"Now, that project is directly connected with a futures orientation. Another way, of getting involved would be if in my reading I see some opportunities for us. I would go directly to the department head and say 'I'd like to chat with you and your people about some ideas I have.' And those ideas would be fed into the decision process.

"Another way is that one of our departments might be thinking of going into a new line of business. They might send me their proposal at some stage and say: 'From a futurist point of view, what are your comments on this, how do you read this?' For example, when we were considering going into a health maintenance organization—HMO—they sent me their proposal and asked me whether from my perspective, it appeared to be a sound business move.

"Another major way of involvement is our training programs. I've spoken at most of them providing a session on the future. Another is that I have this kind of a dissemination role, sensitizing people about the future both within the company at conferences and at outside meetings. I do around 20 a year, at agency conferences, professional meetings, and so on, speaking about the future—where we're going and what we need to do to help shape that future."

"How does one 'read the future'?" I asked Darrow.

"There are a number of rather specific techniques that have been developed including cross impact analysis and other types of statistical and sophisticated technological forecasting. As a one-man shop, what I do is what is known derogatorily in the trade as 'genius' forecasting. Essentially I try to synthesize the material that other people produce in a primary way. Therefore the emphasis is on critical thinking and critical application of logic to the concepts of others.

"To do this you must rely heavily on reading—books and periodical publications. As you can see I subscribe to 43 different periodicals which are scanned to see if they have anything dealing with implications for the future.

"Then too there is an industry committee, an industry service where over 60 publications are monitored for the implications for the future. That is the program coordinated by the American Council of Life Insurance. We have 130 monitors from over 100 companies who submit abstracts dealing with future implications."

"Do you also monitor the arts? What else goes into this business of looking at the horizon?" I inquired.

"Well, I've got 110 files that I've been pouring stuff into over the last 10 years, and it goes from the implication of arts for the future all the way out to various 'values' files. It covers biology, medicine, institutions, politics, economics, war, outer space, and much more. I tend to read these materials very quickly and put them into files. Then when an issue develops, I go back to the file and work on a build-up of over 10 years. You end up with a lot of material that you can put your hands on quickly.

"Plus I'm involved in various groups, the so-called invisible colleges, such as the Doxiadis Group in Athens. I put in five years on the U.S. Chamber of Commerce Council on Trends and Perspectives, and there have been a number of other groups like that."

My next question to Darrow was, "Are you in a position to offer any general conclusions on the threat to the corporation from various sociopolitical forces in the future as a result of your work? Can you see stronger assaults coming over the hill, or is that behind us?"

"I think we're going to see a continuation for at least the next 20 years of the growth of the power of the state vis-à-vis the other sectors and institutions of the society, largely because of the continuation of the impact of technological/scientific developments on a modern society. Because the level of performance of government may not improve very much, we are, I think, going to have a muddling through in which more and more problems will be thrown at government despite poor past performance just because there is no other obvious place to go.

"I think much of the alarm about this development is naïve because the key to understanding power relationships is 'for whom is the power being used?' I think we have to ask what kind of power and leverage large corporations will have in the face of some of the changes. I don't see the corporate powerlessness that some other people see every time they envision an expansion of state power. I think what typifies this issue is what's happening in the regulatory agencies, where you have agencies that have fairly broad powers, but the powers are used in ways that were perhaps not intended by the original ideologues. These agencies are using regulatory power really to help some of these industries function better rather than regulating them from an adversary position."

"But aren't there large and important voices being raised, suggesting that relationship become an adversary relationship?" I asked.

"I think that's true. But to what degree are the regulatory agencies going to be power sources within the economy? I think that the environmentalist movement as well as the consumerism movement are going through the early stages of rhetoric. On the major thrust of consumerism—fairness in the marketplace—corporations certainly have no problems living with that. When we get into some of the disguised critiques that are being offered under the name of consumerism, the destruction of the corporate form or the mixed enterprise system, you're dealing with a very small minority.

"Most of the people who are in the consumerist movement are for the reform of the abuses in the marketplace and not for the elimination of corporations.

"There is a separate issue that's also sometimes handled under the guise of consumerism, and that is the internal government of corporations. I think the opponents here are again a very small group. They have used the marketplace as a lever, and as the marketplace reform takes place, as it will continue to, these other issues will tend to sort of dry up. They won't go away, but they won't have the same compelling thrust to them.

"The same thing holds for the environmentalists. Of course, some of the die-hard resistance that business makes to what are essentially acceptable ideas should also disappear. It becomes very hard to argue that you can't design a certain kind of engine when someone has already done it and is selling it on the market."

"But there are dislocations in situations like that that have to be dealt with," I said.

"That's why we're going to muddle through. I think that things are just going to get screwed up. We're not going to deal with them well. We will deal with them in the same sloppy way we deal with a lot of things. I don't see a millenium before the year 2000. I see that the dislocations will then lead to rather abrupt breaks, with a lot of unhappy people. I don't think we have the leadership in many major institutions, nor that we know how to make these changes. The reason is essentially the underlying model that we operate by—the growth model. We just don't know how to handle balance and real trade-offs. If everything is growing, we know how to handle that. We know how to handle more kids—we build schools. We know how to handle more old people—we build more nursing homes. But when we start getting into population shifts where maybe we're getting less kids and more old people, we really don't know how to shift our resources in society."

"What do you see as the future of the corporate futurist?" I asked.

"I thought that this was a fad that would disappear some time ago. I'm surprised at the durability of it. Thus, my first forecast—that the corporate futurist would by now have disappeared—was wrong, which doesn't really help my track record! I think the current indications are that futurists will be a part of more and more large corporations because of the higher and higher degree of uncertainty that we will be operating under.

"I think the uncertainty is going to be there. One of the reasons the systems are becoming more and more complex is that there's a greater degree of fragmentation of our institutions and in our values. This is going to continue for some time, and there will be a general reluctance to try to institute major change because of the difficulty of foreseeing all the consequences.

"There are two major ways of handling that kind of uncertainty. One is *not* to give any thought to trying to monitor what's going on around you because it's too hard—and because you're going to get a feeling of hopelessness about being able to make any predictions. The other is *because* it's harder, to try to do it better, and thereby be able to take advantage of shifts.

"Thus, I think one kind of corporate reaction to uncertainty could be to revert to know-nothingism. But I think the more likely reaction will be to *plan* to operate more effectively in an uncertain future, with the emphasis on keeping options open but being able to take advantage of opportunities and to avoid disaster—above all, don't get locked in.

"Therefore the monitoring of the emerging threats will become more important."

"Do you think the corporation will survive and succeed?"

"I'm sure of it," Darrow answered. "Its ability to change with the times, roll with the punches, and so on is demonstrated. I think it's more adaptable than most of our other institutions, although that's not very high praise. Institutional adaptation is exceedingly difficult. I think corporations, more than any other of the major social institutions, innovate. It's a rare corporation that has as a proud banner 'we are conservative, we do not believe in change, we believe that what was good 150 years ago is good today,' which some of our other institutions would say. Some of the recent struggles within universities were based on how the university should change its structure. I think a good corporation will have to be innovative, progressive, responsible. I'm not suggesting that it buy change for change's sake, except under certain circumstances. Sometimes we *do* put in changes for change's sake, where people are beginning to go stale. Change will shake them up.

"I think essentially you've got to look beyond the rhetoric to see what are the levers of power and who has power within societies. Then try to develop scenarios in which the corporation could become powerless. I think you can do that but they tend to be very, very low probabilities in alternative futures.

"On the other hand, if you look at alternative futures with continuous growth of corporate influence, it's very easy to develop scenarios with higher probabilities."

Not all corporate futurists operate quite like Mort Darrow.

At the General Electric Company, for example, a sophisticated system of environmental analysis for use in strategic planning has evolved during the past decade. Ian H. Wilson, a veteran of about 10 years in a variety of GE public relations assignments, now coordinates the company's environmental monitoring function. Wilson is Staff Associate, Business Environment Research, in GE's Corporate Strategic Planning Department. He has written a number of revealing and instructive descriptions of GE's approach to "corporate futurism."

The following passages are reprinted from Wilson's "Corporate Environments of The Future: Planning for Major Change," a special study published in 1976 by The Presidents' Association of the American Management Associations:

> In a society as complex and diverse as that of the United States, the population cannot be slotted at one level only, for

there are people operating at *all* levels. A profile of the population makeup, with its various modes of living will thus be needed to represent the full range of values; and future changes in this profile will be indicative of shift-value systems.

. . . the correlation seems to exist between need levels and levels of affluence and education. Both intuition and the available evidence suggest that there is a table of relationships along the following lines:

| Need Level | Income Level[a] | Education Level |
|---|---|---|
| 1 | less than $3,500 | Eighth grade or less |
| 2 | $3,500–7,500 | Some high school |
| 3 | $7,500–15,000 | High school graduate/some college |
| 4 | more than $15,000 | College graduate |
| 5 | ? | College graduate |

[a] Expressed in constant 1970 dollars.

. . . It is possible to predict that by 1985 there will be fewer people in the poverty/low education class, and thus a reduction of emphasis on survival and safety needs nationally. At the other end of the spectrum, increasing affluence, more education, and the changing composition of the labor force will mean a rise in the number of high-income individuals, college graduates, professional and managerial personnel and thus an increase in emphasis on social, ego and self-fulfillment needs.

. . . A graphic illustration of some of the elements of this shift was attempted in a 1969 study by General Electric's Business Environment Studies staff. . . . What the shifting "values profiles" do suggest (Figure 9-1) is (to use another historical analogy) a "New Reformation"—a major re-formation or reordering of our public and private values.

. . . During this period of transformation, society might be said to be rewriting its "charter of expectations" of corporate performance, and defining the parameters within which business may operate.

One [definition of the purpose of the corporation] we have discussed at General Electric comes in two stages. Stage 1 states: "The corporation is a creation of society whose purpose is the production and distribution of needed goods and services to the profit of society and itself. . . ."

. . . Stage 2 of this definition extends the business-society

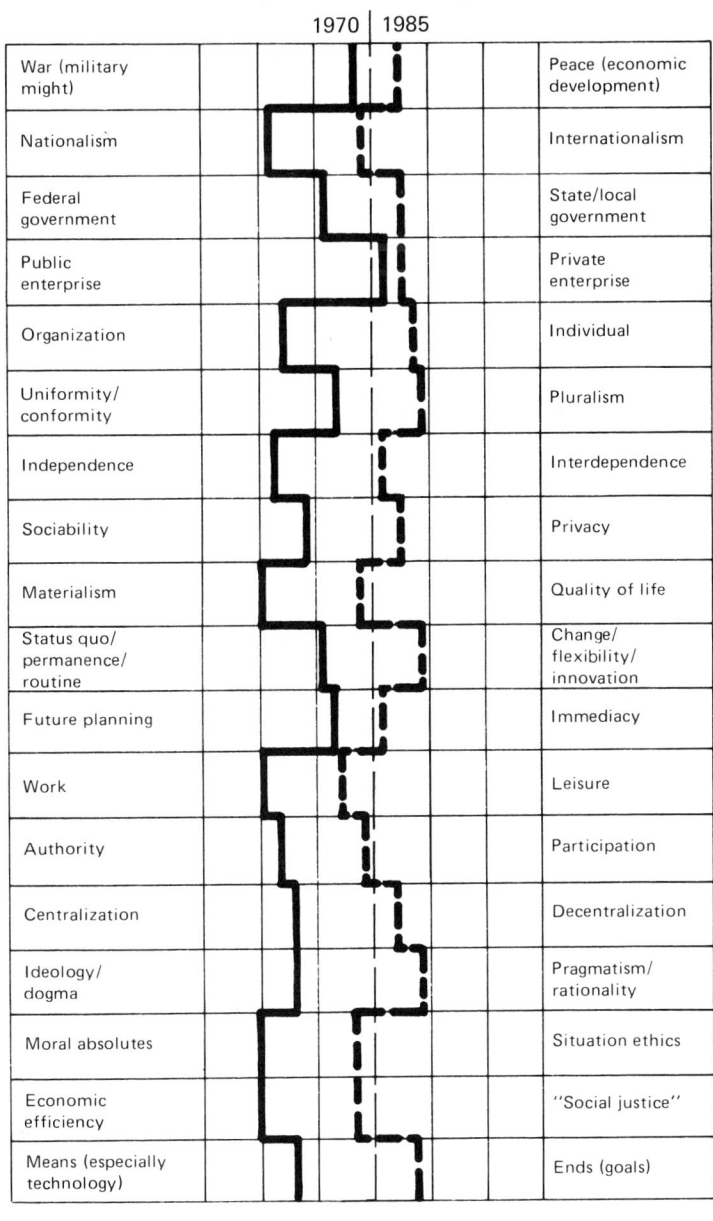

**Figure 9-1**

relationship a step further: "As a microcosm of society, a corporation must reflect *all* of that society's shared values—social, moral, political and legal, as well as economic." The corporation, in other words, is not, and cannot be, a purely economic institution. It must change as society changes, but, as a dynamic institution, it can also seek to influence the ultimate form and expression of these changes.

. . . in the final analysis, the corporation must always act from signals, often faint and confusing, that society sends out to indicate its needs and expectations.

In the past, corporate performance *has* responded to the shifting requirements of social expectations. . . . In each instance, society looked to business for the technology, the resources, the organizational know-how to meet these special goals—to provide jobs, supply consumer goods, build up weapon systems, catalyze the space program. Thus, society has a way of making known its goals for business, and business has had the flexibility to respond to these changing goals.

There are also some underlying goals that remain relatively constant—the goals, for instance, of a free society, a stable society, a prosperous society, and an equal-opportunity society. Corporations have an enlightened self-interest in these goals, for they represent the basic conditions for the successful conduct of business, as well as for the peaceful progress of society.

For the future, we may reasonably conjecture that the new challenge to corporate responsiveness will be in the qualitative sector of public expectations. We are seeing a broadening of the horizons of our social concern.

### Identifying Major Impact Points

It was to assess more precisely the totality of these impacts, as well as to arrive at some ordering of priorities for corporate action, that the Business Environment Studies staff of General Electric attempted a systematic analysis of the vast array of current and prospective societal pressures that beset modern corporations. Prepared for the Public Issues Committee of the company's board of directors, this analysis used as its starting point a comprehensive inventory of social demands on business, grouped in eight categories.

Marketing and financial power
Production operations
Employee relations and working conditions
Governance
Communications (including advertising)
Community and government relations

Defense production
International operations

In each area the social pressures were defined in terms of the major charges and complaints that are made about business performance. Although this approach may seem to be too negative, the reason for taking it was quite simply that these are likely to be the most clearly defined and the most intense pressure points as far as business is concerned. From the first stage of this inventory it was then possible to identify the major demands likely to be made on corporations. These are, in effect, the proposals advanced by a variety of pressure groups to deal with perceived flaws in the business system as they view it. Added to this list were a number of hazards that companies might face as a result of inadequate response to these social demands. All told, the inventory produced a total of 97 different demands and hazards confronting the modern corporation on the social front. . . .

It is not, of course, suggested that this exact inventory will be equally applicable to every company, only that the discipline of producing a comprehensive listing of social pressures is a useful exercise and a necessary first step in setting corporate priorities.

The priority analysis stage of the project consisted, first, of ranking these 97 demands/hazards according to their "convergence" with some of the expected major societal trends of the next decade. The questions asked here were: What will be the effect of these trends on each of these demands? Will the tendency be to reinforce or impede the realization of the demand? Instead of giving just a generalized answer to this question, the decision was made to score each of the 97 demands against each of the 13 trends, on a scale of 1 to 10, positive or negative, according to the assessment of the degree of "convergence" or "collision" between the demand and the trend. This scoring process was undertaken by a number of individuals, and thus the aggregate convergence score for each demand became a measure of collective judgment of the extent to which it seemed to be "in tune with the times" (and the future).

In addition to the convergence factor, we also developed a measure of the degree of pressure behind each demand, since, as already noted, not every demand is pressed with equal fervor, or by the same groups. Fourteen corporate constituencies were identified, and each demand was again scored, this time on a 4–3–2–1 basis, according to our estimate of whether it fell in the top, second, third, or bottom quartile of each group's demands and interests.

Admittedly, this scoring process is imperfect, and still reflects subjective judgments, though on a consensus basis. It does, however, approximate a systematic and objective selection process; and while the numbers (scores) are only a means to an end, they do force some hard thinking about a large series of microjudgments which, in total, can reasonably be said to have greater validity than a single overall value judgment.

On the basis of these two scores, it is then possible to plot each demand on a matrix (Figure 9-2), one axis of which is convergence (with trends), the other, intensity and diffusion of pressure. This plotting, in turn, suggests focusing corporate attention on those demands that fall in the upper right quadrant of the matrix, that is, those that have *both* high convergence and high intensity/diffusion.

## Overall Assessment of Major Demands on the Corporation

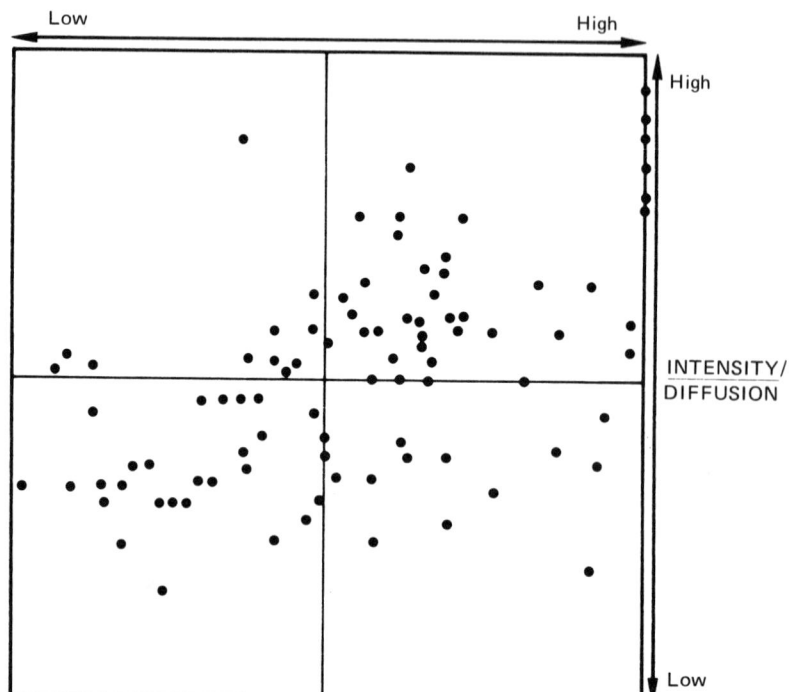

**Figure 9-2**

This preliminary analysis indicated that the high-priority demands gravitate toward one of six major areas of future challenge to the corporation:

1. *Constraints on corporate growth:* a spectrum of issues ranging from national growth policy through economic controls and environmental protection to questions of antitrust policy and industrial structure.
2. *Corporate governance:* including matters of accountability, personal liability of managers and directors, board representation, and disclosure of corporate information.
3. *Managing the "new work force":* dealing with the growing demands for job enlargement, more flexible scheduling, more equality of opportunity, greater participation and individualization.
4. *External constraints on employee relations:* the new pressures from government (EEO, health, safety, "federalization" of benefits), unions (coalition bargaining), and other groups (class action suits, encouragement of "whistle-blowing").
5. *Problems and opportunities of business-government partnership:* including a redefinition of the role of the private sector in public problem-solving.
6. *"Politicizing" of economic decision making:* the growing involvement of government and other groups in corporate decisions through consumerism, environmentalism, industrial reorganization, inflation control, land use planning, and so on.

The purpose here is not to discuss in detail either the merits of this process of "prioritizing" issues or the ramifications of the specific issues uncovered by this particular exercise. Rather, the point is to demonstrate the wide range of impacts on business created by the transformation we are undergoing (if corporate social responsibility encompasses all six—and more—areas, how can we any longer consider it a peripheral rather than a focal matter for corporate policy-making?), and to suggest that each company should undertake its own comparable disciplined examination of societal pressures, with the concurrence (and, preferably, the participation) of the chief executive officer.

### Challenges to Business Values

It would be reasonable to predict that the future holds for business the prospect of a major restructuring of its mission, its "style," its modus operandi, its system of governance. . . . The totality of these impacts amounts to a shaking of the "seven pillars of business," those basic values that we have up to now considered to be the eternal verities undergirding our business system—growth, technology, profit, the concept of private property, managerial authority, "hard work," and "company loyalty." It is not so much that these values will be totally rejected for a set of opposite values. Rather, we face the more uncertain outcome of a redefinition of the operational terms of these values, of a new balance being struck between these and other values to which we are giving a new emphasis. (1)

Mort Darrow and Ian Wilson are not alone.

A 1975 study published by AMACOM, a division of American Management Associations, provided one of the first indications of just how much corporate futurism has grown. The study, *1974-75 Exploratory Planning Briefs (Planning for the Future by Corporations and Agencies, Domestic and International)*, by W. W. Simmons, offers descriptions of planning sections in some 48 domestic and foreign corporations and associations. (2) Although it is difficult to discern exactly how many are into societal monitoring in addition to traditional corporate planning, many of the entries leave no doubt of the growing corporate commitment to such analysis.

Two examples from the AMACOM study are:

> *Ford Motor Company:* The primary concern of long-range planning at Ford Motor Company is to survey and analyze the changing business environment. Focus is on social change . . . its implications, and how it will affect the corporation.
>
> *Western Electric Company, Inc.:* Among its activities, the Corporate Planning staff has developed a Corporate Environmental Scanning Program. This is a formal attempt to gather and analyze future trends and development in business, society, science and politics that might be relevant to company long-range planning.

Actually, it would be fair to say that corporate futurism, an identifiable subsection of the futurist movement in general, has helped spawn a mini-industry. Many of the corporate futurists help to support and participate in studies conducted by universities, foundations, and commercial "think tanks" and consultants. *Planning Briefs* lists some 107 such organizations hard at work on futures, not including many governmental agencies both here and abroad.

Among the private organizations listed by *Planning Briefs* is Hill & Knowlton, the world's largest public relations firm. In the summer of 1976, *Jack O'Dwyer's Newsletter of Public Relations* reported that "PR people . . . were 'futurists' long before the word came into vogue. A few PR people are now attempting to peer into that chasm beyond one year—and as far as 10 to 25 years in advance. Some even unblushingly call themselves 'futurists' and say that futurism could be one of PR's better growth areas." (3)

American corporations active in futurism, or those contemplating such activity, may be interested in a profile of how seven Swedish companies have approached such work. Table 9-1 is reproduced from an article on the subject in the November 1975 issue of *The Environment Monthly*, which in turn was based on an analysis originally written for *Sweden Now* by that publication's associate editor, Ruth Link. (4)

Lest all of this lead the reader to believe that by undertaking a few futures studies, every corporation can attune itself to all the demands to be placed on it, we once again quote Wilson's study, *Corporate Environments of the Future: Planning for Major Change*:

> At least a couple of caveats are in order. First, it should be obvious that with the pace of change being what it is, such an evaluation cannot be considered as other than a "snapshot," valid perhaps as a picture of reality at that moment, but not as a permanent guide for corporate policy. What is needed is more like a moving picture, a continual—or, at least, a repeated—monitoring of the social and political environment to determine the shifting pattern of social priorities, the emergence or the disappearance of significant demands and pressures. Such an activity can be done "in house," or the company may choose to subscribe to a service such as Corporate Priorities provided by Yankelovich, Skelly and White, Inc.
>
> A second caveat is that one should not focus on the high-priority issues and demands to the exclusion of other items plotted on the matrix. For one thing, as just noted, today's low-priority demand may become tomorrow's burning issue. For another, the lesson of the matrix is that of the *need for differentiated strategies*.

One of those differentiated strategies may well relate to the problems of corporate *product* planning, especially in those industries strongly tied to changing fashions.

In a fascinating article on the subject in the November-December 1975 issue of the *Harvard Business Review*, Dwight E. Robinson, professor of business, government, and society at the Graduate School of Business Administration, University of Washington, makes these points:

> To the businessman who is baffled or frustrated by the problem of rapidly shifting tastes, I would say that product planning does not have to be a guessing game. . . . Evidence is at hand on which to base two principles about the way in which

Table 9-1
How Long-Range Planners for Top Swedish Firms Pick
Great Future Impacts—Plus Their Forecasting Tools

| Corporation | Great Impact, Past Ten Years | Great Impact, Next Ten Years | Main Background For Forecasting |
|---|---|---|---|
| KEMA-NORD (chemicals) | Oil crisis<br>Rachel Carson's *Silent Spring* | North Sea oil | Marketing feedback<br>Public opinion<br>Internal information bulletin |
| ASTRA (pharmaceuticals) | Acceleration in change<br>Awareness | Society's attitudes<br>Scientific discoveries | Marketing feedback<br>Cross-fertilization with other firms<br>Special literature |
| VOLVO (vehicles) | Oil crisis<br>Changed attitude to car<br>Ralph Nader's *Unsafe at Any Speed*<br>Rising demands of developing countries | Shift in world wealth<br>Decreased rise in energy consumption<br>Information systems<br>North Sea oil<br>Industrial democracy and "job quality"<br>Growing equality between sexes, nations, classes<br>Internationalization of trade union movement | Special studies<br>High-level contacts (both Swedish and international seminars) |

| Company | | | |
|---|---|---|---|
| SAAB-SCANIA, Aerospace Div. | Environment debate<br>Oil crisis | Communications<br>North Sea oil<br>Cybernetics | Defense Department<br>Political contacts<br>Special studies<br>Public opinion |
| JOHNSON GROUP (industrial conglomerate) | Oil crisis<br>Club of Rome-type thinking | Employee decision-making<br>Relations in developing countries<br>A new economic order<br>New energy crisis | Contacts in international organizations<br>Futurology literature<br>Special studies |
| SANDVIK (metal products) | Meadows' *Limits of Growth*<br>The stagnation of air traffic | Economic models<br>Superpower recall of plutonium<br>Raw materials crisis<br>Demands for relocation in developing countries | Marketing feedback<br>Special studies<br>General reading |
| PLM (packaging) | Environment discussions<br>Protectionism<br>Back-to-nature trend<br>Energy crisis | Raw materials shortages<br>Sociological revolution (job power) | International contacts<br>Public opinion<br>Marketing contact |

fashion works: (1) fashions follow an inexorable cycle, and (2) because they are inexorable, fashion cycles must be as independent as any force to be found in social change.

. . . fashion change is sufficiently intelligible and predictable that its study and application to product planning can enormously reduce the risk of costly errors of judgment and may even contribute positively to successful new designs . . . the potentialities for using [fashion] to improve product planning could easily amount to many billions of dollars annually.

No planner, short- or long-term, should concentrate his attention on what producers and their professional engineers are doing to the exclusion of what amateurs (collectors, hobbyists, sports enthusiasts and buffs) are doing. Hobby magazines, for one thing, are treasuries of information. . . . For example, such journals pick up on antique crazes for period styles of a variety of articles whether they are clothes, furniture or cars. It is sociologically unthinkable that if millions of people are opting for Edwardian men's suits and women's dresses, Tiffany glass or Art Deco, or Dusenbergs and Bugattis, such associations are not going to have some effect on what people are looking for in new products (in terms of shape, texture, ornamentation, and all the rest). (5)

. . . I believe . . . that fashion is a behavioral phenomenon, probably growing out of status competition. In jockeying for position of higher social status, people seek to demonstrate the extent of their purchasing power. One way that they do this is through the acquisition and possession of things that are comparatively scarce—and therefore, so much harder to get. Fashion creates that scarcity by discarding old forms.

. . . Once a new fashion trend is set in motion, there is little—whether it be technological innovation, political edict, functional change, even basic economics—that can be done to stop it or change its course. Therefore, specialists in these fields are of limited use to style policy.

Finally, here are some thoughts on "youth watching" as presented by Paul A. Wagner, a former senior vice president of Hill & Knowlton, in *Critical Issues in Public Relations*:

Since much of the demand for social change will originate from certain sectors of American youth, it will become the prime responsibility of the public relations counselor to alert his clients to the demands being made; to distinguish at an early date a fad from a significant shift in attitude; and to trigger a fast reaction to any demands that might affect the client in a serious way.

This is a big order . . . what is needed is a youth watcher,

... one who is ... willing to glean those special inputs that can be gained only by close observation of the youth scene. (6)

Wagner says that serious youth watchers will monitor books on the college best-seller lists, the films most popular with young moviegoers, professional and intellectual journals, college newspapers, films produced by students, and the cultural, mystical, and religious interests of youth groups.

In a delicious analogy that underscores the importance of "youth watching," Irving Kristol has suggested that America has recently produced a "New Populism," with today's young, disenchanted college-educated class as its army and Ralph Nader (succeeding William Jennings Bryan) as its leader.

The corporate futurists—one very hopeful sign that the corporation will anticipate social change and prepare for it.

## REFERENCES

1. Wilson, Ian H. *Corporate Environments of the Future: Planning for Major Change* (New York, N.Y.: The Presidents' Association of the American Management Associations, 1976), pp. 18–38.
2. Simmons, W. W. *1974–75 Exploratory Planning Briefs* (*Planning for the Future by Corporations, and Agencies, Domestic and International*), (New York, N.Y.: AMACOM, a Division of American Management Associations, 1975), pp. 5, 13.
3. *Jack O'Dwyer's Newsletter of Public Relations*, September 8, 1976, p. 3.
4. *The Environment Monthly*, November, 1975, pp. 8–9.
5. Robinson, Dwight E. "Style Changes: Cyclical, Inexorable, and Foreseeable," *Harvard Business Review*, November–December 1975, pp. 121–131.
6. Wagner, Paul A. "Youth a Fractionated Audience," in *Critical Issues in Public Relations* (Englewood Cliffs, N.J.: Prentice-Hall, Inc., 1975), pp. 145–154.

# 10

# *Toward a New Workplace*

> *"Our parents lived to work. We work to live."*
> —advertisement describing readers of
> Psychology Today
> October, 1976

Nowhere in the corporation are society's changing values having more impact than in the workplace. Fittingly, it is here that the corporation's ability to adapt is best being illustrated.

The workplace of tomorrow is already well under development. In addition to reflecting the advance of technology, it will, more importantly, reflect the progress the corporation is making in its relationship with its employees. To be sure, this progress has been somewhat fitful. Delayed by the recent economic downturn, it is nevertheless inexorable.

In this chapter, we will briefly describe the changes sought, and the corporate response to date, in two basic aspects of work—the restructuring of working time and the reorganization of work itself. What all these changes add up to is, in the words of an informed observer, "recognition of the dignity of the worker rather than the dignity of work."

First, however, it is necessary to deal with the contention that the new employee demands are only transitory, that given a good stiff dose of increased unemployment, such demands will fade. John Hoerr has addressed himself to this contention. "For the first time in their working lives, workers who grew up in the 1950s and 1960s—a generation noted for rebelliousness on the job—have now tasted the bitterness of a prolonged economic slump," he wrote in a May, 1976 issue of *Business Week*. He says further:

A new concern for job security has tamed their restiveness, but underlying generational conflicts remain. Employers and unions must still learn to cope with the markedly different social values of the post-World War II generation. . . .

Some authorities on worker behavior believe that the new stress on job security is only a temporary diversion from the main thrust of the young workers' revolt. The major social and political upheavals of the 1960s . . . imbued the postwar generation with cultural values far different from those of older generations. These values are not reversible. When the job security issue begins to fade as the economy recovers, employers and unions will be confronted once again by demands for more rapid change in the workplace. . . .

Within a few years the postwar generation will make up a majority of the nation's work force. The pressures for change then may become overwhelming unless corporations and unions find ways to make work more meaningful and rewarding. Research by psychologists Daniel Yankelovich and Raymond A. Katzell has shown that most managers and union leaders believe that, for all the exaggeration of the "assembly line blues," worker dissatisfaction is a reality and the quality of working life must be improved. They say this can be done with increased productivity, although no single technique will work in all industries. (1)

It is happening right now. Such change is in place, as experimental or fully tested procedure, in companies large and small across the country. And in the years immediately ahead, the ranks of such companies will grow as an unusual form of corporate competition—the competition for the more satisfied, more productive worker—takes root.

That is one of the main propositions of a seminal book on the subject, *The Future of the Workplace* by Paul Dickson. In an early and fundamental passage in the book, Dickson writes:

In general terms, this movement that began to make itself felt in the United States in the early 1970s has to do with prospecting for new ways to work which break away from long-established trends not seriously questioned before. New premises are being offered that include:

- Treating workers as educated adults.

- Allowing those at all levels to have greater involvement in decision making.

- Increasing the opportunity for individuals to use their minds on the jobs.

- Substituting individual responsibility for heavy-handed discipline.
- Giving working people greater individual identity.
- Removing a layer or two of supervision.
- Giving people greater control over time.
- Taking jobs that have become fragmented and rebuilding them into new jobs with coherence. (2)

Before taking a closer look at how corporations are reconstituting jobs, let's deal briefly with *why* they are undertaking what is, after all, a monumental task.

The first response to "Why?" is the obvious one, "Because employees and potential employees are demanding such changes." But there is a much more interesting and more characteristic answer to why corporate managers are thinking this way: A body of evidence is now accumulating that with values evolving as they are, it can be much more productive—and therefore much more profitable—to restructure the workplace.

It is important to see this up front so that we avoid the trap of thinking that altruism alone has fueled this movement. If it had, as Ackerman and Bauer have pointed out (see Chapter 9), the long-term future of the movement would be shaky at best. No, there is something much more fundamental at work here—the growing belief that this is both humanistic *and* capitalistic, and that those motivations are by no means mutually exclusive.

## RESTRUCTURING WORK TIME

Let's look at what is happening to the corporation's concept of employees' time on the job. This concept involves not only the shorter week but also such matters at "flexitime," sabbaticals, and new definitions of vacations. The root of all of this re-evaluation of work schedules is, once again, society changing and the workplace trying to keep up with, or get ahead of, such social change.

Consider the work force of the late 1970s as compared to that of even 25 years ago. It has more formal education, it has at its command sophisticated communications media undreamed of a few decades ago, and—perhaps most important—it is increasingly female. How could a work force *not* be seriously affected when half the country's population is experiencing a profound change in outlook and opportunity?

The assaults on traditional work schedules are truly fundamental.

We are now dealing not only with new concepts of the work*day*, we are dealing with new ideas concerning the work*life*.

## The Shorter Work Week

The shorter work week has been a gleam in organized labor's eyes for several decades, and with chronic national high unemployment, there are new pressures to "spread the work around." The most common form of the rearranged work week seems to be the four-day 40-hour schedule, but there are many variations.

Riva Poor, a Cambridge, Massachusetts, management consultant, is widely thought to be the best-informed observer and advocate of the shorter work week. In the summer of 1976, she estimated that several thousand corporations, employing about a million workers, had converted to the four-day work week. (3) These companies seem to vary considerably in size, nature, and location. One of the largest and best known is the Equitable Life Assurance Society of the United States which in 1976 had an estimated 75 percent of its 7,000 home office workers on rearranged work schedules. Similarly, the John Hancock Mutual Life Insurance Company at that time had about 2,500 of the 6,000 employees at its Boston headquarters office on a four-day week.

Not all companies who have tried the four-day work week have stayed with it. But those who have cite increased output, lower production costs, better utilization of capital equipment, and reduced absenteeism as justifications for this schedule.

In the fall of 1976, the United Auto Workers seemed to strike a blow for a shorter work week for production workers when negotiating its new contract with the Ford Motor Company. Basing projections on Federal Energy Administration statistics, the UAW argued that although the industry's production levels in 1990 will be 47 percent above 1976, employment will increase only 5 percent because productivity will be improving. For this reason, the UAW argued, shortening work time "will require the private sector to fulfill social responsibilities in reducing the levels of mass unemployment." Ford didn't buy that argument, and the best the UAW could get was discussion of additional paid holidays. But the union, well known for foot-in-the-door bargaining strategy, will undoubtedly be back next time with an even stronger shortened work week position.

The union's arguments were not overlooked among thought-leaders. A *New York Times* editorial stated:

> The modest opening toward a four-day work week made by the Ford Motor Company strikers ushers in what could be a crea-

tive quarter-century in American labor-management relations. . . . The important question is whether the new generation of union chiefs will . . . recognize that genuine improvements in living standards and job security depend on cooperation between employer and unions to insure a healthy, productive economy and an equitable sharing of its fruits among all elements of society.

That question is especially pertinent to the impending shortening of the work week, a development that is almost certain to spread in the next few years from the Big Three automobile companies to many other branches of industry. . . . A younger, better educated work force has been exhibiting restiveness under the constraints of routine, repetitive jobs. . . . What is needed, however, is some assurance that the full achievement of a four-day, 32-hour timetable will not simply mean, in industrial terms, an inflationary increase of 20 percent in labor costs with no offsetting gains in productivity. (4)

The unusually cold winter of 1976–77 served as an unforeseen stimulus for the four-day work week when President Carter urged industry to consider such scheduling as a meaningful energy-conservation policy.

### Flexitime

Flexitime has many variations, but basically it allows employees to start and stop work at times more convenient to them than the traditional 9:00 A.M.-to-5:00 P.M. or other strict-shift schedules. Generally, it provides for core hours when everyone is expected to be on duty and an unchanged total of hours worked during a week.

Originated in Europe and applied in limited degree in recent years in major urban centers to decrease traffic congestion, flexitime has, understandably, become a favorite demand of women's groups. An estimated 100 companies had tried it by the spring of 1976, according to testimony presented to the House Committee considering whether to authorize a full-scale flexitime test among federal workers (the House subsequently did authorize such a test and the Senate is expected to do so in the 95th session). Both private companies and federal agencies that have experimented with flexitime seem pleased with the system as a means of increasing employee morale and adding flexibility to the work force without reducing productivity.

Many other personnel programs to tap the vast potential of women as workers are being tested. Most involve some sort of special-arrangement work schedules, shared tasks, or split-location (home and office) work. The readiness of an increasing number of corporations to try such programs seems to indicate that in this area of challenge the corporation is indeed flexible enough to meet social change head on.

### The Changing Worklife

In recent years, there have been some well-publicized new programs on sabbaticals for employees interested in doing public service work. Actually, these represent only one of a number of changing worklife programs now being offered by the American corporation. Others include encouragement of second careers and the six-month work year for those preparing for retirement. And there is a new liberalism emerging on vacation policies. More companies are allowing employees to "bank" vacation time instead of having to take vacation time within a calendar year. In short, the corporate work*life*—like the workday—is on the brink of substantial change.

### REORGANIZING WORK

How the employee's time is arranged is important, of course, but far more important is the matter of just what he/she does on the job. Here we get into the various plans for worker participation in the operating decision-making processes, as opposed to demands for employee representation on the corporation's board of directors (for more on *that* demand, see Chapter 5), as well as the concepts advanced under the general heading of job enrichment.

The worker participation movement has been well tested in Scandinavia. The successes at companies such as Volvo in Sweden and Norway's Standard Telefon og Kabelfabrik (which, significantly, is largely owned by the International Telephone and Telegraph Corporation) have been widely chronicled in American business publications and in the consumer press as well.

Participation developments on the American scene are moving along quite well too. At Herman Miller, Inc., a small manufacturer of commercial and industrial furniture in Zeeland, Michigan, worker participation has been linked to sharing in the benefit of productivity increases. This program has been in place for over a quarter of a century. At Herman Miller, workers elect representatives to work with management in a variety of planning and implementation decisions. Since the plan's inception, an average of 10 percent extra, attributable to worker participation in such decision making, has been added to monthly paychecks.

Participation seems to be coming fastest in the automobile industry. In 1976 Chrysler, for example, gave the assembly workers at its new Windsor, Ontario, Dodge compact wagon plant increased autonomy in setting up job teams, rotating assignments, and taking over many functions normally performed by foremen. The company is moving toward applying such experiments company-wide.

At General Motors it is already policy to try to move responsibility down the employee ladder, and worker participation in many areas of plant operation is growing rapidly.

Other large American companies well into participation programs are Motorola, the Firestone Tire and Rubber Company, and General Electric.

### Job Enrichment

As to *job enrichment* (in many cases, an outgrowth of worker participation in the decision process), here too we find a mini-industry of institutes, foundations, and consultancies ready to lead the very willing corporation to new ground. Organizations such as the Work in America Institute and the National Center for Productivity and Quality of Working Life, very often supported by corporate contributions, are making constant inroads in determining optimum characteristics of enrichment and the best course of action to achieve them. At a recent conference sponsored by those organizations, the rationale for such programs was aptly described by William A. Snow, a psychologist who is director of education and training for Rockwell International: "What is happening is that we have smarter people doing dumber things. . . . Those jobs do not challenge and motivate people to perform at the levels they are capable of achieving." (5)

Dr. Snow and Donald Rand, administrative assistant to the secretary of the United Auto Workers, told the conference about a Rockwell-UAW project that planned a new production facility at Battle Creek, Michigan, and developed job procedures that gave people a complete unit of work to do, let them be responsible for the quality of work performed, and provided them with as much autonomy in their jobs as possible.

At General Electric, a group of psychologists and other in-house consultants has been assigned to upgrading jobs. Among their approaches are educating workers on how their jobs fit into the overall assembly or production system, communicating to workers how their products are used in the outside world, and even taking the employees on trips to see their products installed and in operation. Such enrichment usually results in employees who care more about the products they produce.

Other experimental enrichment programs include roundtable discussions between the top management of a plant and randomly selected employees, temporary employee task forces aimed at solving specific problems, and special programs to groom foremen from the ranks of production workers.

Nor do job enrichment programs have to be limited to production facilities. *The Future of the Workplace* describes a white-collar job enrichment program carried out by the Bankers Trust Company of New York. (6) First in the bank's stock transfer department and later in other departments, employees were freed of needlessly rigid procedures, given more independence and responsibility, and encouraged to make suggestions for a more satisfying and productive work system. The results were so positive that the bank has become an apostle of such programs among other financial institutions.

There are now dozens of companies across the country well into worker participation and job enrichment programs in both blue-collar and white-collar areas. Obviously, such programs are not without problems of their own. But for the 100 American companies estimated to have initiated such activities by the end of 1976, the problems represent a frontier they are quite willing to explore.

For those who doubt that so great a change is possible in the workplace, we suggest a glance over the shoulder at the workplace of 50 or a 100 years ago. The 12-hour day, the six- and even seven-day work week, a despotic supervisory structure, child labor, filth, noise and even danger were all accepted with little or no question from the rank and file. With the coming of new social values, the corporation developed technology and policy to eliminate all these things and increase productivity many times over. It is still happening. All that is needed is for corporate management to be able to read the signals society sends out, and to listen even better to what is being asked.

Fittingly, we end this chapter with what seems to be a particularly apt bottom-line analysis from *The Future of the Workplace*:

> Why is the business community adding to this momentum [of a changing workplace]?
>
> Because carefully considered and executed workplace reform can allow an employer to couple humanitarian and hard-nosed business goals in a single package. As scores of studies and experiments have demonstrated, an organization which changes to make people's work more interesting, meaningful, and responsible commonly makes business gains in terms of lower employee turnover and absentee rates, better quality work, and higher productivity. For leaders of industry and commerce, it provides a rare opportunity to have one's cake and eat it too—that is, to take statesmanlike action against employee alienation and malaise while improving the health, condition, productivity,

and profitability of the organization. As an executive involved in a job redesign effort within a company in the Bell Telephone System put it, "The unbelievable thing is that a successful program can make a manager a hero to both the largest stockholders and the people on the lowest rung of the ladder in the company."

. . . The fact is that what is occurring is the result of a complex set of factors, forces, and influences ranging from an increasing national concern for the overall state of American productivity to a growing proclivity on the part of business organizations to experiment in an experimental age. (7)

## REFERENCES

1. Hoerr, John. "Worker Unrest, Not Dead, But Playing Possum," *Business Week,* May 10, 1976, pp. 133–134.
2. Dickson, Paul. *The Future of the Workplace* (New York, N.Y.: Weybright and Talley, 1975), pp. 16–17.
3. "Moving Ahead With the 4-Day Work Week," *New York Times,* August 20, 1976.
4. "The Four-Day Work Week," *New York Times,* September 17, 1976.
5. *New York Times,* October 24, 1976.
6. Dickson, Paul. *The Future of the Workplace,* pp. 62–68.
7. *Ibid.,* p. 19.

# 11

# *The Environmental Bridge*

Straws in the wind-corporate adaptability dept.: Lately, we're noticing little signs that big corporations are beginning to cultivate a curiously uncorporate perspective of the world around them. We see evidence that some of the biggest growthniks of yesterday are beginning to practice (don't smirk) environmental *husbandry*. Even more remarkable, some of them are acting as if there could be a tidy profit in using stuff they used to throw away (like scrapped cars and chicken manure) and saving stuff they used to ignore (like gasoline and children's minds). (1)

That was a tough-minded, card-carrying environmentalist, William Houseman, while editor of *The Environment Monthly*. (Houseman, having ceased publishing the periodical in December 1976, is now consulting and writing in Wisconsin.) Bill didn't always have such good thoughts about the American corporation. In the eight years that *The Environment Monthly* was published, Houseman repeatedly and justifiably gave good licks to many a firm across the American industrial spectrum; but in 1976, the careful reader of this publication began to perceive a new optimism, a hope that maybe the corporation was indeed stirring and that some kind of societal rapprochement was on the horizon.

I interviewed Houseman at some length in mid-1976. An excerpt of the interview was subsequently published by the *Public Relations*

*Journal* as one in a series of "environmental detente" discussions I held that year:

> "Do you feel that maybe we are at a point where there is sufficient promise for movement of contending [environmental] forces?" I asked.
>
> "Yes. You are quite right. I believe that we can all be grateful, if we are interested in environmental improvement and in the energy crisis. Suddenly fossil fuels, pollution abatement, automobile exhaust, and high prices, all of the technological implications, swirl into a new form; and we must consider, it seems to me, the long-haul implications of these factors that make up the quality of life. I think quality of life, the energy crisis, and environmental integrity now form a coherent foundation on which to rethink the purpose of corporate activities. I think the price of an object now has a different significance than just its dollar value.
>
> "It seems to me," he continued, "that we're on the verge of a new ethic, a new set of values on which to make corporate decisions, to make bureaucratic decisions, to make personal decisions as they relate to quality of life."
>
> "Have you seen any signs of increased cooperation between business and conservation groups—are they talking to each other a little more fruitfully than they did, say, five or 10 years ago?" was my next question.
>
> "Generally, I don't believe so," Houseman responded. "I really don't believe so. I think the loggerheads still exist. I think that when it comes to confrontation, the values are black and white.
>
> "When we hear the plea, as I do in news releases every day, from major corporations that we need less regulation, I can only think of how monstrous the problems would be without the increased amounts of regulations in matters of environmental quality. The point, in fact, is that compliance with regulations is our best practical hope. Companies that readily comply after having fought a good fight at public hearings, and done their lobbying and all of the other things that they will do and should do—after all this contention and the battles are over, then compliance is the way to go.
>
> "But it is those companies which cheat, which shave matters, which put out releases claiming that they will be bankrupted by adding their scrubbers—these are the companies I have no patience with whatever because, as you know, the record indicates that practically no companies with an economically healthy foundation have suffered critically by complying with environmental quality standards."
>
> "Do you think that these problems can be solved within the

context of the free enterprise system as we know it, or will solution require some radical adjustment?" I queried.

"I don't think that there is any really serious argument with that. With or without these changes, the free enterprise system can be modified every day. There are all sorts of evidence of it.

"The professionals, for example, are coming under heavier and heavier fire to conform to certain ethical expectations, competitive expectations. The very fact that corporate survival seems to be more and more dependent on what David Reisman first characterized as the coming together of birds of a feather, in order to protect their self-interests—that's a concession by the free enterprisers themselves to the need for collectivism. It seems to me the real alternative is to replace the empty, money mentality with a different kind of analysis of materials and services needed by our society. And this is evolving."

"How about the pressure for change from the conservation and environmental groups? Is it declining? Has it plateaued? Some people think that it will just erode. Are they kidding themselves?"

"Well, of course, it won't erode and go away," he began.

"It won't go away because corporations and politicians are not yet sufficiently responsible. It would go away only if corporations and government leaders began to understand the new ethic which says that growth cannot go on forever, which says that fossil fuels are not only a kind of ridiculous way to keep the industrial society going but also damaging in every way. I think that the string is running out on old-type industrial production."

"But all of these actions cost something. Do you see these costs becoming natural costs of doing business?"

"Well, sure," Houseman answered. "After all, when Union Camp or Georgia Pacific gives to the Nature Conservancy acres of land, admittedly with a few strings attached and with some tax breaks, they are providing a leading-edge indication of what the future may hold.

"I do believe that the so-called free enterprise system is under heavier and heavier fire and under greater stress than it has ever been. Teapot Dome was nothing compared to this present corporate difficulty. After all, the businessman does rate pretty much at the bottom of the pecking order in public esteem."

"You sometimes seem to be saying that the environmentalist, the conservationist, has 'bigger questions' to ask than the questions that deal strictly with the environment. You're talking about product selection and marketing and questions that might normally be thought of as *business* questions *per se*. Correct?" I asked.

"The environmentalist has not only the right but the obligation to evaluate on sound terms the utilization of nonrenewable resources in our society. This is a new issue, it is a new argument. I think even high school and grade school children now have intuitively, as well as through environmental education, a basis for challenging a company with sound social-environmental arguments."

"On the 'frivolity' of a product?"

"No, no. On the utilization of nonrenewable resources. It is the best way to torpedo frivolous products. To argue the merits of how they are produced and packaged and marketed in terms of their impact on society measured by the emerging quality-of-life standards."

He continued, "This is why I said at the outset that the quality of life, ecological integrity, energy, and economics all now conspire to provide the public and political leaders and corporate leaders with a new equation for evaluating that which we decide to do."

"Is it possible to identify specific environmental issues that are going to be in the forefront in the next 25 years?"

"Yes, I think some are possible. For example, I think one of the towering issues will be that of who owns, manages, controls the power—literally the power.

"The question is whether in the interest of a safer, saner and perhaps in the long run, more productive environment—in those interests—can we alter the political and economic stranglehold a few people have on the production and delivery of energy. Because they are only investing Mickey Mouse research in alternate energy deals. This is one of the major issues, and it can't be minimized."

"Are you hopeful at all?"

"Oh, sure," Houseman answered. "I think the very, very wild idea that a businessman might even get votes in the next election because he is not ashamed to say he is religious is an interesting straw in the wind."

"It means that all things are possible then?"

"I think so." (2)

Similarly, in early 1976 I discussed the prospects for environmental detente with Russell E. Train, then administrator of the US Environmental Protection Agency (EPA).

"There is, obviously, mistrust or misunderstanding of EPA among some industry executives. Is there anything that can be done about that?" I began.

"I think you can improve on this. After all, we are a regulatory agency. We do necessarily have to deal with those whom we regulate. Of course, it would not be appropriate under our system to have some hand-in-glove relationship with the regulated parties."

"In a way, the adversary relationship is valid?"

"Well," he replied, "I think that the adversary relationship is really inherent in the system. I would also say, based upon a good many years of experience, that it is inherent in the American way of doing things.

"But I think that we have to insure that we don't get polarized, that we at EPA take the initiative, wherever we appropriately can, to invite a full range of opinions on issues. I think that is true on the other side too, but I think we have a responsibility in this regard, and I think we are doing this through advisory group sessions.

"I have done a lot of this since I have been here, the last two and a half years, bringing in industry groups for meetings here with me and my other top administrators in the agency."

"The cost of environmental progress seems to be a matter of great controversy. How should we measure the true cost of such improvements?" I wanted to know.

"I think what you are asking is whether the improvements in our environment are worth the expenditure. The answer in a word: absolutely. Admittedly, the costs and benefits are in some instances difficult to quantify. But we have developed data which indicates, for example, that the annual damage caused by sulfur oxides and airborne particulate matter amounts to $11.2 billion while the cost of controlling those pollutants would be half that amount. The human effects such as longer life expectancy, less demand for health services, and greater worker productivity because of reduced illness—these also are difficult to quantify, but they are certainly enormous.

"And in the development of our pollution control standards, economic impacts on the affected industry are thoroughly and openly considered, and rightly so, as an integral part of the standard-setting process. EPA does some of the best economic analysis to be done by any government department or agency. That's not just my word; it's been said by the Office of Management and Budget, too."

"Returning to communications, public relations professionals have been described as 'the public's representatives within an institution and the institution's representatives to the public.' What can professionals do to foster responsible environmental progress?"

"Well," Train answered, "if we're going to work with that definition of the public relations professional's function, I think there is a great deal to be done. Especially within individual companies.

"I'd suggest that as an important first step, the public relations person represent the company in local environmental programs. . . . Contribute both a point of view, and, as far as possible, resources. And similarly, get the communities' environmental viewpoint back to the company. Really act like a good citizen, in all of its meanings, and at all levels of management and places of business.

"From that kind of beginning, many other 'bridging' activities can develop. And I'd certainly encourage them." (3)

When I sought out a well-known leader of a national environmental organization, Thomas Kimball, executive vice president of the National Wildlife Federation, I found additional reason to be optimistic.

"Do you think that environmental 'detente' between industry and conservation groups is possible?"

"I definitely think it's possible," Kimball began. "I think what makes it possible is that we must solve the problems. Otherwise the decisions will be based on who can amass the most political clout, and that may not be in the best overall public interest."

"Have you seen any progress along these lines?" was my next question.

"Not as much as I'd like, of course, but I think there has been some. A good example is in the problem we are facing in the forestry field—clear cutting, and cutting timber on public land in particular. We realize a need to come together."

"Are we well beyond the 'black-hat, white-hat' polarization of say, five years ago? Are we anywhere closer to detente?"

His reply was, "Yes, I think we're much closer. There's a growing body in the middle that says we've got a problem and the thing to do is to be intelligent in discussing it and collecting data to solve it in the overall public interest."

"Have you experienced any increased industry interest in participation in the Federation in recent years?"

"Oh, yes. I think industry is looking for responsible environmental conservation organizations with which they can deal."

"How do you measure increased business interest? Are there more cooperative programs or increased membership in the Federation?" I wondered.

"There is indeed increased cooperation on projects," he responded. "We've always had a meeting in December of each year where we discuss national issues and we invite business and industry to attend. We're expanding that; we're having more regional meetings and addressing specific issues."

"Is there any hope that in our lifetimes we may see a new

industrial-conservation effort, a genuinely cooperative spirit?"

"I think we definitely will. I think it must come. It certainly will not involve all of industry, or even all segments of a particular industry. But I think the more responsible, alert, intelligent industrial managers will see it as a great benefit, as will the environmentalist organizations." (4)

## THE ENVIRONMENTAL BRIDGE

Is all the foregoing just rhetoric? Not much to support it? I might have agreed until I learned of the efforts of corporate executives and environmentalists to build an environmental bridge on a specific issue. The program is called the National Coal Policy Project and its objective is nothing less than "the development of a working accommodation between knowledgeable and respected environmentalists and knowledgeable and respected industrialists." Administered by the Center for Strategic and International Studies at Georgetown University, the project came into being in 1976.

The project is developing a set of guidelines, or plan of action, for the development of the United States coal resources in an environmentally benign fashion. It is then intended that all who participated in the development of the plan will work together to publicize it and promote its adoption and implementation.

A few key paragraphs from the project's introductory document follow:

> The Project proposes to bring together a select group of environmentalists and industrialists. In this case "select" means that they shall be working types rather than theoreticians; not spiritualized environmentalists on the one hand nor doctrinaire laissez-faire industrialists on the other, but just people who have been frustrated trying to get resolution of the coal issues and who are willing to sit down together and have another go at it. Some of them will have served in the "front lines" of conflicts on environmental issues before, and it is believed that this will be an advantage rather than the reverse.
>
> The process which these people will use is a version of the "Rule of Reason" rather than the more common adversary approach, which means that they are expected to negotiate rather than fight it out. They will be challenged to:
>
> 1. Educate each other about their respective positions.
>
> 2. Identify areas of agreement (in layman's terms).
>
> 3. Identify areas of disagreement (again, in terms understandable to the layman).

4. Specify the work needed to resolve issues.

5. Construct an interim working agreement and plan.

. . . The tangible product of the National Coal Policy Project will be a report presenting the guidelines and plan of action for the orderly and acceptable development and use of the nation's coal resources. There will be considerable follow-up to assure that the recommendations in this report are utilized by policy makers: legislators, regulators, and judges, and it is expected that all of the participants will help in this effort.

To do this, it is necessary to obtain fairly widespread publicity and understanding for the results of the Project. One mechanism that is contemplated for achieving this is a series of forums at key locations around the US, probably under the sponsorship of the National Academy of Science.

You may well ask, "Why coal?" The participants have a rather forthright answer: "There are few domestic issues which transcend in importance the reconciliation of future energy needs and environmental protection."

The project is real, not a fairy tale, so all the characters are not exactly living "happily ever after." There have been delays and disagreements. The project may even have collapsed by the time you read this, but the significance is that it was undertaken. And its participants at this writing are encouraged enough to be thinking about a second project—the Oil and Natural Gas Policy Project.

Another kind of environmental bridge is the environmental mediation services that have been springing up around the country. The Environmental Balance Association, for example, is a Minnesota coalition of business, labor, public interest, and environmental organizations. Other similar organizations include the Office of Environmental Mediation at the University of Washington in Seattle and the New England Energy Policy Council in Boston. Their efforts range from simply bringing disagreeing parties together to actually hammering out a binding settlement. Do these organizations really work? Increasingly the answer is yes. And the reason is simple enough—the cost, hassle, and delay of extended regulatory or judicial proceedings is becoming too much for many protagonists.

Still another encouraging development: In what may be an unprecedented display of industry-labor cooperation, in late 1976 Johns-Manville Corporation and the International Asbestos Workers Union agreed that each would donate $250,000 to start a research program at

Mount Sinai Hospital, New York City, to fund an effective treatment for mesothelioma, a cancer linked to excessive exposure to asbestos.

And, finally, perhaps the most tangible of all environmental bridges is the EPA's policy, announced in late 1976, that it would henceforth try to compromise the conflict between two national goals—economic growth and the abatement of industrial pollution. Talking trade-offs, the agency stated its intention to permit industrial growth with attendant new pollution on a replacement basis. New industrial emissions will be permitted in an area equivalent to reductions already achieved in that area, so that there will be no net increase in the area's pollution.

Too, the new policy's emphasis on *all pollutants in an area* replaces the "vertical" regulatory process that evolved largely because Congress tackled various pollution issues one at a time, passing the Clean Air Act in 1970, the Clean Water Act in 1972, and others, culminating in the Toxic Substances Control Act in 1976.

So, after years of costly turmoil, the environment may soon be less a battleground and more a place of accommodation between previously warring factions of society. A bridge between these factions is not just probable. Movement from each shore is already discernible.

## REFERENCES

1. *The Environment Monthly*, August 1976, p. 1.
2. "Environmental Update," *The Public Relations Journal*, October 1976, pp. 1–2.
3. "Environmental Update," *The Public Relations Journal*, March 1976, pp. 25–27.
4. "Environment, Energy," *The Public Relations Journal*, August 1976, p. 37.

# 12

# More Signs of Corporate Stirring

There are many other signals that something is indeed stirring in the corporation. Even as corporate futurists peer at the social horizon and fundamental progress is made in the workplace and in the environment, hundreds of other corporate accommodations to new demands are beginning to fall into place.

I said early in this book that I would not attempt to present the myriad corporate programs undertaken in the interest of social responsibility. There are, however, a number of recent corporate developments that seem significant enough to warrant brief attention in the context of *Will The Corporation Survive?* In offering this selection, I make no judgment as to whether these and similar developments are "enough," because here "enough" is a meaningless concept. Enough for whom? Enough as of what month, what day?

This is, then, an arbitrary snapshot of a process—a process in search of an accommodation.

## THE BOARD GOES SOCIAL

The corporate board of directors will never be the same ("the same" meaning the corporate board model of, say, 10 years ago). Having already been broadened during the late 1960s to include points of view previously excluded—those of women and minority members, for instance—the corporate board is nevertheless still very much in flux.

We have already discussed the emerging demand for employee representation. A more fundamental change—the concept of new importance for the outside director, alluded to in Chapter 3—deserves more attention. The extreme model here is the restructuring of the board of the Phillips Petroleum Company in the wake of the 1976 payments controversy.

Phillips, as part of a settlement of the suit brought against it by the Center for Law in the Public Interest (see Chapter 3), turned over control of its board to independent outside directors. The structure of the Phillips board was changed from one composed of eight "inside" (management) directors and three "outside" directors to one with nine outside directors and eight inside directors.

In addition to gaining majority, the Phillips outside directors were given sweeping powers over the company's audit functions and future nominations to the board. Of the six outside directors added to the board, the Center for Law nominated three and mutually nominated a fourth with the company. The two additional outside directors were nominated by the company with the Center's agreement. Future vacancies on the Phillips board will be filled by outside directors until 60 percent of the members are outsiders.

The Phillips board restructuring served as a model for Lockheed Aircraft Corporation when that company switched the weight of board control to outsiders in April 1976. Lockheed added four new directors to bring the total of outsiders to 10. The Lockheed board also has seven inside directors. The new structure and board members were subject to prior review by the Securities and Exchange Commission, which had just completed a negotiated settlement with Lockheed on its foreign payments policies.

In the Phillips board restructuring, new weight was given to the board's audit committee. The new board was required to appoint an audit committee composed entirely of the outside directors, to recommend outside auditors, and to review their work as well as that of the internal audit staff. In decisions to hire or fire auditors, only outside board members can vote, and the audit committee will have complete authority to order investigations into Phillips business activities by outside or internal auditors.

The concept of board outsider audit committees with muscle seems to have taken hold in the wake of the payments controversy. The New York Stock Exchange, prior to making a September 1976 request that companies establish such committees as a requirement for listing, surveyed Big Board companies and found that 966 of the 1,163 respondents had already set up such committees or were taking steps to do so (see Chapter 3).

The Exchange, in its audit-committee regulation, was responding to a request by Roderick M. Hills, then SEC chairman who had cautioned:

> In our review of corporations who have revealed questionable foreign and domestic payments, we have found an almost universal use of misleading financial records to conceal such corporate practices from outside auditors and directors and corporate counsel. The existence of an audit committee that meets privately with the outside directors to discuss the scope of the audit, questions arising during the audit, including disputes with management, and that has access to the corporate financial information, is an important part of our effort to maintain the credibility of our system of corporate self-regulation. (1)

Incidentally, there are some interesting variations on the corporate outsider audit committee. For instance, at Chatthem Drug and Chemical Company, Chattanooga, the audit committee is comprised of *stockholders*. The idea is that stockholders, the owners of the business, may well have even greater motivation than total outsiders in monitoring the corporate management.

There are many other ideas being advanced on the subject of the proper role of the board member in this era of social change. Courtney C. Brown, dean emeritus of the Columbia University Graduate School of Business and himself a member of numerous corporate boards, proposes a clear separation of board and management and the end of the "rubber stamp" board. In *Putting the Corporate Board to Work*, he suggests that the senior management officer should not report to the chairman but to the board of directors as a whole. (2) The board chairman would be, in large part, an "external communications officer" relating to the "new" corporate constituencies.

Edward Hallan Tuck, a partner in the blue-chip New York law firm of Shearman & Sterling, in reviewing Dean Brown's book in *Business and Society Review*, offers some additional useful commentary on the need for rethinking the nature and structure of the corporate board:

> It is also perhaps obvious that there should be different kinds of directors on each board—management and "outside"— to perform different functions. . . . The argument for management members on the board is that they know the business and that having decisions made at that level can be important. But management members cannot realistically be expected to measure and reward their own performance, ask themselves embarrassing questions, or fire their own president.

It is less difficult for the "outside" director to be independent and objective. In view of the current hostility to business, it would seem useful for many corporations to give more emphasis to the board and to having outsiders on it. Fear of the invisibility and uncontrollable power of the corporation surely lies at the root of much antibusiness feeling. . . .

Finally, if the system is to have fewer critics, management should not be encouraged to consider that handling "internal" problems is "getting down to business" and handling "external" problems is "getting rid of the gadflies." Problems of the consumer, the definition of work, the safety and health of the worker and of the environment *are business problems. They require as much management attention as any other problems. They are part of the air the corporation breathes* [emphasis added]. (3)

Christopher D. Stone thinks that in cases of "demonstrated delinquency" and for "generic industry problems," a type of "limited public director" might be worth a try. In the March–April 1976 issue of the *Harvard Business Review*, he suggested that a limited public director, especially one who by training is expert in a key "social" problem of the corporation, might, among other things, ensure that all laws in his area of special competence are being obeyed in good faith, act as a conduit to public agencies in proposing and reviewing administrative standards, audit the effectiveness of various systems such as environmental monitoring, and serve as the receiver of notice, from anyone within the organization, of anything seriously wrong that ordinary organizational systems were not uncovering. (4)

One more comment on changes in the boardroom. It would be a mistake to overlook the accomplishments of the women and minority-member directors added to various corporate boards in recent years. One of many possible examples: Since the Reverend Leon H. Sullivan, black pastor of the Zion Baptist Church in Philadelphia, was added to the board of General Motors Corporation in 1971, the company has increased its help to black businesses appreciably. Also, during Rev. Sullivan's term on the GM board, the company had, by mid-1976, increased its advertising in black publications considerably, opened an account in every one of the nation's 84 black-owned banks, and placed $2.5 billion worth of insurance with black underwriters. And GM purchases from black manufacturers of parts and supplies increased from $2 million to $50 million annually during the 1971–1976 period. More modest progress has been made in increasing black dealerships and white-collar employees, mainly because of the disastrous 1974–1975 slump in car sales.

## COURAGE TO ASK—AND TELL— "HOW ARE WE DOING?"

There is still a crying need for standards of measurement of social responsibility performance. And there is just as much need for more current standards of disclosure—what will the corporation tell, when, and to whom?

### Measurement

Not long ago a number of expert observers were predicting that the corporation would have to provide the public with full-scale social audits as detailed and empirical as the standard financial audits. Consultants presented any number of methodologies for reaching a social bottom line. None has won general acceptance by management, the accounting profession, or the public at large.

A different form of measurement is emerging. Often called a social performance review, or a process audit, it too has many variations. Most of these attempt only to measure progress of *individual* social responsibility programs against prior objectives and/or current public demands. They do not try to arrive at a bottom line, mainly because it is not possible to establish common-denominator values for activities as diverse as pollution control, affirmative action, product safety, and any number of other socially oriented activities.

Within this context, however, social measurement activity is increasing. In 1974, George A. Steiner reported that in a study he conducted in cooperation with the Committee for Economic Development, 46 percent of the respondents thought that some kind of social performance measurement would be required in the future. "A surprising 52 percent of those who thought it would be required accepted it," he said. "An additional 44 percent said they accepted it with some reservations." (5)

The AMA study offers this additional information on social performance measurement: 81 percent of the 644 companies responding have *not* conducted a special comprehensive study of social responsibilities and how well they are being met. Again, larger companies—understandably—seem to have done much more in this area than smaller companies; among companies with 10,000 or more employees, 50 percent of the respondents said that they *had* conducted such measurement studies.

Raymond A. Bauer was present at the creation of the social audit concept in the early 1970s and has kept a wary eye on all related developments since then. With Robert Ackerman, he has identified and summarized the latest social accounting trends in their book, *Corporate Social Responsiveness*:

If we take 1971 as a baseline, we may say that by 1976 a number of things had changed.

1. The necessity of *some* form of stock taking on social performance is accepted at the top of virtually every large corporation.
2. The reasons are practical and immediate rather than concerned with the devising of some ideal method of "social accounting."
3. There is a rapidly widening appreciation of the inevitability if not the desirability of disclosure of information on corporate policies and actions that a few years ago were regarded as confidential. This has come in part from the actions of the SEC, of the courts, and generally from the success of activists in getting the information they are after.
4. There is a less wide but growing appreciation that assessments of social performance cannot be limited to special programs and activities but must include—in principle at least—the impact of all the organization's activities. There now exist internal monitoring and/or auditing systems for reviewing the impact of various regular business activities. To some extent, these are extensions of traditional monitoring systems such as quality control, but they are explicit recognition of new expectations of accountability for corporate performance.
5. Some elements of what might have been considered a "social audit" a few years ago have become components of a changed system of control and information. For example, it is now commonplace for equal opportunity employment [sic] information to be reported for each meaningful operating unit on a quarterly or even a monthly basis. Less widespread, but identifiable, are attempts to create a regular flow of information to monitor the performance of operating units on pollution control, OSHA, community relations, and consumer relations.
6. Our notion of a management process audit seems to be gaining embryonic acceptance as it becomes clear that one can specify the sorts of management and ad-

ministrative arrangements that facilitate policy implementation.

On the whole, the area of activity which was labeled social auditing several years ago has quickly developed into one of practical concern directed to the two major objectives of internal control and external reporting. (6)

## Disclosure

Surely, on the corporate sensitivity scale, internal control is one thing and external reporting is something else again. Many corporations are wrestling with the gut problem of what to tell, when, and to whom. BankAmerica Corporation is among the leaders in developing some answers. A. W. Clausen, chairman of BA, outlined the bank's progress in a fascinating article, "Voluntary Disclosure: Someone Has To Jump Into the Icy Water First," in the June 1976 issue of *Financial Executive*.

Essentially, BankAmerica has developed a *voluntary disclosure code*. The step was taken, Clausen says, to offset the public perception that for the nation's blue-chip corporations "payoffs, bribes, influence peddling, book-juggling, falsification of records and miscellaneous other hanky-panky are somehow a normal part and cost of doing business." (7) A special BA task force of seven senior executives were given the code development job.

Five underlying principles that the task force was asked to bear in mind throughout their deliberations serve as a useful public disclosure guide. As published in *Purview*, a supplement of the newsletter *PR Reporter*, the principles are:

1. *Usefulness*—provide information that helps people understand how the company works.

2. *Confidentiality*—protect customers' privacy and company proprietary data whose release would impair its competitive position.

3. *Misinterpretation*—try to present the important information about the company in a form that can be easily understood by the general investing public, as well as by professionals.

4. *Speculation*—do not disclose information that would lend itself to speculative activity in company stock.

5. *Cost*—select high value information commensurate with the high costs of data collection, storage, and retrieval. (8)

Based on these principles, BA is now disclosing information in all areas of its activities, including domestic and foreign lending, credit policy, relations with government, and remuneration of directors.

## MORE HOPE FOR THE EMPLOYEE

In Chapter 10 we covered some of the broad corporate policy changes that will shape the workplace of tomorrow. Here we present several additional recent employee-relations programs, none momentous, but each contributing to a pattern that offers hope for increased industrial concord.

### The Corporate Ombudsman

The concept of a corporate ombudsman has not exactly taken off. Only a handful of American companies are known to have established such positions, but those who have—companies such as General Electric and Xerox—generally give the idea high marks.

(The December 1976 Supreme Court decision denying women temporary medical benefits for pregnancy is bound to give corporate ombudsmen new headaches.)

Frederick H. Dunn, who held the title for two and a half years in General Electric's Aircraft Engine Group, has given this description of what was expected of him in the ombudsman role:

- Review the methods for handling complaints from employees and develop programs to correct any deficiencies.
- Improve communications between management and employees to eliminate cases where complaint is unfounded but derives from the company's failure to explain its policies adequately.
- Work to reverse unfair decisions when valid complaints are made.
- Assure an impartial outlet for employee grievances. (9)

Dunn is candid on what an ombudsman *cannot* do:

- Please people whose idea of justice is having their own way even when it is objectively wrong.
- Change managerial styles, even when they could objectively be considered wrong.
- Replace the vital need for an employee and his manager to be honest with each other. (9)

## Affirmative, Affirmative

Two programs designed to improve the position of minorities and women in the work force caught my eye during 1976:

1. The National Fund for Minority Engineering Students, funded largely by corporations, is beginning to make a real dent in the problem of low minority enrollment in, and graduation from, engineering schools. The Fund is well on its way to achieving its goal of a tenfold increase in the number of minority engineering graduates—from about 400 in 1976 to about 4,000 by the mid-1980s.

2. The securities industry formed a special ad hoc committee to correct an employment pattern that has allowed white males to dominate jobs in that industry. Goals included providing employers with material on their legal responsibilities, developing a recruitment program, and setting up a talent bank of minority and female job applicants. Far more important than the need to protect the industry from harmful litigation, publicity and settlement costs, said the committee, is the need to correct an employment pattern which has developed over the years.

These are arbitrary selections out of many possibilities. Think about similar programs you have heard or read about. They are numerous.

## Security and Privacy

IBM has two employee relations policies that deserve to be studied.

**The No Lay-off Policy** • How do they do it? By giving the policy high priority and doing a lot of planning to make it work. Admittedly, few companies have the resources of IBM. But more important, only a few companies have as yet developed the commitment to maintaining a loyal and stable work force through total job security. IBM retains workers no longer needed in one job and assigns them to others. Over 5,000 IBM employees have traveled such career bends. Some part of the company is always growing, and IBM has made the commitment to retrain its own people to staff up those growing functions. It is not easy to maintain this corporate-wide program of balancing manpower, but IBM feels that it is well worthwhile.

**The Employee Privacy Policy** • Former IBM chairman Thomas Watson, Jr. once wrote that "if we respected our people and helped them to respect themselves the company would make the most profit." By "respecting the people" IBM also means respecting their privacy.

Developed as a matter of company initiative, the IBM employee privacy program is now being studied by many other companies that have come under attack on the issue from consumerist and employee groups.

By "privacy" IBM mainly means personal information about employees and who has access to it. First, there's the limitation on personal information requested at the time of job application (questions on date of birth, mental disorder, or arrest records are no longer asked). Personality and intelligence tests have been de-emphasized (they use instead school records or other documentation of achievement). Then there is periodic purging of obsolete personal data from the files. Finally, only those insiders who genuinely need to know may inspect an employee's personal file; and many requests from outsiders must first be approved by the employee in question. (10)

### Helping with Employees' Problems

***Alcoholism*** • A growing number of companies have set up programs to help employees overcome alcoholism. The Department of Health, Education, & Welfare reports that in mid-1973 there were 621 such programs in public and private work organizations and that the number continues to grow.

Why? For many employers, it is a matter of self-interest. Production losses attributable to alcoholism total some $10 billion annually, according to HEW. McDonnell Douglas, which has had a "troubled employee" program since 1970, estimates that it has gotten well over $3 million in added productivity from recovered alcoholics in return for an investment of about $1 million. And the $3 million is exclusive of the dollars saved in not having to hire and train alcoholic employees who would have been fired.

***The Ministry to Industry*** • The Washington Group, Inc., a mini-conglomerate that owns 17 textile mills and operates 60 food stores and ice cream shops, has provided a full-time minister for its employees. It is not alone. One estimate is that there are now between 50 and 100 such full-time industrial chaplains. R. J. Reynolds (since 1949) and Holiday Inns of America are among the other companies having chapplain's offices.

Once again, altruism has little to do with the corporate decisions to establish such ministries. The companies reason that a happy, well-adjusted worker is likely to be a productive worker. And as if to prove that such chaplaincies are permanent (if not eternal), there is now a professional association of such clerics, the National Association of Business and Industrial Chaplains. For *part-time* industrial chaplains, there is the Institute of Industrial and Commercial Ministers. (The virtues of specialization have not escaped the ministers.)

*Transportation to Work* • More down to earth, perhaps, but very real, is the problem of fast and cheap ways to get to work. The energy crisis, with its attendant increases in gasoline prices, has increased the seriousness of the problem. A growing number of companies have organized van pools to help solve it. By the middle of 1976, according to the Federal Energy Administration, some 43 companies had undertaken such programs. The companies ranged from Prudential Insurance Company in New Jersey to the 3M Company in Minneapolis-St. Paul to the Continental Oil Company in Houston. The basic approach is the same in all the companies: The riders split the expenses to reimburse the company for its nonprofit investment. Each rider saves a good bit in transportation costs (the driver travels free), and the company gets happier employees while making a contribution to energy conservation.

*"Worker Capitalism"* • They are controversial and certainly imperfect, but they are increasingly popular. We mean employee stock ownership plans (ESOPs). Hundreds of companies have set up ESOPs, and a greater proliferation is expected during the rest of the 1970s. An amendment to the Tax Reduction Act of 1975 granting an extra 1 percent investment tax credit to companies establishing ESOPs ignited corporate interest, and it is likely to be some time before it is extinguished.

Basically, an ESOP works this way: a corporation seeking to raise cash establishes an employee trust. The trust borrows money from a bank and buys stock in the company. The company invests the money in new plant or equipment or services and, in time, generates enough profit to pay back the loan. The employees get the stock free when they retire, and the company is allowed to deduct both the principal and interest from its taxable income.

Supporters call ESOPs great instruments for capital formation and —with less documentation—stimulants to improved employee efficiency. As the ESOPs spread, there may well accumulate a body of evidence to determine if employee attitudes do indeed change when they own a piece of the corporation. By 1980, when the ESOP program comes before Congress again, a fuller assessment may well be in hand.

There is, however, a temptation to go off the deep end on the "workers capitalism" description of ESOPs. Realistically it must be remembered that such plans are, for the most part, fringe benefits not unlike pension plans. The workers usually cannot vote the stock, receive dividends during employment, or buy or sell any part of their holdings or borrow on such holdings. These are features that it is hoped may be considered in the next generation of ESOPs.

*Employee-Education Frontiers* • Many corporations have traditionally encouraged employees to take courses and even pursue degrees in career-related areas. Now comes Kimberley Clark Corporation's plan to keep employees mentally stimulated by encouraging studies in areas of purely *personal* interest. The company sets aside $480 a year in a "bank account" that an employee can use for such courses. K-C employees have availed themselves of such funds to study languages, painting, psychology, biology, and a host of other subjects. The program has a useful side effect: pumping money into local educational institutions.

## STRUTS FOR THE ENVIRONMENTAL BRIDGE

There is more good news on the environmental front:

*Antipollution Capital Spending Rises* • McGraw-Hill Publications Company reported that American business planned to spend about $9½ billion on pollution control in 1976, 23 percent more than in 1975. Some $5.17 billion, according to McGraw-Hill, was earmarked for air pollution control while another $2.17 billion was allocated for water pollution control. The remainder, about $1.12 billion, was aimed at solid waste cleanup. But the McGraw-Hill report noted that the estimated $9½ billion 1976 expenditures represented only about one-third of what would be required to make United States business facilities conform to 1976 standards. The report expected such spending to peak in 1977 or 1978 and decrease somewhat in 1979, presumably when most of the standards would be met.

One sizable chunk of such pollution control spending will be laid out by the United States Steel Corporation. In October 1976 US Steel ended an extended dispute with environmental control authorities when it announced that it would spend $600 million to bring its Clairton, Pennsylvania, coke works—the world's largest—into compliance with pollution control laws. The corporation said it would clean up and modernize the plant by 1983. As part of the settlement with Allegheny County and Pennsylvania environmental control agencies, the corporation also said it would contribute $750,000 to a study of environmental problems in Allegheny County.

Similarly, Chicago's Calumet River has benefited from an estimated $100 million spent on water pollution control since 1970 by riverside industries, mainly four steel mills. In fact, some observers claim that industry has far outdistanced the city's sanitary district in meeting effluent standards.

### Taking the Initiative

An increasing number of companies are not waiting for environmentalists or government regulators to come knocking on the door before they deal with environmental problems. Some are emulating Union Carbide, which seems to have come around about 180 degrees from its 1971 defensive position when it was charged with "environmental blackmail" for having threatened to lay off 625 employees at its Marietta, Ohio, plant to offset pollution control costs. Union Carbide has developed a computer-assisted plant evaluation system to spot and correct pollution problems early. Under this Environmental Impact Analysis program, each plant continuously records data on every aspect of its products and processes. The data are evaluated by the corporate environmental management section. Depending on how such data correlate with established criteria, the plant may continue on its present course, or have to come up with an action plan to correct a pollution situation, or—in the extreme instance—shut down.

Although the main goal of the Union Carbide plants' materials analysis program remains environmental control, it is also providing commercial bonuses such as the recovery of valuable raw materials from the waste stream. And the data are useful to Carbide engineers seeking additional details on some of the manufacturing processes as well as providing new input for improved design of future Carbide plants.

The Carbide experience tends to confirm the Ackerman-Bauer contention (Chapter 8) that many corporate activities undertaken primarily because of social pressures can also produce commercial benefits.

At some corporations, it goes even beyond that. Dow Chemical Company, for instance, has developed new *businesses*—new product lines—as a result of its commitment to pollution control. At the 3M Company, pollution *prevention* has become an integral part of the corporate philosophy. So committed is 3M that it has showered all of its divisions with video cassettes, personal presentations, brochures, and awards to get personnel to stress product reformulation, equipment changes, process modification, and materials recovery. The central thesis is: If you don't discharge pollutants, you won't have to pay to clean them up.

Representatives of about 200 companies met in Chicago in January 1977 at a two-day interindustry conference jointly sponsored, interestingly enough, by the Environmental Protection Agency and the Commerce Department. What brought them together was the interest in studying case histories like that of 3M in the hope of moving pollution control from the red to the black side of the ledger.

### The Sweet Confluence

Sometimes the profit motive and environmental improvement blend *perfectly*. It is rare and therefore an especially sweet confluence when it occurs. One of the best examples is the steadily growing aluminum can recycling program. Begun in 1967 with a single recycling center, the program has long since become a national resource. By mid-1976 there were over 2,000 such voluntary aluminum can recycling centers across the country; the centers recycled about 5 billion cans during calendar 1976.

The Americans who returned the aluminum cans reduced litter and made money as well. That's because it makes great good sense for the aluminum industry to pay about 15–17¢ a pound (approximately 23 cans) for the aluminum. The industry can process the cans back to molten metal with only 5 percent of the energy used to make aluminum originally. And, of course, they conserve resources in the process.

The whole program makes so much economic sense that the industry is now building on its can recycling experience and recovering automotive aluminum from what used to be called "junkyards," recycling lawn furniture, old siding, and other discarded aluminum products at specially constructed recycling centers; and negotiating sizable contracts for the recovery of aluminum from the municipal solid waste (garbage) processing plants springing up across the country.

## CARE FOR THE CONSUMER

Is the corporation serious about minimizing consumer dissatisfaction?

Maybe the best answer is that in only a few years of existence, the Society of Consumer Affairs Professionals (SOCAP) in Business had developed a membership of 600 by mid-1976. Members represented virtually every industry directly or indirectly reaching the American consumer. Corporate vice presidents of consumer affairs are not unusual among the SOCAP membership; neither, of course, are the "troops" in corporate consumer affairs departments.

SOCAP estimates that one-quarter of its members are in senior management positions. A Conference Board study concluded that in 62 percent of the companies that have separate consumer affairs departments, the department reports directly to the president or another top general manager.

Mary Gardiner Jones, formerly a Federal Trade Commissioner,

now vice president for consumer affairs at Western Union Telegraph Company, recently told *Business Week* that her "mandate feeds right out of the president's office which is the only way the consumer thing can work," and her aim is "to get those complaints and use them as an early warning system." (12)

Corporate consumer affairs professionals are busy designing and implementing a wide variety of programs aimed at improving the quality of products and services and being generally responsive to consumer demands. My favorite example of progress in consumer affairs is the action by a number of companies—most notably, banks and insurance firms—to rescue the English language from their legal departments. Slowly, a variety of legal and para-legal documents is becoming understandable. Simply put, some companies have had the courage to ask themselves why documents such as insurance policies, promissory notes, stock prospectuses, and product warranties have to be incomprehensible. The answer, of course, is that they don't. In a sense, plain language is a manifestation of openness and, it is hoped, honesty. Redrafting of such documents has occasionally revealed inconsistencies long overlooked, not to mention obsolete phrases, sentences, or paragraphs.

This is an example of how cleansing changed a section of a St. Paul Fire & Marine Insurance Company insurance policy:

> *Old:* No action shall lie against the company with respect to any one occurrence unless as a condition precedent thereto, the Insured shall have fully complied with all the terms of this policy.
>
> *New:* We're not obligated to pay for your loss unless you do all of this.

Neither Edwin Newman nor E. B. White could have said it any better.

### AND A BIT OF MISCELLANY

Here are a few additional recent examples of activity which generate optimism concerning the future of the corporation:

### Lending a Hand

**To States and Cities** • Since 1970 the Economic Development Council of New York City, Inc., an independent, nonprofit group of business leaders, has been tackling the managerial problems of the Big Apple on a voluntary basis. The EDC studied the city's court system, its human resources department, its public schools and its middle income housing. Its efforts have resulted in estimated annual savings to the city of $80 million. In 1975, New York's Mayor Abraham Beame established the Mayor's Management Advisory Board to help bring business management techniques to that beleaguered city's municipal government. Since then, the city agencies have clearly stated goals, regular review of progress toward those goals, and evaluation of results—in short, management by objective.

Volunteer task forces of business leaders are catching on. Companies concerned with fast-rising tax bills and antibusiness public opinion are investing executive time in the hope of increasing government efficiency and reducing the cost of government. In Colorado a group of business volunteers helped work out a "sunset law" requiring certain government agencies to go out of existence unless they are periodically renewed by the legislature (partly as a result of the Colorado experience, a national sunset law has been getting increased interest). And in Pennsylvania, savings resulting from the work of business volunteers are said to have reached $120 million annually.

It all requires commitment and follow through. In addition to cutting the cost of government, the business volunteers also achieve something else—an appreciation of the *complexities of government*. In late 1976, *Public Relations News* reported that a just-issued study by The Business Roundtable urged "more personal involvement by businessmen in urban affairs." (13)

**To the Schools** • Several years ago, Standard Oil Company (Indiana) began an ambitious program to help improve the quality of secondary education in its headquarters city, Chicago. In 1974 a consortium of 20 of the largest companies and financial institutions in Boston decided to do much the same thing but on a coordinated basis. Their goal, while improving educational quality generally, was to upgrade the career-preparatory efforts of selected public schools so that graduates could move directly into the Boston work force with minimum difficulty. Some of the specific involvements were a pilot program for a computer curriculum and a course entitled "Introduction to Data Processing"; a work exploration program in which high school students are matched with insurance company employees, one-on-one, for a day on the job; and a student administered remedial reading program.

The Boston program, like so many others we have referred to, is based on one part altruism and three parts self-interest. One of the Boston executives involved in the program explained his company's motivation this way: "The fact is that the public school system is not providing us with adequately trained people for jobs, and this is a way of overcoming that problem."

Similar programs have been undertaken in Detroit, New York, Philadelphia, and Minneapolis, among other cities.

***Clean Political Action*** • The corporate political action committees (PACs), which became popular in 1976, seem to have a dual potential—canceling a negative (the temptation of illicit campaign contributions) and constructing a positive (a broader, more open involvement in public affairs).

After a landmark ruling by the Federal Election Commission in 1975, corporate PACs began to blossom all over the country. By late 1976, according to the Public Affairs Council, there were about 400 such organizations in place or in development. (In addition, 800 labor PACs and 200 other PACs had been formed.)

If the corporate PACs do nothing other than to legitimize all corporate campaign contributions, they will have been well worthwhile. As already noted, in recent years nothing has hurt the American corporation as badly as the hundreds of admissions of questionable or illegal corporate payments. Although most such payments were made abroad, payments made to American politicians represented some of the more sensational cases. In terms of public opinion, the American corporation will be paying heavily for such actions for years to come.

There is another side to corporate PACs. Their positive potential lies in the opportunity they present for the corporation to activate its natural constituencies—mainly employees and shareholders—in public affairs. The short-to-medium-term result may well be the election of more legislators who are understanding of, if not sympathetic with, the interests of these corporate constituencies. The long-term potential is the personal activation of more employees and shareholders in local, regional, and national politics.

There are many variations on the corporate PAC theme. A number of good books on the subject are expected shortly. Here we are interested primarily in the *reasons* for establishing such units. Those reasons appear to boil down to what might be called "reach." A candidate who has received financial assistance is likely to be accessible to those who have helped. Access is one thing; agreement, of course, is something very different.

Still, some ask why should a corporate president have more access than, say, a welfare mother? In the democratic ideal, they are equal. However, you can support access for all and still maintain that a corporate president—or a labor leader or the head of a large consumerist agency—who may well represent the interests of *thousands* of people, merits some appointment priority, with or without contributions.

Also, a word in favor of such advocacy contact: Legislators and their staffs share with all the rest of us the human failings of limited knowledge and experience. They need to receive informed points of view if they are to legislate intelligently.

In any event, the lobbyists are here to stay, and some of the most effective, such as Common Cause, often represent points of view in opposition to corporate interests. Fair enough. Let the marketplace of ideas work. Let the many interests collide and compromise. Out of all this chaos—somehow—comes consensus.

The corporate PACs—and, in a more centralized way, the recently energized Business Roundtable—represent instruments for delivery of the business point of view in this maelstrom. That is a genuine improvement over the hands-off-politics attitude that has existed for years in many executive suites.

Remember the scene?:

Earnest young assistant: "Sir, Do you think the experts are right in attributing the low voter turnout to ignorance and apathy?"

Harried chief executive officer: "I don't know and I don't care."

In most corporations that will survive, those days are gone forever.

## REFERENCES

1. *New York Times*, September 3, 1976.
2. Brown, Courtney C. *Putting The Corporate Board To Work* (New York, N.Y.: Macmillan and Company, 1976).
3. Tuck, Edward Hallan. "Board Members: Inside, Outside or Upside Down?" *Business and Society Review*, Summer, 1976, pp. 82–83.
4. Stone, Christopher D. "Public Directors Merit a Try," *Harvard Business Review*, March–April, 1976, pp. 20–156.
5. Steiner, George A. Paper presented at the "Conference on Business Ethics and Social Responsibilities: Theory and Practice," University of Virginia Graduate School of Business Administration, Charlottesville, March 28, 1974.
6. Ackerman, Robert and Bauer, Raymond. *Corporate Social Responsiveness: The Modern Dilemma* (Reston, Va.: Reston Publishing Company, Inc., a Prentice-Hall Company, 1976), pp. 229–230.
7. Clausen, A. W. "Voluntary Disclosure: Someone Has to Jump Into the Icy Water First," *Financial Executive*, Vol. 44, June 1976, pp. 20–26.

8. "Corporate Integrity Requires More Voluntary Disclosure or Information—Some Guidelines," Purview, a supplement to *PR Reporter*, August 9, 1976, p. 1.
9. Dunn, Frederick H. "The View From the Ombudsman's Chair," *New York Times*, May 2, 1976.
10. "IBM's Guidelines to Employee Privacy," *Harvard Business Review*, September–October 1976, pp. 82–90.
11. "Doing Well in Consumer Affairs," *Business Week*, August 16, 1976, p. 120.
12. *Public Relations News*, November 29, 1976, p. 1.
13. "Boston In a Business And School Partnership," *New York Times*, August 24, 1976.

# *Will the Corporation Survive?*

# 13

# Relating With the Public

> "The skillful propagation of poor policy would merely intensify error."
>
> —Alexander Kendrick in Prime Time, The Life of Edward R. Murrow. (1)

Still, the question persists: Will the corporation, as we have known it, survive?

As we draw near the end of this book, it may be helpful to recast the question. Let's put it this way: Will the corporation relate successfully to its publics in an age when public opinion can make or break an institution?

"Relating to its publics" is not simply a matter of "telling our story," although that is certainly a part of it. It is a matter of reaching out and drawing in the many disparate opinions that exist in a constantly changing society; of listening well, the way the corporate futurists listen; of formulating and implementing policies based at least in part on what society seems to want (and, if such accommodation is impossible, being prepared to explain why); and only then carrying out a well-planned, ongoing communications program. In short, relating with the public (and *true* public relations, as defined by Rea Smith, executive vice president of the Public Relations Society of America) is the sum of everything a corporation does.

For those who feel that I am overemphasizing the power of public opinion, I offer two reminders—Watergate and Vietnam. Admittedly, the corporation is not likely to become involved in such dramatic, vital issues (although the corporate payments controversy is only a step or two down the critical issues ladder). Nevertheless, the way Americans formed opinions on these historic events—and the role of media in that opinion formation—offers dramatic evidence of what an aroused American public can do.

I will never forget that Saturday in October 1973, the night of the "Saturday Night Massacre" of special prosecutor Archibald Cox and his Justice Department superiors William Ruckelshaus and Elliot Richardson. Somehow the news of the White House action galvanized the American public on Watergate. Historians may suggest other turning points, but for me the outcome of Watergate was inevitable once Americans were outraged by what appeared to them to be a breach of faith, a heavy-handed power play, a fundamentally unfair White House action. (Yes, thank God, we are still idealists, and "fairness" still matters.)

There was that flood of letters and telegrams and, of course, the attendant news coverage. The American people had spoken—almost as with one voice—and their elected representatives in Congress finally felt emboldened to take vigorous action. The impeachment effort was given genuine impetus, and the next special prosecutor got safeguards for independent action.

Vietnam offers a very different lesson on public opinion. The long agony generated no single dramatic event to galvanized Americans (although some might make a case for the news of the My Lai massacre). It was more a matter of slow buildup to "critical mass." Over the course of 10 years most Americans moved almost 180 degrees from a Cold War-generated policy of "Pay any price to protect freedom" to "Why are we imposing ourselves on these people?" And once again, when Washington got the public opinion signals, those signals helped to formulate a different Vietnam policy.

Certainly few will contest the role of the national media in bringing the horrors of the Vietnam War home to Americans. Most of us know that all war is, indeed, hell; but to have such hell packaged and delivered into our living rooms every night and our breakfast rooms every morning—that, plus the frustration of a seemingly can't-win position—well, it became inevitable that antiwar activists would prevail.

Some say that Watergate and Vietnam notwithstanding, public opinion is just not that critical in the day-to-day workings of the nation: "Power blocs is where it's at. Influence. Especially in Washington. Go directly to the seat of power. The majority of Americans could not care less about most of the problems facing business. Convince your Congressman and Senator, and the rest will fall into place."

That position is not difficult to attack. There is no denying that most Americans do not have time to grasp all the nuances and stay on top of all the key developments of, say, a complex environmental or public health issue. And it is true that you can fool all of the people some of the time. But the public eventually catches up. And the elected representatives care, and care very much, how the folks back home feel about an issue. The representative wants to know what media in his or her district are reporting, what editorial positions are being taken, and what pubic response is being generated. In other words, government relations and genuine public relations programs can, and indeed should, be coordinated.

If public opinion is so important to the survival of the corporation, it would certainly be useful to understand how public attitudes are formed and diffused. There are a number of theories. A mountain of literature, built by giants in the social science field including Lazarsfeld, Katz, Roper, Abelson, Schramm, Howland, Janis, and Kelley, has accumulated in recent years.

Scott M. Cutlip and Allen H. Center have provided a valuable service to all interested in the formation of public opinion by distilling much of this knowledge and presenting it in their book, *Effective Public Relations*. Here are a few excerpts:

> The term *public opinion* is a slippery one. Our ability to measure it is greater than our ability to define or manipulate it.
> . . . *Public opinion* is difficult to describe, elusive to define, hard to measure, impossible to see. For this reason, the concept is utilized less and less in the growing precision of social psychology, sociology, and political science. Most writers agree that the force of public opinion is perceptible, though the concept is vague. Some scholars doubt that there is a field of public opinion separate from the psychology of attitude formation and change. . . .
>
> There are two main streams of thought with respect to the determination of man's attitudes: (1) one school assumes man to be an irrational being with limited powers of reason and thus susceptible to emotional appeals; (2) the second assumes man to be a rational being with strong powers of reason and discrimination. . . .
>
> Each individual accumulates his predispositions to think or act in a certain way from many places, many sources. A person's attitudes remain latent until an issue arises for the group to which he belongs. An issue arises when there is conflict, frustration, or anxiety. Thus confronted, the individual takes his stand and voices his opinion. . . .
>
> Research in the social science has brought, in recent years, some tentative principles of persuasion. . . .*

---

\* These principles are condensed from a number of sources, including Herbert I. Abelson, *op. cit.*; Schramm's *Process and Effects of Mass Communications*, a reader; Katz and Lazarsfeld's *Personal Influence, op. cit.*; and Carl I. Howland,

1. To accomplish attitude change, a suggestion for change must first be received and accepted. "Acceptance of the message" is a critical factor in persuasive communication.
2. The suggestion is more likely to be accepted if it meets existing personality needs and drives.
3. The suggestion is more likely to be accepted if it is in harmony with group norms and loyalties.
4. The suggestion is more likely to be accepted if the source is perceived as trustworthy or expert.
5. A suggestion in the mass media, coupled with face-to-face reinforcement, is more likely to be accepted than a suggestion carried by either alone, other things being equal.
6. Change in attitude is more likely to occur if the suggestion is accompanied by other factors underlying belief and attitude. This refers to a changed environment which makes acceptance easier.
7. There probably will be more opinion change in the desired direction if conclusions are explicitly stated than if the audience is left to draw its own conclusions.
8. When the audience is friendly, or when only one position will be presented, or when immediate but temporary opinion change is wanted, it is more effective to give only one side of the argument.
9. When the audience disagrees, or when it is probable that it will hear the other side from another source, it is more effective to present both sides of the argument.
10. When equally attractive opposing views are presented one after the other, the one presented last will probably be more effective.
11. Sometimes emotional appeals are more influential; sometimes factual ones are. It depends on the kind of message and kind of audience.

---

Irving L. Janis, and Harold M. Kelley, *Communication and Persuasion* (New Haven: Yale University Press, 1953). All of these sources are the research of many people in arriving at these "principles." These books cite also the original research upon which they are based.

12. A strong threat is generally less effective than a mild threat in inducing desired opinion change.
13. The desired opinion change may be more measurable some time after exposure to the communication than right after exposure.
14. The people you want most in your audience are least likely to be there. . . .
15. There is a "sleeper effect" in communications received from sources which the listener regards as having low credibility. In some tests, time has tended to wash out the distrusted source and leave information behind. (2)

Another approach to describing the process of attitude change is Elmo Roper's "concentric circle theory." Roper has postulated that ideas penetrate the public slowly, moving downward, as if by osmosis, through several tiers: Great Thinkers to Great Disciples to Great Disseminators to Lesser Disseminators to the Politically Actives to the Politically Inert. The Roper theory and others like it serve as the foundation for a number of communications programs aimed primarily at "influentials"—those members of society who have an impact on the opinions of others. Teachers, writers, artists, journalists, legislators, clergymen (to a decreasing degree as the influence of organized religion declines), and celebrities are among the "influentials" of our society.

Columnist Joseph Kraft has written that public opinion, although influenced by media, depends primarily on personal experience.

Certainly the importance of public opinion has not been lost on business executives. In *Ethics and Profits* Leonard Silk and David Vogel conclude: "If one theme dominates the concerns of business executives these days, it is their inability to communicate adequately with the public. It is hard to exaggerate the importance executives attach to this problem. More than any other . . . the failure of communications is defined as the basic threat to the enterprise system. Its solution is held critical to solving all other business problems." (3)

Silk and Vogel offer a subsequent passage that is most valuable in understanding the depth of business leaders' feeling about this failure:

> Executives seem *personally*, not just politically or economically, concerned about their low public esteem; one gets the impression that they would be just as upset even if they were convinced that public disfavor had no adverse policy impact. The chief executives of corporations constitute America's upper class. Unlike the upper classes of pre-capitalist societies, they are

not a leisure class; they feel that they are competent and creative people upon whose judgment and effort rests the economic welfare of millions of individuals in this country and all over the globe. They regard their high financial rewards and privileged lives—both on and off the job—as the consequences of their great contributions to productivity. (3)

That may well be how executives feel, but being realists they must know that what matters is how the American public feels. And the American public still doesn't feel all that confident about the corporation and corporate leaders.

In recent years, we have been exposed *ad nauseam* to the findings of surveys of public attitudes toward business. Most of these surveys seemed to conclude that business ranks very low on the list of public approval, a notch above or below politics.

The *U.S. News & World Report* survey on the subject released in late 1976 is nevertheless of interest on at least two counts—it was an in-depth study conducted by a *national consumer newsweekly*, and it illustrates how recent events have affected public attitudes.

For example, 80% of those heads of households surveyed agreed with the statement "Overseas payoffs and political handouts are widespread"; on this subject, however, it is interesting to note that the same percentage felt that "Government has known about overseas 'bribes' for years."

Some 72 percent of the respondents to the *USN&WR* survey agreed with the position that "U.S. oil companies have been the main cause of high gasoline prices" (67 percent thought that Arab oil nations have been the "main cause").

The statement "Monopolies are growing" was supported by 75% of the heads of households responding, but only 33% felt that "government should limit profits." Similarly, while 62% supported the contention that "Regulation is the best way to ensure safe products" and 74% agreed that "Regulation is needed to maintain safe working conditions," a solid 72% nevertheless felt that "Competition is better than regulation to assure that the public gets what it pays for."

Finally, the American public still seems to overestimate corporate profits. The average respondent estimated such profit as 19¢ on the dollar; when asked how much profit a company *should* make on a dollar, responses averaged 17¢. (4)

There are other disquieting signs of continued public confusion, concern, and unhappiness with business. A 1976 national "consumer satisfaction" study concluded that many Americans believe that most products and services are not as good as they were five or 10 years ago.

The study, conducted by R. H. Bruskin Associates, found that only three out of 15 products or services on the survey list were thought to be comparable in quality or better than their earlier counterparts. The Associated Press in reporting the study commented that "the survey findings are in line with other studies that indicate that consumers are concerned about the quality of products they buy and are not convinced that industry is doing all that it could."

Discount, if you will, such attitudes as largely romantic longings for the good old days, which in reality were often not all that good. However, some senior management officials take such studies quite seriously. William Ellinghaus, vice chairman of AT&T, in the fall of 1976 told the Society of Consumer Affairs Professionals in Business that, "It is the weak spots in our performance that sparked the consumer movement in the first place. To make no visible effort to eliminate practices and procedures that work against customer satisfaction is to add to that dissatisfaction. . . . Consumers want to be treated like people, not market shares . . . they want human decency, courtesy . . . and enough information to make intelligent buying decisions." (5) (Paradoxically, consumer dissatisfaction exists even though, according to a recent Gallup Poll, Americans seem considerably more satisfied with their quality of life than most Western people. The poll, which sampled 90 percent of the non-Communist world's population, indicated that Americans are happier than most Western people with family life, health, leisure time, housing, work and education.)

However, much more important "polls" of American public opinion took place in November 1976— the "polls" at the polls. Shortly after the results were in, the Consumer Federation of America said that 79 of the 82 members of the House of Representatives it endorsed won re-election. The CFA also said that five of the seven candidates it endorsed for election to the House were successful.

Perhaps more significant than candidates for office was "the other election of 1976." Some 300 initiatives and referenda items were presented to voters in states across the country, most of the items relating to economic, energy, environmental, or consumerist issues. Each issue required grassroot petitioning by at least several thousand citizens before it could be put on the ballot. And even those issues that were defeated accomplished certain educational objectives. Many will be back on the ballots in the years immediately ahead, and there will be additional issues for voters to reflect on as well.

I said early in this chapter that it is the sum of everything the corporation does that will determine whether it survives in an era of changing social expectations. In earlier chapters, I have described many of the newer policies and programs adopted by corporations to stay abreast of such social demands. Here I will offer a brief analysis of various *communications* policies, programs, and challenges that seem particularly relevant and will use a rather broad interpretation of the word "communications."

The first key point to be made is that effective communications requires a *listening* capability as well as a capability for projection. Effective corporate listening involves not only the collection of other points of view but also how the corporations' statements and actions are being perceived by others. (Have you ever seen a radio announcer cup his ear with his hand while talking into a microphone? That's so *he* can hear how his voice sounds to *others*.)

As corporate listening devices, public opinion surveys are becoming increasingly sophisticated. The corporation can now commission specially tailored, independent surveys or subscribe to an ongoing service such as the Yankelovich, Skelly & White, Inc.'s "Corporate Priorities" series, or the Opinion Research Corporation's "Caravan" program. Either way, it is now increasingly popular to get *data* before making social policy decisions.

There are also some rather creative individual listening programs in use. One that seems particularly valuable is the "Business Executive in Residence Program" managed by the American Council of Life Insurance. By the end of 1976 this program had placed some 30 high-level life insurance executives in residence for at least a week at 20 college campuses across the country. The executives listen and talk to college students almost anywhere on campus—in classrooms and coffeeshops—on just about any subject the students want to discuss.

James A. Attwood, executive vice president and a director of the Equitable Life Assurance Society, has written about his participation in such a program at Mount Holyoke College:

> The course started with two introductory sessions on the corporate role in general and different views of corporate social responsibility. But the foundation of the course was built on ten case studies. . . . Real understanding occurred when students acknowledged the complexity of the issues. Our purpose is certainly served when students (as well as all of our other publics and constituencies) realize that solutions to business problems are often the result of extremely difficult choices which involve compromise, balance, pragmatism and realism.

Attwood's group, after considerable give and take, was able to agree on "Consensus Guidelines on Corporate Social Responsibility." (6)

A related approach to communicating with college and university students is the establishment of a chair to develop courses and activities designed to promote economic education. The first such Chair of Private Enterprise was established at Georgia State University in 1963. By early 1976 there were 12 such chairs in existence or planned at American colleges and universities.

The respected newsletter *Corporate Public Issues* has offered this commentary on the need for business communication with colleges:

> The Issue:
> A Question of Survival
> . . . Justice Lewis F. Powell wrote: "No thoughtful person can question that the American economic system is under broad attack. . . . The overriding first need is for businessmen to recognize that the ultimate issue may be survival—survival of what we call the free enterprise system, and all that this means for the strength and prosperity of America and the freedom of our people."
>
> CPI comment . . . Start where you live. As chief executive officer, or close advisor to him, offer your services now to the nearest college or university dean of business administration as an adjunct professor or guest lecturer to economic and business courses. . . . Don't preach. Discuss. Listen. The students will respect you and emerge with a clearer understanding of their own future. (7)

*Listening* also means solicitation and appraisal of opinions from some natural corporate constituencies—shareholders and employees. Eastern States Gas and Fuel, Boston, has periodically surveyed its shareholders on their attitudes concerning the company's social responsibility policies. It has even compared the shareholder attitudes with those of college students who had been asked for their opinion of such policies. However, by and large, shareholders have not been asked for opinions on corporate policies and have not been active publicly in support of corporate objectives (although they *are* being asked increasingly to contribute to corporate political action committees).

In fact, Brooks McCormick, president of International Harvester Company, told a 1976 Business Roundtable meeting that shareholders "have been blinded to their own interests in the antibusiness climate of today, and failed to use their political power to protect the interest of the corporations they themselves own . . . capitalists have helped cripple capitalism." (8)

Similarly, the employee is only now beginning to be recognized as an important ally on social issues. After some very worthwhile pioneering work by a team of researchers at Syracuse University a few years back, employee attitude surveys have gone no great distance, even though employee attitudes can be critical to the success of new corporate social policies.

Employees *have* become involved in lobbying, however. Many corporations and trade associations have organized "grassroots impact" programs wherein employees, aware of the possible impact of legislation on their jobs, have communicated effectively with legislators at the state or federal level. Some observers feel that the employees of Pan American Airways were instrumental in saving the company in 1973 when they waged an independent campaign for better public understanding and federal subsidies. They achieved the public understanding and built an environment in which it was possible for the government to help Pan Am in a number of important ways short of subsidies. Since then, employee campaigns have been instrumental in the oil divestiture debate, the nonreturnable beverage container issue, and a number of other federal and state legislative issues. Significantly, Dow Chemical Company has developed "It's Your Government Too!", a series of seminars for Dow people focusing on the workings of the legislative and executive branches of the federal government and has successfully "marketed" the program for use by other business organizations.

There is ample evidence that the employee is becoming more important as a target for corporate communications. Many employee publications that used to concentrate on births, deaths, and bowling scores are being upgraded considerably. The reason is that there is an increasing corporate awareness that the employee can be a particularly valuable ally by virtue of his or her reach in the community and because neighbors tend to regard an employee as "in the know" on matters involving the company.

Many experts look for a veritable explosion of interest and activity in the employee communications field as more and more corporations realize the potential of employees who are well informed on issues vital to the firm. One model for such a communications program exists at the Polaroid Corporation. A keystone of the Polaroid employee communications program is the Polaroid *Newsletter*. (9) For candor and interest, *Newsletter* may be unparalleled in corporate journalism. It presents bad news as well as good, plunges into meaty, issue-oriented subjects, and is a forum for the free expression of employee opinion of corporate policy. A related concept well worth watching is the *employee annual report*, undertaken in recent years by a few corporations to provide employees with vital information on the firm's progress and problems.

If corporate executives must consider new listening capabilities, they must also weigh the need for increased *candor* in their public statements. BankAmerica has broken through in the area of candor concerning internal operations. Candor is also a major building block for credibility on broad business-in-society issues as well. I know several chemical industry executives who privately condemned the manner in which the Kepone environmental tragedy occurred but who would never speak out publicly. And very few business executives condemned their peers who broke the law in issuing illegal payments.

Arthur Schlesinger, Jr. has asked some embarrassing questions about the lack of candor:

> How does the business community react to the squalid record of business malpractice—the bribes and payoffs and kickbacks, the tax dodges and insiders' deals, the illegal political contributions, the shoddy products, the systematic destruction of the environment? . . . If any of these bodies [business organizations] have condemned by name firms and people engaged in business malpractice, they must have done it in the dead of night. Instead, our business leaders give us pontifical talk about the sanctity of private enterprise, interspersed with fulminations against the licentious press . . . as if newspapers had invented these scandals when all they have done is to bring them to light. (10)

It may well be that corporate leaders, realizing that they cannot control everything that happens down the line in their own organizations, will not condemn transgressors on the basis of "there but for the grace of God go I."

In *Ethics and Profits* Silk and Vogel describe this attitude as follows:

> There is great reluctance among business executives to "name names" or publicly criticize other businesses for illegal actions—whether because of fear of a loss of business, concern about "washing our dirty linen in public," anxiety about being "kicked out of the club," or loathness to claim moral superiority and the right to censure others. Yet there is recognition that businessmen's silence on the transgressions of other businesses has contributed to a general public belief that "they're all alike" or "they're all in it together."

A few corporate executives *have* spoken out. Thomas A. Murphy, chairman of General Motors, told the September 1976 meeting of the Associated Industries of New York that:

> the increasing regulation by the government was a reaction to the mood of a large segment of the public that is disappointed,

dissatisfied and disenchanted with the everyday performance of American business, especially big business. . . .

Credibility requires that we in business should not ignore or excuse demonstrated instances of misleading advertising, misrepresented warranties and other questionable practices. We cannot overlook the admitted wrongdoings of some of our country's largest and most respected corporations. No one believes that business is blameless in every respect. For us to try to make it seem to be is worse than ineffectual; it only deepens disbelief. It suggests that we in business can no longer distinguish between what is right and fair and honest and what is not. . . .

I want to contribute a note of urgency—that the clock is running on free enterprise and it is later than we think . . . much of the public's antipathy toward big business is rooted in the American consumer's own bad experiences in the marketplace. To the extent that it is rooted there, it can be remedied only there. (12)

## UNDERSTANDING MEDIA

I think I understand media. Having been an editor for a national business newsweekly for four years and having spent the last 17 years in public relations, I have certainly had plenty of opportunity to observe how print and broadcast people think and how they do their jobs.

I don't understand *everything* media people do. Reporters and editors, like even corporate executives (yes, and public relations people) sometimes have a bad day and do off-the-wall things. But by and large, newspapers and magazines, radio and television stations and networks, wire services, and newsweeklies all have a simple but mighty heavy role —to inform 220 million Americans about what is happening to this crazy, wonderful world. To accomplish this, all they have to do is stay on top of everything, all the time, and present it to us in as arresting a format as good taste and professional ethics will allow.

(Incidentally, I am going to avoid what could be a lengthy discussion on what "press" means versus what "media" means. Suffice it to say that there are distinctions important to the folks in the news business.)

This is not going to be any learned dissertation on the ROLE OF MEDIA in our society. There are any number of foundations and university communications departments pawing over that ground continuously. This will be only a well-intentioned attempt to comfort corporate executives who have felt estrangement from journalists and journalists who distrust corporate executives.

A few theorems:

## Media Reflect Not Life But a Slice of Life

Be honest. When you pick up your newspaper or magazine or tune in on your favorite newscaster, you're attracted to the unusual or the significant. It's only human. The commonplace is a turn-off.

One of the better analyses of "news" that I have come across was formulated by Dick Dalton, a member of Dow Chemical Company's Corporate Communications Department: "It's an old truism that good works are good news and good news, unfortunately, is 'no news.' News, indeed, is all things counter, strange, striking or shocking, things people are avid to learn about. News, generally, is all things a company is *not* about." (13)

To buttress this position, I report an experience I had recently with a producer of a major network television "magazine of the air." I learned that the program was researching a story on herbicides. I volunteered a good deal of background material, offered interview subjects, and waited for the producer to react. A few weeks later I called to check on the status of the story. "We've killed it," the producer said. "We've checked it out top to bottom, and the product is environmentally clean. There's no story."

There's no story in clean products, only in dirty products. And there are many, many more clean (no-story) products and clean (no-story) people than the other kinds.

There are, of course, some upbeat stories that get into print and on the air. Sometimes goodness, or happiness, *is* news, but it has to be *unusual* goodness or happiness. Then it can be positioned as a change of pace in the normal flow of the other stuff.

Theodore White, author of *The Making of the President*, was quoted on the subject:

> There's no collective or conspiratorial abuse. But so many good things are happening in this country. You don't make your reputation as a reporter, and I did not make my reputation as a reporter, by praising anybody. You make your reputation as a reporter by gouging a chunk of raw and bleeding flesh from this system. And I did that, all young reporters do that. You gotta be able to prove you can snap your jaws for the kill. But maybe we've gone too far and maybe there should be someone to call us to account for this also. (14)

All this is fair enough as long as everyone understands the rules. Unfortunately, many Americans haven't thought enough about it to realize that "slice of life" is all we normally get in the media.

Also, there's the matter of media "appetite." It must be fed not three times a day, but constantly. On a slow news day, some rather questionable events become "news." Conversely, when terrorists seized buildings in Washington, D.C. in March 1977, media blanketed the story and all but ignored President Carter's reports on a new training program for young, jobless Americans, a phased withdrawal from South Korea, and progress toward "elimination of atomic weapons from this earth."

### Media Magnification Makes a Subject Bigger Than Life

I think of three types of media magnification.
- The first is the tendency toward melodrama.

Former Senator William Fulbright, writing in the *Columbia Review of Journalism*, touched some raw journalistic nerves when he wrote:

> If once the press was excessively orthodox and unquestioning of government policy, it has now become almost sweepingly iconoclastic. If once the press showed excessive deference to government and its leaders, it has now become excessively mistrustful and even hostile. . . .
>
> The crucial ingredient, it seems to me, is scandal—corporate, political, or personal. Where it is present, there is news, although the event may be otherwise inconsequential. Where it is lacking, the event may or may not be news, depending in part, to be sure, on its intrinsic importance, but hardly less on competing events, the degree of controversy involved, and whether it involves something "new"—new, that is, in the way of disclosure as distinguished from insight or perspective. . . .
>
> We really must try to stop conducting our affairs like a morality play. . . . Bitter disillusionment with our leaders is the other side of the coin of worshipping them. If we did not expect our leaders to be demigods, we would not be nearly as shocked by their failures and transgressions. . . .
>
> The press has always played up to our national tendency to view public figures as either saints or sinners. . . .
>
> Because the press cannot and should not be restrained from outside, it bears special responsibility for restraining itself, and for helping to restore civility in our public affairs. (15)

Just how well Fulbright's advice will go down with journalists remains to be seen. There are influential journalists calling for still more accusatory journalism. For example, John L. Hess, a veteran *New York Times* reporter, wrote in the March 1976 issue of *MORE*:

> Perhaps the most imminent threat to civil liberties today is the notion that the media pose a threat to civil liberties. . . .

The campaign is, in a way, flattering. It suggests that the media are so hungry for scandal that they let no consideration of justice stand in their way. Well, Lord knows we have our faults, but an excess of investigative zeal is not one of them. . . .

"Everyone is innocent until proven guilty." The statement is at once an absurdity and the glory of our judicial system. . . . our courts must act *as if it were true*. . . . Apply this principle to the press and we are dead. (16)

- Next, consider whether television news is almost a world in itself. For one thing, the very presence of a camera crew and an interviewer creates an event or at least magnifies its significance. Some of the activst groups learned this early. Intrinsically, a handful of demonstrators doing their thing on a street corner is not very different from a tree falling in the proverbial uninhabited forest. Enter the camera crew and that same handful, strategically deployed to construct a media event, can be seen across the country on the evening news. But it is still a handful of people, and most likely only a miniscule minority of those who have a position on the issue.

Paul Weaver, an associate editor of *Fortune* magazine, has offered readers of the *New York Times Magazine* some observations on how television journalism impacted on the 1976 presidential campaign:

> As I watched the networks' coverage of the 1976 primaries, my main impression was not of particular events and people, but of being drawn into a world that is different from the one we know from everyday experience. This other world is based on real people and events, but the constant intervention of the television newsman—with his unremitting efforts to select, highlight, summarize, explain and above all to tell a story—drains it of its characteristic humdrum and endows it with the magic intensity of myth and fairy tale. This is the world of television news, and in it things from the real world take on new qualities and meaning. . . .
>
> In the world of television news . . . the diversity, complexity and uncertainty of the real world become all but invisible. They are replaced by the false simplicity and clarity of what TV news, assuming a posture of omniscience, pretends to know. (17)

Well, you're saying, what would you *expect* from a *Fortune* editor, a *defense* of broadcast journalism?

All right, let's look at a statement on the "distortion through compression" of broadcast news made by a very different kind of commentator. Broadcast news programs, this expert said, "fall far short of presenting all of the news needed by a citizen to intelligently exercise his franchise." The speaker? Walter Cronkite at a mid-December 1976 meeting of the Radio and Television News Directors Association. (18)

Severe time constraints. Tell a *story*. Entertainment. Ratings. These are the very burdensome aspects of television journalism.

Paddy Chayefsky, the former television playwright (*Marty, Bachelor Party*), stepped right into the middle of the television journalism controversy when he wrote *Network*, a late-1976 hit film that portrayed television news as a business heavily related to the ratings game. Chayefsky's main indictment seemed to be that if the American people want Roman circuses, television news is prepared to give it to them. "Television," he said in discussing the film, "is democracy at its ugliest. Give the people what they want."

There are television critics who have begun to say somewhat the same thing. Edith Efron, a columnist in *TV Guide*, in 1976 used a couple of her columns to attack the accuracy and emphasis of television documentaries attempting to link cancer with environmental pollution.

Similarly, Elizabeth Whelan, who holds advanced degrees in epidemiology and demography from Harvard and Yale, offered these opinions in the November 15, 1976, issue of *Barron's*:

> After viewing all three broadcasts [CBS and NBC documentaries linking cancer to environmental pollution and food], one could scarcely fail to conclude that the United States is in the midst of an industrially produced cancer epidemic, surrounded by a sea of carcinogens, at the mercy of an array of noxious chemicals peculiar to the American environment.
>
> The average viewer was doubtless unaware that these reports contained inaccuracies, served to confuse known cancer risks with hypothetical ones, cleverly used emotionalism and horror stories to establish guilt by association and innuendo, and sought to suggest that we are all victims, rather than the beneficiaries, of industrial civilization. . . .
>
> . . . Dan Rather told us that "environmental pollution may account for up to 90% of the causes of cancer in this country." "Environmental pollution" is a highly misleading term. Actually, it is *environmentally related* causes which most scientists believe play a major role in 80% to 90% of human cancers. Even more important was Rather's failure to note that the majority of medical and public health scientists now feel that it is cigaret smoking and imprudent dietary habits . . . which make up the great bulk of the "environmentally related" total. . . .
>
> Television can and should play a major role in informing the public about cancer trends and advising them of recent findings in cancer research. But the approach should be constructive —one which meticulously separates out emotion and politics, leaving factual, balanced accounts. If we are truly interested in

preventing cancer, we should no longer accept without protest such polemical offerings. Or, as an alternative, perhaps we should demand that they carry with them the warning: "This TV special may be hazardous to your health." (20)

Whelan has formed the American Council on Science and Health "to provide public health education based on balanced, scientific evaluations (avoiding scare tactics and sensationalism) and extensive consideration of benefit-risk ratios on a variety of subjects related to man's relationship to the artificial and natural chemicals in the environment."

Television news and documentary producers have countered such criticisms by saying that what they present on the air is based on facts and opinions offered by recognized "experts" (it's true—you can find a scientist somewhere to support almost any position on the *possible* effects of substances in the environment); that much of the criticism is a matter of splitting hairs; and that some of the critics represent "vested interests" (we'll have more on this later in the chapter). What happens when *media* are accused of being a public health hazard? According to MORE, the media magazine, "Federal Agents investigating the presence of carcinogens in the nation's pressrooms have been barred by such newspapers as the *New York Times, New York Daily News,* and *Chicago Tribune* from inspecting their plants." (19)

One more note on television-type news: it may be coming to some newspapers. Newspaper readership in the decade ending in 1976 is estimated to have dropped about 4 percent, or 2.5 million readers. In an effort to turn that tide, some publishers are turning to consultants brought in by the newspaper marketing or circulation departments. Some of the consultants are the "designers" of television news programs. Again, "ratings" (circulation) seems to be the dominant factor. The marketing and circulation people seem to be saying, "Let's ask the reader what he/she wants and give it to them." Editors respond, "Let's retain our sense of news and give the reader what we think he/she needs." Undoubtedly, many papers will compromise.

• I think that it is also possible to make a case for the proposition that we may have evolved a system of *over*communication. Consider what can happen when several media repeat the same theme. A few years ago, it was fashionable for sports reporters to tell the fans how dumb a certain ballplayer was. The first impression on reading, say, the morning newspaper, might well have been, "Gee, that fellow must not be too sharp." The afternoon paper comes out with another anecdote (some were apocryphal), and the reader progresses to, "That guy is really dumb." By the time the late evening newscast makes its contribution to the destruction of the ballplayer's IQ, the fan has been led to the conclusion that "that guy is one of the dumbest clowns around." All that on a day when the unfortunate ballplayer may not have uttered a word.

### The Winds of Change are Beginning to Cool Media, Too

Clarence Kelley, director of the Federal Bureau of Investigation, said in 1976: "If there is an institution in our society with power that approaches unlimited power, that institution is the news media." (21)

Walter B. Wriston, chairman of Citicorp, suggesting that the press hold itself more accountable, said, "History teaches that when any sector of our society grows too powerful, it is only a matter of time before that power is curbed." (21)

Wes Gallagher, outgoing chief executive of the Associated Press, told the 1976 AP annual meeting: "Too many readers are beginning to look upon the press as a multivoiced shrew, nitpicking through the debris of government decisions for scandals but not solutions. . . . Readers and viewers are being turned off." (21)

There is under way something of a re-evaluation of the rights and duties of the media in a free and democratic society. For example, the recent court cases wherein newsmen and newswomen went to jail rather than divulge their sources present a bit of a social conundrum. Most people understand the necessity for the press to preserve confidentiality if it is to be an effective agent for social reform. Watergate might never have been adequately pursued if it were not for the famous but still unidentified "Deep Throat." But how can a defendant in the court of public opinion adequately defend himself or herself if an accuser is shrouded in the veil of confidential source? The reporter or editor who chooses to protect the source accepts a heavy burden; if the source is inaccurate, unnecessary, and perhaps irreparable, injury can be incurred. Even the Supreme Court has been somewhat ambiguous on this clash of constitutional rights. And newsmen have gone to jail rather than reveal sources.

What sort of redress should media make when they have, in fact, damaged a person or an institution by sloppy or biased reporting or editing? Media people themselves are beginning to come up with some suggestions. One is the editorial ombudsman. Another is an attempt to admit error more openly. A third is expanded coverage of unpopular or unconventional points of view as well as opinions opposing those of the media carrying them.

By mid-1976, some 30 newspapers were known to have established editorial ombudsmen. Their role is to be a representative for the dissatisfied reader and an in-house critic of what appears in their papers.

Charles B. Seib, the veteran journalist who is ombudsman at the *Washington Post*, recently told *U.S. News and World Report* that about half of the complaints from readers involve "some element of overreaching in the story," overstating the facts of a situation to make the story seem more important or dramatic than it really is. (21)

Correcting erroneous stories is admittedly still a very sensitive operation at most newspapers, but the number of papers running correction boxes in the same spot every day is growing. And the *Charlotte News and Observer* has gone so far as to give corrections the same "play" as the original story. Other papers are studying other techniques.

Opening up to unpopular or opposition points of view normally means an expanded letters-to-the-editor page or an opinion page where the points of view can be expressed at some length. According to one recent estimate, about 90 major dailies had instituted such "op-ed" pages in the past few years.

It is much tougher to build a satisfactory forum for dissent and criticism in radio and television. However, some CBS executives have taken to the road to appear before local audiences to answer questions and respond to criticisms. Then CBS airs tapes of the meetings locally.

### The Great Majority of Journalists are Honest, Objective, Hard-working Professionals

It is self-defeating for corporate executives to think in terms of black-white adversary relationships with reporters and editors.

Just as a small minority of business executives dispensed illegal or improper campaign contributions, so too there is a relatively small percentage of lazy or sleazy journalists. By far the greater number of journalists are reasonable people willing to listen to anyone they consider credible and whose opinions are supported by facts.

However, journalists have personal opinions like anyone else. They support progressive change and are suspicious of vested interests. They are successful as journalists to the extent that they keep their personal feelings out of their professional efforts. Their stock in trade is facts; but it is naïve to think that having collected all the facts available and having reached a *professional* conclusion, they will offer only a recitation of facts.

The entire question of journalistic objectivity is being re-evaluated. Although journalistic tradition has enshrined objectivity, *U.S. News and World Report* has noted some serious slippage recently:

> For nearly a century, "objectivity" was a reigning word in the list of journalistic imperatives. Young reporters were told that a story, first of all, must be fair, give all sides of a contro-

versial issue and let the reader reach his own conclusions on the basis of the facts given him. Today, such a creed is under attack by some journalists as unrealistic and simplistic. Important news, they say, is becoming far too complex for the reader to unravel for conclusions on his or her own.

At its minimum, this interpretation of the journalist's role is summed up in the statement of WTOP–TV newsman Pat Collins, in Washington, D.C., describing his philosophy of news: "I don't think there's such a thing as an objective story. So be honest with people. Tell them what you think the truth is and then let them decide for themselves."

At its maximum, interpretive reporting plunges into "advocacy journalism," which insists that words are weapons and that reporters must clearly delineate the "right" and "wrong" sides in a public controversy. (22)

When objectivity reigned supreme, most respected journalists labeled commentary and reportage as such. Advocacy journalists reject such distinctions and claim an even longer tradition dating from Tom Paine and the pamphleteers of the Revolution to the abolitionists and muckrakers and even on up to the activist press of the 1960s.

## "WHAT SHOULD WE DO—
## JUST SIT THERE AND TAKE IT?"

Many corporate executives are understandably frustrated when the media attack. It seems as if the press has all the cards. After all, to paraphrase A. J. Leibling, "Freedom of the Press belongs to all those who own a press." Almost, but not quite.

First, it is helpful to understand how and why media people think and operate as they do. Perhaps the paragraphs above will help, but there is even more help available within most corporate organizations. I am referring to the many ex-media people—former reporters, editors, or broadcasters—who have become corporate employees. Very often they are in the public relations or public affairs departments. Sometimes they are in employee communications. It doesn't matter so much where they *are* as where they've *been*—on the editorial "side." The Public Relations Society of America is building "dialog" relationships with media-counterpart organizations such as the Associated Press Managing Editors, the Society of Professional Journalists and the Radio and Television News Directors Association.

Next, and most important of all, is that vast ongoing challenge of getting, and keeping, the corporate house in order. If there are social vulnerabilities within a company or an industry, in this day and age they are likely to come out. Before the corporation can expect a "good press" it has to be sure that it is not generating its own "bad press." Joseph Nolan, while professor of journalism and public affairs at the University of South Carolina, said it quite well in the *Harvard Business Review*:

> The essence of improving the business image rests not in trying to conjure up a good story when performance fails, but in sharpening corporate perceptions of emerging social and political trends and in adjusting performance so there will, in fact, be a good story to tell. In short, doing a plastic-surgery job on the business image is no substitute for reforming some substantive business practices. (23)

Further, with increasing disclosure—voluntary or required—"regulation by public opinion" is going to increase. Competing for public acceptance may well be as important as any competition the corporation engages in.

What about some of the practical communications problems? What follows is only one man's opinion. It is certainly not meant as pontification. It will serve its purpose if it stirs a bit of discussion in corporate board rooms and communications departments.

### Taking the Initiative

Our AMA survey found that only a minority of companies initiate communications about their social responsibility programs. Asked whether their organizations actively communicate news of their social responsibility concerns and/or programs to the general public, 71 percent of the respondents said no. But among the minority (29 percent) who *do* actively communicate such information to the public, 62 percent perceived positive public response to such information; 36 percent have noted "no response to speak of"; and only 2 percent say that they have experienced negative public response.

Of course, social responsibility programs are not the only reason to communicate with the public. Just about every corporate objective has within it the seeds of a communications program to target audiences. But that's another book.

### Attacked? Reply!

There is a school of thought that keeping a low profile is the best policy in the face of a negative story. I say any story that contains error or misinterpretation should be answered. The answer may not get adequate—or any—"play"; it certainly isn't likely to get the same play as the original story. Nevertheless, it is worth the effort. The life of published misinformation is inversely related to the vigor of the effort to stamp it out as soon as it appears.

This suggestion doesn't apply, of course, if the story is unflattering but *accurate*. Then it's back to Nolan's advice.

### Asked for an Interview? Cooperate

There is disagreement on this too, but I believe that in most cases it is in the interest of business to cooperate fully with the media—to be available for interviews, to operate in good faith. Those who disagree cite instances of misquotation, sloppy editing—especially of television film or tape—and other media misdeeds that have embarrassed the cooperative company or executive. There *is* that risk.

However, to refuse to be interviewed can be even more troublesome. In most cases, the story will be published or broadcast anyway, and the lack of cooperation is read by many in the public as having "something to hide."

A modest suggestion for the wary executive: If there is concern about the reporter's possible use of remarks inaccurately or out of context, tape the entire interview. Few reporters will object when conducting an "on the record" interview, although you may hear a grumble about "reduced spontaneity."

What to say? How to say it? Dozens of schools to train executives in handling media interviews have sprung up in recent years. Many are very helpful. Their instruction: Be relaxed and concise; use terms the public can understand and relate to; and be accurate and informed. A. O. Sulzberger, *New York Times* publisher: "Is the press antibusiness? . . . No. Is the press antidullness? . . . Yes."

Irving Kristol, Henry Luce Professor of Urban Values at New York University, has an interesting suggestion for corporations—or anyone—who feel wronged by media. He says that they should take chapter and verse to jounalistic peers.

> . . . journalists, whatever their media, do like to think of themselves as professionals—i.e., as observing professional standards of accuracy and truth telling. Though most are biased in a "liberal" direction, only a few are intellectually dishonest. They may not give a damn what the business community thinks of them, but they care very much what kind of professional reputation they have among their peers. . . .
>
> What has to be done to set the record straight [when a corporation is victimized] is a public rebuttal—detailed, polemical, and sharply phrased so as to challenge the reporter's (or newscaster's) professional integrity. And this rebuttal will have to take the form of paid advertising in that media which the re-

porter and his colleagues read. . . . The purpose of such advertising is not to affect public opinion directly, but to influence journalistic performance over the longer run. (24)

### Practical Advice on Strategy From a "Radical"

The juxtaposition of Irving Kristol, "conservative," and Saul Alinsky, "radical," on this page strikes me as rather unusual, but Alinsky, too, has some interesting words on communication:

> Communication with others takes place when they understand what you're trying to get across to them. If they don't understand, then you are not communicating regardless of words, pictures, or anything else. *People only understand things in terms of their experience, which means that you must get within their experience. Further, communications is a two-way process. If you try to get your ideas across to others without paying attention to what they have to say to you, you can forget about the whole thing* [emphasis added]. (25)

### This Is the Age of Communications Feedback

Alinsky refers to two-way communication. Why do you suppose citizen band radio has spread like wildfire? People are tired of being talked *to* and want an opportunity to respond as well. Radio call-in talk shows are all the rage for the same reason, and President Carter's use of this communication device says something of its potential value.

A number of interesting "dialog" communications experiments have been attempted in recent years. In the fall of 1976, the management of the New York Rangers and New York Knickerbockers invited fans to telephone and talk to the general managers of the hockey and basketball teams. Similarly, an organization called CAST—Council for Agricultural Science and Technology—has conducted three *national* telephone "dialogs"; consumers and students have been invited to dial toll-free telephone numbers and talk to scientists about environmental and public health concerns relating to agriculture. And the Agricultural Council of America has maintained an *ongoing* "dial-og" capability, inviting consumers to call toll-free to farmers to discuss food prices and the food production and distribution process.

Arco (Atlantic Richfield Company) did something similar in print advertising. To mark the Bicentennial, it launched a major advertising campaign inviting Americans to express themselves on their hopes and desires for an improved nation. Then Arco ran many of the ideas in subsequent ads across the country.

## What About All Those Economic Education Campaigns?

First, let's listen again to Irving Kristol:

> Today there are more programs in "economic education" emerging from the business community than one can keep track of. . . . They all derive from the supposition that corporate executives would have a nicer reputation if only people understood the rudiments of business enterprise and the relation between the prosperity of the corporation and the well-being of the citizenry. . . .
>
> Advertising is precisely the wrong vehicle for *any* kind of education. Education, properly understood, induces a growing comprehension of abstract ideas and concepts; advertising, properly understood, aims to move people to do something definite and unambiguous. Education is always raising questions; advertising is always giving answers. . . .
>
> Moreover, favorable or unfavorable attitudes to business seem to have little or no correlation with the taking of courses in economics. . . . There are plenty of radical economists, after all, and even more "liberal" (i.e., anti-business) ones. These people don't have to be told what "profits" are. . . . They have nothing against profits in a purely accounting sense. They just don't see why control over these profits should be exercised by corporate executives rather than by, say, professors of economics or higher civil servants. . . .
>
> . . . popular attitudes are often provoked, to begin with, by experience. In recent years, it has been the experience of inflation that may well have been decisive. Inflation *always* elicits anti-business attitudes from consumers, for obvious reasons. (26)

Kristol notwithstanding, I believe that there are many undecided persons out there up for grabs. In recent years, I have admired the Textron and General Motors economic education advertising, mainly because they have used *employees*—not polished-but-obviously-purchased actors—to speak to the general public.

Just a word about "profits." There has to be a more engaging way to explain the word and tie it to social imperatives. Try these on:

John Hill, a public relations pioneer and chairman of the world's largest public relations firm: "We need to convince [people] in their terms and by our actions, that private enterprise wants just what they want—to make ends meet and have something left over." (27)

Fletcher L. Byrom, Chairman, Koppers Company: "Profits are to a corporation what breathing is to a human being. We cannot live without breathing and a corporation cannot live without profits. But breathing is not the sole purpose of life, and profits are not the sole purpose of the adventure that we call business." (28)

One more thing on economic education. Could we, once and for all, inter Adam Smith's "invisible hand"? Have you ever heard a less comforting term to those who are insecure about their welfare within the apparent chaos of the marketplace?

### Finally, Stop Crying Wolf, Wolf!

Whether dealing with the media or with legislators and regulators in Washington, corporate leaders are going to have to stop crying wolf! wolf! if they are to build credibility. It is common negotiating strategy to develop an opening position and a fall-back position. However, if the opening position is "You are going to drive us right out of business with this proposal," you had better be able to document the charge.

Stanley Marcus, chairman of Neiman-Marcus of Dallas, told executives of his industry that all of business has much to reflect on in the area of crying wolf:

> Americans . . . have a quarrel with that majority of businessmen who have fought and obstructed and delayed every piece of progressive legislation enacted during this century.
>
> Who among the business community today would seriously propose that Congress repeal our child labor laws, or the Sherman Antitrust Act? The Federal Reserve Act, the Securities Exchange Act? Or workman's compensation? Or Social Security? Or minimum wage? Or Medicare? Or civil rights legislation?
>
> All of us today recognize that such legislation is an integral part of our system; that it has made us a stronger, more prosperous nation—and, in the long run, has been good for business. But we can take precious little credit for any of the social legislation now on the books, for business vigorously opposed most of this legislation.
>
> I wonder sometimes if we really believe in the free enterprise system. When those who have the greatest stake in it often turn out to be its greatest enemies, I wonder if free enterprise can survive. (29)

This is by no means a suggestion not to resist burdensome government regulation. However, in offering such resistance, corporate executives must carefully circumscribe the field of discussion, scrupulously analyze the real costs involved, and effectively communicate to both government and the public what those costs are likely to be and who is likely to pay them (ultimately, of course, it is the public).

Americans have great good sense. When they've had enough, they will take the necessary action. There is no better example than the compulsory harnessing of American automobile drivers that was promoted by public interest organizations. Aggravated by someone telling them that they *had* to harness up before their new cars would start (someone who knew better what was good for them), they simply threw off the yoke. With it went a lot of public interest organization influence on other issues as well.

## SCIENCE IN THE PUBLIC INTEREST

Many Americans seem to have gotten the impression, mainly through media, that only antiestablishment scientific spokesmen are operating in the public interest. A few years back, one public interest group gained the initiative by naming itself Scientists Institute for Public Information (SIPI). Media love to report what such scientists have to say about a host of corporate practices that "create possible dangers."

I have encountered many scientists in industry and government who are frustrated by the low esteem they feel they have among the general public. Part of the reason for the lack of credibility of scientists who work for industry is that they are not very visible and are, therefore, largely unknown to the public. They are competing with the "visible" scientist, a new breed of scientist-media expert recently described by A. Rae Goodell, then a research associate at the Massachusetts Institute of Technology. Goodell contends that a number of highly visible scientists play a critical role in how the public perceives science and science policy issues. She says: "Dramatic changes in science and in communication are forcing changes in science communication and, in the process, the kind of scientist who gets communicated." (30)

Goodell says that the "visible" scientist circumvents the traditional channels of scientific communication and goes straight to the public. She says that today's most visible scientists are not known for scientific discoveries but rather for these characteristics: each is controversial and articulate, has a topic and a colorful image, and, as a result, has credibility. Among the "visible" scientists Goodell studied are Barry Commoner, Paul Ehrlich, Linus Pauling, B.F. Skinner, Margaret Mead, and William Shockley.

Several things may happen to the visible scientists. One: They can be confronted "on the media trail" by scientists who have a different viewpoint; media now seem ready to accept such counterspokesmen as representing new and interesting opposition. Two: The scientific community can speak out against all who circumvent the traditional scientific channels and avoid peer review and publication in scientific literature. Three: Media can do a better job of checking to see whether a visible scientist has, indeed, presented his theories for peer review and decide that without such review, the claims are totally unsubstantiated and therefore like many other tips that reach the newsroom, unconfirmed by a second source.

What is likely to happen is that media will continue to report the "juicy" claims of visible scientists. That is all right if they will grant equal time to scientists who disagree. Again, let everyone be heard and let the marketplace of ideas operate.

The trouble is that too many journalists still suffer from the vested-interest fixation. They question whether a scientist who gets direct or indirect support from industry can retain integrity. In other words, they question such a scientist's ability to maintain professional objectivity. Ironically, most *journalists* work for profit-making organizations and have no problems in maintaining *their* professional integrity. The only way to handle the vested-interest fixation is to confront it head on. A personal note: Having represented a variety of chemical and other corporations and trade associations, I can state unequivocally that I have never been asked to compromise *my* professional standards in such relationships.

A confrontation of sorts occurred on this issue at the 1976 annual meeting of the American Association for the Advancement of Science (AAAS). In an all-day meeting on ethics and the corporate scientist, Alan C. Nixon, former president of the American Chemical Society, said, "I believe the scientist has a responsibility to bring to the attention of the American public any problems in his field of science . . . it remains very difficult for a corporate scientist to speak out—often if he does, he is either fired or transferred, to a less desirable assignment." However, Dr. Arthur Bueche, who *is* a corporate scientist (vice president for research at General Electric), had another point of view: If in the course of his or her work, a scientist discovers problems, he or she should first discuss the problems with management—and be willing to resign if a public attack seems warranted. (31)

On the other side of the "vested-interest" coin, you run into the appealing argument that the "activist" scientist—for that matter, all activists—has nothing to gain by advocating a certain position. To the contrary, he or she has everything—everything that matters in his or her ethic—to gain. In this case, "everything" is the successful transmission of an idea. For many activists, that is the whole professional ballgame.

None of this should be construed as suggesting the activist scientists should be muzzled. Like all activists in recent years, these dedicated people have created a healthy tension that has caused many a needed re-evaluation of standards. Much good has come of such re-evaluation. The problems arise only when the factual structure for such attack is flimsy. And only the scientific community itself can make that determination.

In October 1976 major meetings of the scientific community heard appeals for scientists to play a more active role in promoting better public understanding of scientific issues. The American Association for the Advancement of Science, with 113,000 members and 300 affiliated societies, announced a broadening of activities in this direction. And at a symposium the National Academy of Sciences sponsored in conjunction with the General Assembly of International Council of Scientific Unions, an international panel of scientists challenged their colleagues to help guide the world away from nuclear war, famine, and exhaustion of raw materials.

### A Scientific "Supreme Court"?

Facts. Empirical data. There's the rub. Many of the attacks on products and manufacturing processes as potential causes of disease and death *are* based on facts, on research conducted in respected laboratories. The unfortunate truth is that on most environmental and public health questions you can find scientists who will *interpret* the data differently enough so that society is more confused than instructed.

Remember the 1976 conclusion of the California State Assembly Committee on Resources, Land Use and Energy after 15 days of testimony from 120 "imposing" witnesses? "The questions involved require value judgments and the voter is no less equipped to make such judgments than the most brilliant Nobel Laureate." When this happens, very often "political toxicology"—who can get the most support for one of two conflicting positions—occurs. Many scientists would say that a number of products that have become synonymous in the public mind with villainy—DDT, cyclamates, red dye #2—were more the victims of political toxicology than strong scientific evidence. Political toxicology relies greatly, of course, on how the media play the respective points of view on a controversial issue.

James P. Lodge, a consultant in atmospheric chemistry, has offered some interesting observations on the effect of science reporting, the importance of dosage in scientific testing, and the tragedies of public panic or ignorance of scientific analysis of products:

> Too often, what began as appropriate—indeed necessary—scientific questioning is assumed to be scientific fact. The attendant publicity tends to be in direct proportion to the extent that the original question carries "doomsday" implications. (Why is the continuation of the world so much less welcome news than the end of the world? Are our consciences troubling us?)

All too often a scientist's statement that "under highly unrealistic laboratory conditions, I have a small amount of evidence to suggest that lifetime exposure to elephant hide could, with 5% probability, cause cancer" becomes "Scientist says elephants cause cancer." . . .

In areas that concern public health and consumer products, the risks are compounded. An easily frightened public reacts to publicity, and pressure for government action grows. . . .

Recently it has come to light that some women had abortions because spray adhesives, since shown to be harmless, were suspected of causing birth defects. As a scientist, I find that kind of reaction chilling. . . . I do not deserve that sort of life-and-death power.

But what of the opposite situation, such as the thalidomide scandal? Certainly that case illustrates the need for new areas of pharmaceutical testing. (32)

Lodge suggests two types of solution: Approach each case by making an initial assessment of the risks and the costs involved, and enlist the media to report more accurately the full context of scientific announcements, as it did in 1977 when FDA proposed a ban on saccharin.

Such concerns have led to the suggested "impartial scientific supreme court." There are variations in detail, but in essence the court would be composed of several eminent and impartial scientists who would attempt to weigh carefully the scientific facts behind a controversial national issue and offer a prestigious scientific "advisory" on it. The "court" might be placed within the National Academy of Sciences, which is frequently called upon to advise the government, or it might be an independent, quasi-judicial agency. There are impressive arguments pro and con on the "court" proposal. If it is attempted, it will provide only an additional set of inputs for the ultimate court in American society—the court of public opinion.

In fairness, examples of careful, incisive journalistic reporting on community or scientific issues should not be overlooked. For example, on April 30, 1973, the *New York Times* offered this editorial comment:

> Obviously no saving in meat prices can justify a real risk of cancer in the food Americans eat. But how real is the risk from which the F.D.A. has now begun to protect the community? The F.D.A. has reported that its extremely sensitive analytical equipment has detected DES on the order of magnitude of 120 parts per trillion in the animal tissue examined. Such sensitivity in measuring infinitesimal quantities is a respectable scientific feat, but how meaningful is it as a guide to the public? Is there a significant—even an appreciable—risk of anyone getting cancer from eating meat containing so tiny a quantity of DES? How

does the "risk" the F.D.A. has moved against compare with the risk of breathing normal polluted air in Manhattan or downtown Washington, D.C.—or with the risk of having a chest x-ray or smoking a single cigarette?

The point is that the Delaney amendment is an all or nothing affair, and presumably would have applied if the analytical equipment had found only one thousandth of a trillionth part of DES. This sounds more like fanaticism than intelligent public policy. Would not Congress be well advised to consult the scientists on what meaning, if any, the law should give to infinitesimal quantities? [In 1977, the *Times* repeated its attack on the Delaney clause in connection with FDA's move against saccharin.]

### And Other Courts

A final note on courts as they relate to scientific disputes involving the corporation (and here we mean the courts that already exist in the American judicial system): Most people do not understand that there are inherent difficulties in attempting to apply legal processes in reaching answers to questions of great scientific complexity. The Pacific Legal Foundation, a nonprofit organization that has specialized in such work, has offered an analysis of such difficulties.

> The legal method is based upon the adversary presentation. Such a method is in direct conflict with the scientific approach to the resolution of problems. Indeed, in such a hostile atmosphere many scientists find themselves restricted in the presentation of their views. They do not appreciate the evidentiary limitations which they often feel distorts their presentation. They feel that such proceedings are not a search for truth, but a game. This runs contrary to all of their training and belief and discourages many of the most capable from appearing in such proceedings.
>
> There is a more fundamental defect in trying to apply legal methods. The legal system is based on the concept that adversary proceeding will produce the pertinent facts, and based upon these facts, a reasoned and accurate determination can be made. In contrast, in a pesticide hearing, the decision is not necessarily based upon facts, but rather upon opinions, projections, predictions, and unfortunately at times on mere wild speculation. . . .
> To further complicate the problems of the decision maker, he is faced with alternate choices, either of which involves substantial risk. On the one hand there is the threat to the health and well-being of the people if an injurious pesticide is allowed to be used. On the other there is the danger of famine which society will suffer if needed chemicals are unjustifiably withdrawn from use, for this will result in substantial decreases in the production of food as well as increases in heretofore controlled diseases. . . .

> This committee [EPA's Pesticide Advisory Committee] may well wish to review the entire regulatory system now operating to control the registration of pesticides in order to suggest a more effective method of evaluating and resolving scientific problems. (33)

Milton R. Wessel, adjunct professor at New York University's School of Law, in his book, *The Rule of Reason, A New Approach to Corporate Litigation*, offers a great deal of useful insight on the subject. Wessel feels that "a new 'rule of reason' approach to the resolution of disputes generally, not just 'litigation' in the narrow sense, is essential to corporate success and even corporate survival in its present form." (34) Among his many useful suggestions and observations are these:

> The trouble with industry's present approach to litigation—in contrast to the approach of many of its adversaries—is that it fails to recognize that the key disputes have changed radically in recent years. . . . The civil rights, environmental, and consumer movements of the fifties and sixties gave rise to a quite different type of dispute: that calling for the "risk/benefit" analysis. In this new type of case society as a whole, rather than any of the traditional litigants, must be considered the main party of interest. . . . Safety is a typical risk/benefit issue of this kind. How safe is safe? Nothing is totally without risk, from driving a car to sleeping quietly in bed. (35)

One of the key objectives of environmentalist litigation, Wessel feels, is:

> . . . education of the public and consequent public support . . . with one key trial tactic being to cast the opposition in the role of obstructing the public's right to know the facts. . . .
>
> The rule of reason demands complete consistency between public statements, public positions, and even the most intimate internal corporate discussions and actions. Even if ethics and morality were not a consideration, one can no longer rely on *anything* remaining secret or confidential in the giant corporate structure of today. . . .
>
> . . . calls for maximum disclosure of facts and opinion and trial and decision at the earliest possible time.
>
> . . . seeks to pursuade by emphasizing the affirmative benefits to be achieved, and by using every proper tool to maximize effective communication of technical and scientific matters to laypersons. (36)

## THE NEW CORPORATE MANAGER

In 1972 I wrote an article for the *Public Relations Journal* (circulation about 10,000) in which I offered this thought: "From time to time, studies appear on how company presidents climbed the corporate ladder. In the past, we've seen trends in lawyer-presidents, accountant-presidents and engineer-presidents. With the importance of social responsibility firmly established as a corporate function, it's not difficult to imagine presidents who have primary training in corporate social responsibility." (37)

I didn't get a single response—not a letter, telephone call, or candygram. It was as if the article had never been published. I concluded that readers felt the point of view to be so off the mark that it didn't deserve to be dignified by comment.

About a year later, I wondered aloud about this to a top executive of an oil company. He replied: "The trouble with that article was that it was closer to being a truism than to being controversial. Look at the chief executive officers of a lot of companies. They may not have come up the ranks in personnel or public relations, but they have had to take courses, or attend institutes, or in a number of other ways get immersed in the strategies and tactics of the corporation-in-society. The heads of utilities, energy companies, and consumer products companies especially get training in these issues; if they didn't they'd never be able to lead such organizations."

S. Prakash Sethi, visiting professor of management at Boston University's School of Management, has suggested that top management can best rely on revitalized corporate public affairs departments for support in these areas. In a 1976 address to the Public Affairs Council, as reported by *PR Reporter*, he suggested that the corporate public affairs department is best geared to carry out social responsibility programs, but some changes must be made: "(1) Make sure the public affairs officer is in a position to tell the corporate management what the rest of the world thinks of it and why. . . . (2) Make sure that information relating to social concerns becomes part of the input that goes into corporate decision-making." (38)

Sethi's remarks were comforting to me because I have long felt that public relations professionals, who traditionally have been stationed at the corporate/society interface, are best trained to manage the function at whatever level such management required. Contrary to the many misconceptions of the public relations profession, its roots lie in such responsibility. Edward L. Bernays, a public relations pioneer, in 1923 sketched just such a function when he described the public relations counselor as one who advised his client on policies and practices that meet social goals in accord with changing public desires and demands. In a 1976 article, "Social Responsibility of Business" in the *Public Relations Review*, he reminded readers that "action of business must be based on the public interest." (39)

Apparently the public relations field is producing an increasing number of top executives for corporate and other enterprises. In October 1976, *Public Relations News* editor and publisher, Denny Griswold, honored some 75 public relations professionals who had advanced to or within management positions during the year. Since 1956, *Public Relations News* has recorded 2,009 such promotions. More significantly, Ms. Griswold has identified 22 public relations professionals who have advanced to chairman of the board, 71 to president, and 162 to senior vice president, including promotions to such titles within firms which counsel on, or implement, communications programs.

Equally relevant, I think, is Ms. Griswold's definition of public relations: "The management function which evaluates public attitudes, identifies the policies and procedures of an individual or an organization with the public interest, and plans and executes a program of action to earn public understanding and acceptance."

## ISSUE MANAGEMENT—A CASE HISTORY

I end this chapter with a case history—how the aluminum industry has marshalled and organized its resources to deal with social issues that have serious public opinion and regulatory implications. Its trade association is the Aluminum Association, an association with a number of resources that make it the most practical instrument for many issue management activities.

### Rationale

The *concept* is that by identifying sooner and more clearly the major problems that are *going* to confront us, the better we shall be able to deal with them, to have an impact on their solution.

The *process* is one of maintaining organizational flexibility to deal with issues as they arise, and at the same time neither disrupt normal operations nor proliferate unnecessarily the cross-departmental structures that are developed to deal with individual issues.

The *overriding consideration* is adaptation to the needs for change on an efficient and planned basis.

### The Management Technique

Set up a systematic *early-warning watch* on the people and trends from whom issues may emerge.

Create an *ad hoc unit*, parallel to the traditional structure, but apart from it, made up of: the people whose oxen stand to be gored if the issue in question matures, and people in charge of the functions—legal, government relations, communications, technical, etc.—needed for action.

Develop a set of loose, *flexible procedures* for action that can be tailored to the special needs of a specific issue.

Obtain the temporary but concentrated attention and clout of the very *top people*.

Build in a *self-destruct* mechanism to dissolve the unit as early as possible, once the issue has been resolved or has been institutionalized into the traditional structure.

*Day-to-day coordination* is vested in a team of staff specialists at Association headquarters. We call it our Staff Issue Management Team. It meets once a month to consider new issues and to determine who should do what about them, if anything. It also considers what issues have run their course and can be phased out.

It is composed of the individual issue managers, most of whom have this as an additional duty while performing primary responsibilities within the organization. This team is supported by staffers responsible for specific disciplines, many of whom are also responsible for specific issues:

    Technical

    Statistical and Economic

    Business Management

    News Bureau

    Information and Education

    Government Relations

## *Issue Roster*

### *"Issue" Criteria: Test Questions*

Does it:
1. Cut *across* traditional *lines?*
2. Have *public* implications?
3. Have potential *government* implications?

Is It:

4. *Proper and appropriate* for Association action?
5. *Susceptible to intervention* by the Association?
6. *Significant* enough to warrant industry action?
7. An aluminum problem *that wouldn't be handled adequately by others* without us? And/or

8. A *multi-industry problem* in which our industry's participation is necessary?

*Class I—Active List* • (issues actively being pursued by a designated Association group).

1. Environmentalism   a. Clean Air
   b. Clean Water
   c. Containers
2. Energy
3. Job Safety & Health
4. Product Safety & Liability

*Class II—Monitor* • (issues being monitored actively by the Association with action of some sort being taken or under consideration by the Association or someone else*).

1. Energy   Nuclear*
   Northwest*
2. Anti-Business, Anti-Profit Attitudes*
3. Equal Employment Regulations
4. Business Credibility
5. Material Availability   a. Bauxite Alternatives*
   b. Stockpile
6. Capital Availability*
7. Consumerism and Product Quality
8. Materials Competition

*Class III—Files* • (issues on which files are collected by staff members against the possibility of action ultimately being required).

1. No-growth, Back-to-nature, Anti-technology Attitudes
2. Advocacy Journalism
3. Work Force and Work Attitude Changes
4. Business Accountability and Ethics
5. National Planning

*Class IV—Watchful Waiting* • (issues of potential but remote apparent importance to this industry. No formal files or action required at this time).

1. Third World Pressures
2. Anti-Business Terrorism
3. Productivity
4. Class Action Suits
5. Demographic Changes (youth, elderly)

The team is headed by the Vice President for Public Affairs.

Adding it all up, how far has corporate responsiveness to new public expectations come? One very useful appraisal has been provided by the man who has been monitoring the matter for years, Raymond Bauer of the Harvard Graduate School of Business. In a July 1976 summary Bauer wrote: "Corporate responsiveness as a field of study has expanded so fast and increased so greatly in complexity that the Business School program, despite its findings and publications, can scarcely begin to exploit the research opportunities now at hand." (40)

## REFERENCES

1. Kendrick, Alexander. *Prime Time, The Life of Edward R. Murrow* (Boston, Mass.: Little, Brown and Company, 1969), p. 465.
2. Cutlip, Scott M. and Center, Allen H. *Effective Public Relations* (Englewood Cliffs, N.J.: Prentice-Hall, Inc., Fourth Edition, 1971), pp. 125–131, 151–152.
3. Silk, Leonard and Vogel, David. *Ethics and Profits. The Crisis of Confidence in American Business* (New York, N.Y.: Simon and Schuster, 1976), pp. 104–106.
4. "Summary Report—1976 Study of American Opinion Concerning Public Attitudes Toward Business and Government." Copyright © 1976 by U.S. News & World Report, Inc., pp. 3–10.
5. *PR Reporter*, October 11, 1976, p. 4.
6. Attwood, James A. "The ABCs of Responsibility," *Business and Society Review*, Summer 1976, pp. 75–76.
7. *Corporate Public Issues*, Vol. 1, Number 16, November 30, 1976, pp. 2–8.

8. *New York Times*, October 15, 1976.
9. Dickson, Paul. *The Future of the Workplace* (New York, N.Y.: Weybright and Talley, 1976), p. 199.
10. Schlesinger, Arthur, Jr. "Eloquent Silence," *Business and Society Review*, Summer, 1976, p. 78. (Article reprinted from the *Wall Street Journal*.)
11. Silk, Leonard and Vogel, David. *Ethics and Profits*, p. 227.
12. *New York Times*, September 25 and October 10, 1976.
13. Dalton, Dick. "Upbeat," Memo 5689K, in *Time Marketing* (New York: Time, Inc.).
14. *Long Island Magazine* of *Newsday*, June 6, 1976, p. 33.
15. Fulbright, J. William. "Fulbright on the Press," *Columbia Review of Journalism*, November–December, 1975, pp. 39–45.
16. Hess, John L. "The Real Danger To Civil Liberties," *MORE*, March, 1976, p. 28.
17. Weaver, Paul. "Captives of Melodrama," *New York Times Magazine*, August 29, 1976, pp. 6–57.
18. *New York Post*, December 13, 1976.
19. "Poisoned Presses?" *MORE*, February, 1977, p. 10.
20. Whelan, Elizabeth. "'Stop The Technology'–TV Networks Persistently Air A Distorted Picture," *Barron's*, November 15, 1976, p. 7.
21. "America's Press Under Fire," *U.S. News & World Report*, August 2, 1976, pp. 20–24.
22. "America's Press Under Fire," *U.S. News & World Report*.
23. Nolan, Joseph. "Protect Your Public Image With Performance," *Harvard Business Review*, March–April 1975, p. 135.
24. Kristol, Irving. "On 'Economic Education'," *Wall Street Journal*, February 18, 1976.
25. Alinsky, Saul D. *Rules for Radicals* (New York, N.Y.: Random House, 1971), p. 81.
26. Kristol, Irving. "On Economic Education," *Wall Street Journal*, February 18, 1976.
27. Hill and Knowlton Executives. *Critical Issues In Public Relations* (Englewood Cliffs, N.J.: Prentice-Hall, Inc., 1975), p. 16.

28. Byron, Fletcher L. *Koppers News,* Spring 1976, p. 1.
29. *New York Times,* December 15, 1975.
30. Goodell, Anita Rae Simpson. "The Visible Scientists," a dissertation submitted to the Department of Communications and the Committee of Graduate Studies of Stanford University, January, 1975. © 1975 by Anita Rae Simpson Goodell.
31. Scientists Discuss Divided Loyalties In Their Work," *New York Times,* February 22, 1976.
32. Lodge, James P. "A Risky Road From Hypothesis to Fact," *Business Week,* June 21, 1976, pp. 14, 16.
33. Pacific Legal Foundation's comments for the public meeting held by the US Environmental Protection Agency's Pesticide Advisory Committee, Sacramento, California, August 13, 1976.
34. Wessel, Milton R. *The Rule of Reason, A New Approach to Corporate Litigation* (Reading, Mass.: Addison-Wesley Publishing Company, 1976).
35. *Ibid.*
36. *Ibid.*
37. Paluszek, John. "Corporate Social Responsibility: PR's Last Big Chance?" *Public Relations Journal,* November, 1972, p. 66.
38. *PR Reporter,* March 1, 1976, p. 2.
39. Bernays, Edward L. "Social Responsibility of Business," *Public Relations Review,* Vol. 1, No. 3, 1976, p. 9.
40. Bauer, Raymond A. "Empirical Research on Corporate Responsiveness," Progress Report to the Division of Research, Harvard Business School, July, 1976, p. 8.

# 14

# The Corporation in a Self-Correcting Society

> "There's a fragility to the American society. Extreme tensions reside beneath the thin skin of stability stretched over our complex ethnic, class and regional structures.
> To keep it all going is the great achievement. Not to know how hard it is to keep it going is the disastrous innocence." (1)

Something lasting seems to have happened to the American society in the fairly recent past. We have experienced a national loss of self-confidence, followed by, at least in the Bicentennial year, a modest rebirth of pride in what this nation, with all its faults, has accomplished. Sometimes it is hard to remember that this is not the first time American institutions have had to deal with new values and the creative tensions that come with the need to adjust. It may be useful at such a time to reflect on how people as far apart ideologically as Alinsky and Kristol have characterized the system in which the corporation functions.

Alinsky says:

> A free and open society is an ongoing conflict, interrupted periodically by compromises—which then become the start for the continuation of conflict, compromise and on ad infinitum. Control of power is based on compromise in our Congress and among the executive, legislative and judicial branches. A society devoid of compromise is totalitarian. If I had to define a free and open society in one word, the word would be "compromise." . . .
> We learn, when we respect the dignity of the people, that they cannot be denied the elementary right to participate fully in the solutions of their own problems. Self-respect arises only out of people who play an active role in solving their own crises and who are not helpless, passive, puppet-like recipients of private or public services. To give people help, while denying them a sig-

nificant part in the action, contributes nothing to the development of the individual. In the deepest sense it is not giving, but taking—taking their dignity. Denial of the opportunity for participation is the denial of human dignity and democracy. It will not work. . . .

Dogma is the enemy of human freedom. Dogma must be watched for and apprehended at every turn and twist of the revolutionary movement. The human spirit glows from that inner light of doubt whether we are right, while those who believe with complete certainty that they possess the right are dark inside and darken the world outside with cruelty, pain and injustice. (2)

Kristol, writing in the *Wall Street Journal* on "What Is Social Justice?" has some remarkably similar opinions about our free society:

> Social justice is a loaded phrase: It blithely suggests that "society" ought to determine the distribution of income. This assumption is now so common that few people realize how controversial its implications are.
>
> The social order we call "capitalism," constructed on the basis of a market economy, does *not* believe that "society" ought to prescribe a "fair" distribution of income. "Society," in this context, means government—"society" is voiceless until the political authorities speak. . . .
>
> A distribution of income according to one's contribution to the society—to the "common good"—requires that this society have a powerful consensus as to what the "common good" is, and that it also have institutions with the authority to give specific meaning and application to this consensus on all occasions. Now, when you have such a consensus, and such authoritative institutions, you do not have—cannot have—a liberal society as we understand it. . . .
>
> A liberal society is one that is based on a *weak* consensus. There is nothing like near unanimity on what the "common good" is, who contributes to it, or how. There is not utter disagreement, of course; a liberal society is not—no society can be—in a condition of perpetual moral and political chaos. But the liberty of a liberal society derives from a prevalent skepticism as to anyone's ability to know the "common good" with certainty. . . .
>
> The distribution of income under capitalism is an expression of the general belief that it is better for society to be shaped by the interplay of people's free opinions and free preferences than by the enforcement of any one set of values by government. (3)

So, the system is imperfect. It is inefficient and costly and disorderly. And yet that very disorder is symbolic of the freedom we all

## THE CORPORATION IN A SELF-CORRECTING SOCIETY

hold so dear—the disorder that allows—encourages—attack on corporate policy and standards and also allows and encourages internal corporate adjustment and response.

What is good for society? Very few cases are clear-cut. The corporate executive will, more often than not, be able to determine only what is good for his or her constituency and hope that the policy will be socially responsible as well. The executive must adopt and implement such policy and then be prepared to "mix it" with those who may call such adjustment socially inappropriate or inadequate.

Assumption of the new role seems to be well underway. Silk and Vogel report:

> . . . more and more thoughtful business executives, whether because they think it prudent and necessary or because they think it is right, are trying to form a new philosophy or ideology; or, to put it more plainly, to find a new way of conceiving of their job, of their role, of their mission, of their values, that might lead to a better reconciliation of private objectives and public goals. Their hope is to find a means of safeguarding the relative autonomy of private business while helping to solve urgent public problems which large corporations cannot help but affect one way or another—for good or evil. . . .
> 
> The most politically and socially astute business leaders do recognize that, to preserve the system, they must change, their institutions must change and capitalism itself must change in response to new objective conditions and to new social demands. Such conservatives recognize that they will lose all if the system fails—and that excessive rigidity or negativism on the part of business can result in systemic failure. (4)

### THE SELF-CORRECTING SOCIETY

John Kenneth Galbraith, in an address given at Memphis State University in 1975, offered an arresting word picture of America as a self-correcting society, a nation that provides adequate outlet—freedom of expression—for all.

> In the case of Vietnam there was a remedy. It came out of the good sense of the country as a whole. It is in this that we can justly take the satisfaction.
> 
> When before has a great country stopped in the middle of a war, assessed the wisdom of its participation, decided it was wrong, asserted the judgment against all the chauvinistic tendencies aroused by armed conflict, dismissed from power those responsible, and brought its participation to an end?
> 
> The answer is never, for unlike the French before us, we

had a choice. The country corrected the error of its leaders in Vietnam. It was not a defeat but a triumph of good sense. Surely our critics abroad might take more note of this achievement. Does it not say anything for democracy?

However, let us not make the presence of this remedial power a license for any more such mistakes. (5)

A *self-correcting* society. One that eliminates the need for terrorism by providing the means for free expression—for the bearded, unwashed of the 1960s who were way out ahead of the rest of us in protesting the tragic Vietnam involvement as well as for the more conservatively attired corporate executive in the mid-1970s warning that an American welfare state could bring us the dire future now facing Great Britain.

A *self-correcting* society. One that provides freedom for all and an equal opportunity for a high standard of living for all who will make the effort to achieve it.

A *self-correcting* society. Always imperfect, but always seeking perfection.

Can the corporation similarly become self-correcting? Can it, like the society it serves, develop the mechanisms for adjustment in an age of rapid change? Will it hear the voices of the employee, the customer, the community leaders who now, more than ever, influence its future? Given man's natural discontent, his constant need for "more," for "better" and for "new," can the corporation change enough to meet his ever-changing demands?

In short, *will the corporation survive?*

We close this short book as we began it, with Reginald Jones in Detroit in November of 1974:

> . . . we must anticipate public criticism and take the initiative in developing *voluntary* standards . . . and move out front with effective programs of consumer education. . . . The American public, the sum total of all our constituencies, is highly pragmatic. It supports institutions that deliver the goods. . . .
>
> Thus the basic strategy for corporate survival is to anticipate the changing expectations of society, and serve them more effectively than competing institutions. (6)

## A PERSONAL POSTSCRIPT

Reflecting on this manuscript, I have come to believe that its central theses will be rejected out of hand by two types of readers.

"Hard-core" public-interest advocates will call it a (ugh!) "public relations whitewash." They won't believe that the corporation is changing to meet new social demands.

"Old-line" industrialists will call it soft-headed trash. They won't believe that there's any *need* for the corporation to change.

I'm afraid we'll just have to write off both types.

To everyone else, I say, believe.

## REFERENCES

1. Author unknown.
2. Alinsky, Saul D. *Rules for Radicals* (New York, N.Y.: Random House, 1971), pp. 4, 59, 123.
3. Kristol, Irving. "What Is Social Justice?" *Wall Street Journal*, August 12, 1976.
4. Silk, Leonard and Vogel, David. *Ethics and Profits* (New York, N.Y.: Simon and Schuster), pp. 236–239.
5. Galbraith, John Kenneth. "On History, Foolishness and Vietnam," *New York Times*, July 12, 1975.
6. Jones, Reginald H., in a speech to the Detroit Economic Club, November 25, 1974.